Twayne's English Authors Series

EDITOR OF THIS VOLUME

Bertram Davis
Florida State University

Nathaniel Lee

TEAS 270

Seen As Neurotic Genius
*Engraved by John Watts (fl. 1770–86)
from a painting in the Garrick Club
falsely attributed to William Dobson
(1610–46) and published in 1778.*

Seen As Disciplined Artist
*Engraved by A. W. Warren (1781?–
1856) from a drawing by J. Thurston
(1774–1822) and published in 1821.*

Two Depictions of Nathaniel Lee

Courtesy of the Harvard Theatre Collection

NATHANIEL LEE

By J. M. ARMISTEAD

University of Tennessee

TWAYNE PUBLISHERS
A DIVISION OF G. K. HALL & CO., BOSTON

Library of Congress Cataloging in Publication Data

Armistead, J M
Nathaniel Lee.

(Twayne's English authors series ; TEAS 270)
Bibliography: p. 202–13
Includes index.
1. Lee, Nathaniel, 1649?–1692—Criticism and
interpretation.
PR3540.A88   822'.4   79-12130
ISBN 0-8057-6748-7

For Benjamin Boyce

Contents

About the Author

Preface

Chronology

1. The Playwright and His Milieu   17

2. The Psychosis of Evil: *The Tragedy of Nero, Emperour of Rome (1674)*   32

3. Hero as Endangered Species: *Sophonisba, or Hannibal's Overthrow. A Tragedy (1675)*   43

4. Journal Entries: *Gloriana, or the Court of Augustus Caesar (1675/6)*   58

5. Shirt of Nessus: *The Rival Queens, or the Death of Alexander the Great (1676/7)*   67

6. "famish'd Tygers . . . have us in the Wind": *Mithridates King of Pontus, A Tragedy (1677/8)*   80

7. Disaster of Principles: *The Massacre of Paris: A Tragedy (1678/9?)*   94

8. Providence and the Fallen Psyche: *Caesar Borgia; Son of Pope Alexander the Sixth: A Tragedy (1679)*   106

9. Christian Heroism: *Theodosius: or, The Force of Love, A Tragedy (1680)*   122

10. Providential Surgery: *Lucius Junius Brutus; Father of his Country. A Tragedy (1680)*   130

11. A Playwright's Revenge: *The Princess of Cleve (c. 1682/3)*   144

12. Christian Sanity and Social Order: *Constantine the Great; A Tragedy (1683)*   163

13. Lee's Artistry   174

Appendix   180

Notes and References   183

Selected Bibliography   202

Index   214

About the Author

J. M. Armistead received his B.A. from Michigan State University and, as a Woodrow Wilson and Danforth Fellow, his A.M. and Ph.D. from Duke University. After six months of teaching English as a second language in Arlington, Virginia, followed by two years as an army officer, he joined the faculty of Rider College, Lawrenceville, New Jersey. Three years later he moved to his present post at the University of Tennessee in Knoxville. Professor Armistead has held summer research grants from Duke, Rider, and The Better English Fund at the University of Tennessee. He is the editor of *Restoration: Studies in English Literary Culture, 1660–1700* and has published articles on English and American authors in such journals as *SEL, Poe Studies, Essays in Literature, RECTR, Papers on Language & Literature*, and *The Durham University Journal*. At the moment his main scholarly project is *Ten Restoration Playwrights*, which surveys the criticism, from the earliest to the most recent, of prominent professional dramatists, 1660–1700; it will become part of G. K. Hall's Reference Guide Series.

Preface

Enormously popular in the Restoration and eighteenth century, the plays of Nathaniel Lee are, said Allardyce Nicoll, "of inestimable importance in any attempt to divine the quality of the tragedy of his age."[1] For three hundred years the distinguished critics and historians of English drama, with a few exceptions, have agreed, some going so far as to place Lee's works in "the First Rank" and to call them "great."[2] Yet what George Saintsbury noticed in the early years of this century remains true today: "no English playwright of anything like his merit has been so shamefully neglected."[3] Over the past twenty-odd years, since Thomas B. Stroup and Arthur L. Cooke produced their modern edition,[4] a few of his better plays have been newly edited or criticized by reputable scholars like G. Wilson Knight, Eric Rothstein, John Loftis, James Sutherland, and David Vieth.[5] Thus far, however, no full-length critical study has appeared, so that this volume makes at least a start at supplying the deficiency.

It is, to be sure, merely a start. I set for myself limited aims, and these were further limited by the requirements fixed for all volumes in this series. Readers who are curious about Lee's literary relations with contemporaries, his manuscripts (still missing), or the staging and performing of his works,[6] will not be satisfied—though I think a good deal more can be learned about all these matters. Nor will this book satisfy those with a penchant for ranking playwrights in terms of general excellence. I have attempted less to evaluate than to provide the bases for evaluation. My foremost aim was to make Lee's dramatic works more accessible to the modern reader, to do so by analyzing his themes and forms in light of his sources, milieu, major intellectual interests, and literary conventions. His poetry (including his dramatic verse as poetry) I have left for others to analyze,[7] for I discuss it only where indispensable to my central concerns. With some regret I have also passed over the two joint efforts with Dryden, *Oedipus* and *The Duke of Guise*, and not simply because space did not allow me to include them. More to the point, I wished to keep attention focused entirely upon Lee's artistry as maker of whole dramatic designs. Of course, what this subject naturally leads toward is a fuller understanding of how Dryden and Lee shared the artistic successes of their collaborative works, and I shall be turning to that partnership as this volume goes to press.

In the spirit of the Royal Society, I have attempted to work inductively, examining each biographical fact and each play on its own terms. Nevertheless, I freely followed clues to historical and intellectual backgrounds and tried to weave my findings into a contextual apprehension of both Lee's life and his works. The emphasis remains throughout on fact and on the design of specific plays, but these are, I hope, illuminated by associated ideas and events which Lee must have expected his audiences (and biographers and critics, presumably) to share. The overall result has turned out to be more unified than expected. Inductive procedures notwithstanding, there emerged some clear lines along which Lee's artistry seems to have developed. To avoid the implication that these were superimposed, I have kept to a strictly chronological ordering of analyses—where chronology can be ascertained—and have left a discussion of Lee's artistic development for the final chapter. On the other hand, where it can throw light on dramatic technique, I do try to show how each play picks up character traits, motifs, and structural devices from its predecessors, and how it points toward future works.

For whatever I have been able to accomplish I owe debts of gratitude to the research committee at Rider College (Lawrenceville, New Jersey) and to the Trustees of the Better English Fund, established by John C. Hodges at the University of Tennessee, Knoxville. Both groups provided much needed financial support. Equally important scholarly support came from Percy G. Adams (University of Tennessee), Earl Miner (Princeton), Robert D. Hume (Penn State), and G. K. Hall's field editor, Bertram Davis (Florida State), each of whom read the manuscript and made valuable suggestions for improving it. Other senior colleagues who offered special encouragement were Professors Benjamin Boyce and Oliver Ferguson (Duke University), James W. Clark (North Carolina State), Louis Landa (Princeton), and David Vieth (Southern Illinois). Many thanks also to Mr. Henry Gray, Parish Clerk of Hatfield, Hertfordshire, England, who unselfishly shared genealogical information about the Lee family. My studies were reliably guided by the staffs of the University Library at Cambridge, the British Library, the Folger Shakespeare Library, and the Firestone Library (Princeton). I especially appreciate the continuing aid given by the staff at the Main Library of the University of Tennessee: Olive Branch promptly acquired necessary materials, Eugene Abel provided the use of a faculty study, and the reference librarians helped with finding obscure facts and sources. The final typescript of this volume resulted from the generous efforts of Donna Beavers, secretary in the English Department, University of Tennessee, Knoxville, who worked without extra compensation. The following journals graciously allowed me to use substantial portions of essays first appearing in their pages: *Essays in Literature*, IV (1977), 159–73; *Papers on Language & Literature*, XV (1979), 38–51; and *The Durham University Journal*, LXXI (1978), 35–43. Ultimately, my greatest debt for sustained encouragement is to my wife Jane.

Chronology

1645– Nathaniel Lee born sometime between the birthdates of his
1652   older (Samuel) and next younger (Daniel) brothers—in Hat-
       field, Hertfordshire; in Middlesex; or in Walthamstow, Es-
       sex.

c. 1658 Enters Charterhouse, nominated by the Earl of Salisbury.

1665– Attends Trinity College, Cambridge (pensioner, 1665); be-
c. 1671 comes Scholar in 1668, B.A. in 1668/9, and possibly Fellow in
       1669. In 1670 "On the Death of the Duke of Albemarle" is
       included with other poems in *Musarum Cantabrigiensium.*

1671   Moves to London, possibly as protegé of George Villiers, sec-
       ond Duke of Buckingham, who neglects to support him.

1672   Acts the role of Captain of the Watch in Nevil Payne's *Fatal
       Jealousie.*

1673   Plays Duncan in Sir William Davenant's version of *Macbeth*
       (February 1672/3).

1674   *The Tragedy of Nero, Emperour of Rome* opens at Drury Lane
       on May 16.

1675   *Sophonisba, or Hannibal's Overthrow: A Tragedy* opens at
       Drury Lane on April 30. *Nero,* published spring, is dedicated
       to the Earl of Rochester, suggesting that Lee had become one
       of the rake-earl's literary step-children.

1676   *Gloriana, or the Court of Augustus Caesar* performed at
       Drury Lane (c. January 29, 1675/6). The dedication (to the
       Duchess of Portsmouth) seems to reflect depression over
       Rochester's vicious critical attack on *Sophonisba.*

1677   *The Rival Queens, or the Death of Alexander the Great* opens
       at Drury Lane (March 17, 1676/7) with a prologue by Sir
       Charles Scroop. Its dedication shows that Lee has shifted to
       Mulgrave's literary camp and now regrets his former de-
       bauchery. "To the Prince and Princess of Orange, upon Their
       Marriage" and "To Mr. Dryden, on his Poem of Paradice"
       appear, the latter formally inaugurating a lifelong friendship.
       Dryden responds with "To Mr. Lee, on His *Alexander.*"

1678   *Mithridates King of Pontus, A Tragedy* performed at Drury
       Lane (c. February 1677/8) with an epilogue by Dryden.

1678– *Oedipus: A Tragedy*, written with Dryden, performed at Dor-
1679   set Garden (sometime between August, 1678 and February,
       1678/9) in apparent breach of contract with the King's players.
       Hereafter, until the merger of 1682, all of Lee's plays will be
       performed by the Duke's Men. *The Massacre of Paris: A Trag-
       edy*, possibly with D'Urfey's prologue, is forbidden the stage
       probably this winter. *Caesar Borgia; Son of Pope Alexander
       the Sixth: A Tragedy* performed at Dorset Garden (spring or
       summer, 1679) with a prologue by Dryden.

1680   *Theodosius: or, The Force of Love*, A Tragedy performed at
       Dorset Garden (late summer or September) with songs to
       Purcell's music, "the first he e'er Compos'd for the Stage"
       (says Downes). The dedication of *Borgia* suggests Lee's harsh
       treatment by critics and, perhaps, his consternation over the
       banning of *Massacre*. *Lucius Junius Brutus; Father of his
       Country. A Tragedy*, with Richard Duke's prologue, banned
       after three to six nights at Dorset Garden (December).

1681   "To the Unknown Author of this Excellent Poem" is affixed to
       the second London edition of Dryden's *Absalom and Achito-
       phel*. Dryden's prologue to the Oxford revival of *Sophonisba*
       published.

1682   "To the Duke On His Return" and "To the Author & Transla-
       tour of the following Book" (Simon's *Histoire Critique*) pub-
       lished, and in November Drury Lane puts on *The Duke of
       Guise. A Tragedy*, another joint effort with Dryden. *The Prin-
       cess of Cleve* may have been first performed at Dorset Gar-
       den, with Dryden's prologue and epilogue, in December or
       in winter 1682/3.

1683   *Constantine the Great; A Tragedy* performed in November at
       Drury Lane with Dryden's epilogue.

1684– Admitted to the Bethlem Royal Hopital on November 11,
1688   1684. Beginning in January 1685/6 his expenses paid by the
       Board of Greencloth, in response to a petition from his
       brother Daniel. He is discharged as cured on April 23, 1688,
       and takes lodgings on Duke Street, his only known source of
       income a pension of ten shillings weekly from the Theatre
       Royal.

1689   "On Their Majesties Coronation" and "On the Death of Mrs.
       Behn" published. *The Princess of Cleve* published with a ded-
       ication asking Dorset to allow performance of *The Massacre of*

Paris. The latter put on at Drury Lane, with D'Urfey's epilogue (a version of his earlier prologue), on November 7.

1690– Obscurity. Dies in spring, 1692; buried on May 6, in St.
1692   Clement Danes, his grave said to have been next to Otway's.

1730   William Oldys, antiquarian, reports hearing that one of Lee's
        brothers (probably John, in Bigby, Lincolnshire) possessed
        the playwright's considerable literary remains.

CHAPTER 1

The Playwright and His Milieu

WE are separated from Nathaniel Lee's drama by three centuries of intellectual, social, and literary history. During that interval of time, the experiences that he felt were important have receded beyond easy grasp, for they were not merely private episodes for which any reader can find modern equivalents within himself. Restoration men of literature, coddled and encouraged by their monarch, were especially sensitive to the larger world of politics, fashion, and critical thought. Through their plays, poems, and essays the vital movements of society were subjected to ongoing analysis and representation, so that a work of art was also a public record. Yet to us the most interesting and enduring products of such artistry possess qualities that transform them into more than historical documents: an elegant unity, perhaps a peculiar lyricism reflecting their authors' unique styles of apprehending social phenomena. Such qualities make any artistically recreated experience worth acquiring a taste for, worth possessing as part of our aesthetic heritage. Because Lee's plays have this kind of appeal, we should try to part the veils of convention that time has placed between our world and the one he understood in his distinctive way.

I Family and Education

We must begin with what little is known of the man as he carried on the inevitable dialectic with his culture, for out of that dialectic grew his dramaturgy.[1] His family, the earliest form of culture he would have known, was not undistinguished. His grandfather William was a merchant, landowner, and bailiff of Nantwich, Cheshire. One of William's sons started the branch that eventually produced Reverend Samuel Lea, the headmaster who denied young Sam Johnson admission to Newport Grammar School. Another son was Na-

thaniel's extraordinary father, Richard Lee (1612-84/5). Well educated at Nantwich School and at Caius and Peterhouse Colleges,
Cambridge, he seems to have begun dabbling with alternative religious persuasions while still an undergraduate. Dr. John Cosin, Master of Peterhouse, may have guided him, along with his friends Peter
Gunning (later Master of St. John's and Bishop of Chichester and Ely)
and one Nichols, toward Roman Catholicism, and perhaps as a result
he left college in some disgrace. Recovering almost immediately,
however, he set a pattern of resiliency which he was to follow over
the next twenty-five years of seeking preference in the Anglican and
Presbyterian hierarchies.

During these years when the presentation of ministers passed from
the control of bishops to that of parliamentary committees, then back
again to the bishops, Richard Lee somehow managed to please and
impress leaders on both sides of the mid-century religious conflicts.
He was ordained an Anglican deacon in 1637 and spent a few obscure
years as curate and vicar in Derbyshire or Lancashire. But by 1644
he was himself ordaining ministers, not as an Anglican bishop but as
an officially designated "ordainer" on the Presbyterian model, and he
had begun rapidly to accumulate parish livings. These came to include St. Martin Orgar, London (Rector, 1643–45); Walthamstow,
Essex (Vicar, 1643–46); Kingston, Cambridgeshire (Rector, 1643–?);
St. Leonards, Shoreditch, London (Rector, 1644–c.49); and Hatfield, Hertfordshire (Rector, 1646–84). Later on he would become a
controversial Master of Wyggeston's Hospital, the old grammar
school for poor boys in Leicestershire (1650–c.60), and Rector of two
more Hertfordshire parishes, Little Gaddesden (1655–58) and Berk-
hamsted St. Peter (1656–?). By the end of the interregnum he had
gained wide repute as a zealous preacher for the Covenant.

Like the Vicar of Bray, however, Richard Lee could skillfully ride
the waves of political and ecclesiastical change. As General Monck
marched his army through St. Albans on his way down from Scotland
in January 1659/60, Lee greeted him with a sermon, was made an
army chaplain, and probably followed his new patron to London for
the Restoration. In the following December we find him reinstated
at Hatfield, this time as an Anglican rector, and in 1662 he officially
conformed to the Established Church. The penitential sermons he
delivered the next year at St. Mary's, Cambridge, and at St. Paul's,
London,[2] seem to have enhanced his growing prestige, for he was
made doctor of divinity in 1664, notwithstanding Robert Wild's at-

tempts to brand him an unscrupulous turncoat in two doggerel broadsides:

> To CHARLES *the First* I was a bloody Foe,
> I wish I do not serve the *Second* so:
> The only way to make me leave that trick,
> Is to bestow on me a *Bishoprick*.[3]

Indeed, by 1670 he had been offered (and refused) at least one bishopric, an Irish one, and was petitioning for an English deanery, possibly the one at Lincoln which he sought again in 1675. Sometime during this period, moreover, he was made Chaplain in Ordinary to King Charles II, a post he may have held in 1671 when Lieutenant General Lyttleton Annesley records hearing the "famed" preacher at court.[4]

For his family Richard Lee appears to have been as ambitious as he was for himself. His wife Elizabeth (c. 1624–1713/4) bore him at least ten (probably eleven) children, and all but three lived to adulthood. He managed to send five of the six surviving sons to Oxford or Cambridge University. Raising and educating this considerable brood must have pinched finances, for while the eldest son Samuel (c. 1645–?) was expensively schooled at Old Westminster (under Dryden's famous headmaster, Richard Busby), the second son, Nathaniel the playwright, was sent to the Charterhouse, an equally fine institution but one founded for the poor. The remaining sons were prepared for university at home, probably at the local grammar school. Three of them, Daniel (1652/3–?), Richard (1655–1725), and John (1662/3–1730), became Anglican priests, while the youngest, Emmanuel (1667–1725), seems to have continued on at Hatfield, a perennial debtor to his father and elder brothers.

This obviously bright, active family must have provided an intense intellectual and emotional environment for young Nathaniel Lee. No wonder most of his plays explore the burning religious, political, and psychological issues of the day, for these were subjects of conversation at home, if we can judge from Dr. Lee's large private library, which at his death in 1684/5 had grown to well over one thousand volumes.[5] Reflecting its owner's need to reconcile conflicting theologies, the library contained not only the great orthodox Anglican treatises and sermons of Richard Hooker, Lancelot Andrewes, John Donne, Jeremy Taylor, Thomas Fuller, Edward Stillingfleet, Gilbert

Burnet, and John Tillotson, but also major works by the Cambridge
Platonists Henry More and Ralph Cudworth, by Puritan divines like
John Cotton, by Quakers like William Penn, and by conscience-rid-
den men like William Chillingworth, John Wilkins, and Richard Bax-
ter, whose theological agonies would have attracted the ambivalent
Rector of Hatfield.

His son Nathaniel, both as a growing boy and as a mature dramatist
visiting home, may well have gained a great deal from this library,
even if its holdings were considerably smaller in the earlier years. As
catalogued for auction in 1685, it included many publications relating
to each of the five interests which consistently inform the playwright's works: Providence and the infernal powers; the history of
ancient Rome, the Roman Catholic Church, and Renaissance France;
seventeenth-century psychology; political thought; affairs of court
and state.[6]

When the nascent dramatist began to read in this library and converse maturely with his brothers and sisters (Anne, 1658–1724, and
Mary, 1660–?) is open to conjecture, since the date and place of his
birth are not precisely known. He must have been born sometime
between 1645 and 1652, possibly in Middlesex or Walthamstow, Essex, but just as likely in Hatfield. The relevant parish registers reveal
nothing, most lacking entries during the crucial years. But if we can
assume he entered the Charterhouse in 1658, when he was nominated for a vacancy by his father's parish patron, the Earl of Salisbury,
then perhaps he was at that time ten, the earliest age of admission,
and was therefore born at Hatfield in 1648 or 49. After about seven
years at Charterhouse he entered Trinity College, Cambridge (pensioner 1665, Scholar 1668, B.A. 1668/9, possibly Fellow 1669–71),
and spent three to five years among some of the most brilliant minds
of its history: its Master, the renowned Anglican theologian John
Pearson; its Professor of Mathematics Isaac Barrow; and Barrow's
favorite pupil and successor, Isaac Newton (sub-sizar 1661, Fellow
1667, Mathematics Professor 1669), who was already making vital
notes about gravity when young Lee took up residence.[7]

It was a vintage period for stocking the mind of an intellectually
curious undergraduate. In other colleges of the university the Cambridge Platonists Benjamin Whichcote and Henry More were holding forth, and from the presses of London and Oxford flowed key
books on several fashionable subjects: in the new science, Thomas
Sprat's *History of the Royal Society* (1667); in occult thought, Joseph

Glanvill's *Philosophical Considerations concerning Witches and Witchcraft* (1666); in divinity, John Bunyan's *Grace Abounding* (1666) and Henry More's *Divine Dialogues* (1668); and in imaginative literature, the heroic plays of Sir Robert Howard, the Earl of Orrery, and John Dryden; comedies by Sir William Davenant, Dryden, Sir George Etherege, Sir Charles Sedley, and Thomas Shadwell; poems and familiar prose by Abraham Cowley, Andrew Marvell, Edmund Waller, and Dryden; and above all, John Milton's *Paradise Lost* in ten books (1667).

II *London and Fame*

The education that Lee acquired from such books and from experiences in Hatfield and Cambridge would not contribute to dramatic history for several years to come. Possibly he spent 1669–71 as a Fellow in his college, for in 1670 his first known poem, signed "Nathaniel Lee, A. B. Trin. Coll.," appeared in a collection of verses mourning the death of his father's old patron, General George Monck, who had become Duke of Albemarle.[8] Although it is a clumsily written elegy, foreshadowing his mature dramatic style only in its classical allusions and cosmic imagery, it may have attracted the notice of George Villiers, second Duke of Buckingham. A seemingly reliable story[9] suggests that in summer, 1671, when Buckingham made a spectacular visit to be installed as Chancellor of Cambridge, he was attracted to the young poet, brought him along to London, and then promptly lost interest in him. Possessed of little besides energy, good looks, and a resonant voice, Lee apparently turned actor, appearing as the Captain of the Watch in Nevil Payne's *Fatal Jealousie* (1672) and as Duncan in Sir William Davenant's version of *Macbeth* (February 1672/3). But because of stage fright, and perhaps to satisfy a competing desire to compose his own plays, he quit acting after this Shakespearean role and made his next appearance as author of *Nero* (1674).

The few glimpses we get of him between 1674 and his death in 1692 tell a tale of poverty, increasing emotional distress, and insanity—punctuated by brief, airy episodes of social and dramatic triumph. These lighter episodes occurred mainly in the decade 1674–84 when several of his plays enjoyed extraordinary popularity. *Nero* was not among these, and in its dedication to the Earl of Rochester the fledgling playwright asks protection against censorious critics, but *Sophonisba* (1675) was a smashing success and continued to be enthusiastically received during the next century. That it was damned as sentimental "fustian" by John Wilmot, Earl of Rochester[10] may account for Lee's lament in the dedication of the following play, *Gloriana* (1675/6), where he speaks of "blasted . . . hopes" and "unjust fortune."[11] By the next March, however, fortune smiled again, for *The Rival Queens* (1676/7) became an immediate and lasting hit and today is regarded as one of his best works.

In dedicating it to the Earl of Mulgrave, the newly confident dramatist fiercely denounces his former indulgence in "Neronian Gambols"[12] and thus indirectly savages the scornful Rochester while turning for succor to his former patron's greatest literary and social rival. The dedication also highlights Lee's productive association with Mulgrave's famous protegé, John Dryden. Their bond was sealed in the younger writer's poem, "To Mr. Dryden, on his Poem of Paradice," where he commends the "Monarch of Verse" for refining on Milton and urges him next to compose a poetic comparison of Charles II to the "Hebrew King" David.[13] Dryden soon returned the compliment in "To Mr. Lee, on His *Alexander*" (1677),[14] praising the novice author's poetic passion and luxuriant imagery. Over the next five years the literary output of this relationship became considerable: Dryden's prologue and two epilogues to *Mithridates* (1678–81), prologue to *Caesar Borgia* (1679), prologue to the Oxford revival of *Sophonisba* (1680/1), prologue and epilogue to *The Princess of Cleve* (c. 1682/3), and epilogue to *Constantine* (1683);[15] the two dramatists' collaboration on *Oedipus* (1678–79) and *The Duke of Guise* (1682); and Lee's complimentary poem affixed to *Absalom and Achitophel* (though he professed not to know Dryden was the author).[16]

During these years when Lee was writing his best and most popular works, we can suppose that his social and financial status rose to its peak. His friends must have included not only Dryden but also Thomas Otway, his fellow actor and, later, fellow writer for the Duke's Company. And we can easily envision him hobnobbing with Tom D'Urfey, who contributed an epilogue to the 1689 production of *The Massacre of Paris*; with William Wycherley, whose poem about Lee in Bedlam is both compassionate and irreverent; and with Richard Duke (author of the prologue to *Lucius Junius Brutus*) and Charles Saunders (author of *Tamerlane the Great*, 1681), two younger Trinity College men who, like Lee, hovered about their eminent predecessor at Trinity, John Dryden.[17] Lee was now dedicating his plays to the luminaries of the Restoration court, the Earls of Dorset and Pembroke, and the lovely Frances Stewart, Duchess of Richmond, one of the King's most esteemed mistresses. Some of these targets of his flattery probably wined and dined him, if we can credit later anecdotes, and while he gained a reputation as "dedicating Lee," the ladies' playwright, he probably also gained a paunch and the red nose of a tippler. He wrote a conventional panegyric on the wedding of the king's niece to William of Orange,[18] and the royal family sometimes attended or commanded performances of his latest plays.

Mithridates (1677/8) proved another smash hit, as did the first collaboration with Dryden, *Oedipus* (1678–79), the latter produced at Dorset Garden in apparent breach of contract with the King's Company. Hereafter, until the merger of companies in 1682, all of Lee's plays were written for the Duke's players. Perhaps this move had something to do with the banning of *The Massacre of Paris* (possibly that same winter), for the Master of Revels responsible for censuring it would have been Charles Killigrew, manager of the King's Company.[19] At any rate, the gore and anti-Catholicism of *Massacre* appears in Lee's next effort, *Caesar Borgia* (1679), which also seems to have experienced difficulty with the censors, despite its more subtle approach to current political issues. When it failed to attract much notice, Lee apparently decided to resume with variations his proven formula of amorous dilemmas and heroic anxieties, and the result, *Theodosius* (1680), became a century-long success. Unfortunately, his last box-office hit, *Lucius Junius Brutus* (1680), was regarded as a dangerous return to more potent political commentary and was banned after three to six nights, never to be revived in its original form.[20]

As if to emphasize his loyalty, the next year Lee published a tribute "To the Unknown Author" of *Absalom and Achitophel*—the poem where Dryden develops his friend's notion of comparing Charles II to King David—hailing "a Milton" who "the right party chose."[21] And in 1682, in addition to a brief verse compliment "To the Author & Translatour" of Richard Simon's *Histoire Critique du Vieux Testament*, he produced a fulsome ode to the Duke of York "On His Return" from political exile.[22] But despite these efforts to preserve his status as fashionable court poet, Lee's fame began rapidly to fade. Although his second collaboration with Dryden, *The Duke of Guise*

(1682), succeeded after a four-month political prohibition, his own works, *The Princess of Cleve* (c. 1682/3) and *Constantine* (1683), went by almost unnoticed.

III *Insanity and Obscurity*

Within the year Lee became "distracted" and on November 11, 1684, supported financially by his friends, was admitted to "Bedlam," the Bethlem Royal Hospital for the insane. A year later his brother Daniel petitioned the Board of Greencloth, a branch of the royal household serving the newly crowned James II, to underwrite the Bedlamite's expenses. Perhaps because James recalled those flattering depictions of him in "To the Duke On His Return," *The Duke of Guise* (as Henry of Navarre), and *Constantine* (as Dalmatius), the petition succeeded, and from January 1, 1685/6 until the mad author was released, April 23, 1688, his bills were paid by the court. The causes, symptoms, and prognosis of his madness can only be guessed at using the few extant reports by contemporaries. Anthony Wood, the diarist and Oxford biographer, thinks Lee's reason was unseated by a too intense imagination, Gerard Langbaine says alcoholism was an important cause, and Wycherley blames neglect, starvation, and Lee's inherent tendency to lose his temper and rail at friend and foe alike. We may never know the actual causes; nor can we be certain of how Lee behaved and was dealt with in Bedlam. Sir George Etherege, writing from the Continent, supposed the confinement was intermittent, and the anonymous author of "Satyr against the Poets" portrays the institutionalized dramatist as having painful raving fits, as being chained at night and being confined in darkness by day (though some of this information was simply lifted from Lee's own lines 262-268 in *Caesar Borgia*, V.i.). Later sources say his head was shaved and he was placed on a milk diet by Dr. Edward Tyson, physician at Bedlam from 1684–1707 (certainly these were therapies typically used at the time).[23]

Whatever the treatment, Lee "recovered" sufficiently to be discharged in spring, 1688.[24] He took lodgings on Duke Street (now Sardinia Street) close to the Theatre Royal where he went to draw his pathetic weekly pension of ten shillings. In the following December James II fled to France, and when William and Mary were crowned on April 11, 1689, Lee came forth with another unremarkable, if competent, panegyric.[25] Later the same year he again praised the new monarch in a prologue to the newly published version of *The Princess of Cleve*. He dedicated the play to his old patron, Dorset, King William's Lord Chamberlain, and asked the Earl to encourage production of the once-banned *Massacre of Paris*, now deemed politically suitable to the prevailing climate of opinion. The play was duly staged in November, the queen and her maids of honor in attendance. But by now, according to the anecdotists, the formerly handsome and congenial dramatist, with his abundant hair and excellent reading voice, had become red-faced, carbuncular, and corpulent, his milk diet having given way to further episodes of heavy drinking. The pathos of his condition is suggested by his last dateable poem, the apparently heartfelt elegy "On the Death of Mrs. Behn" (1689), in which he seems to long for the oblivion of another world "where I shall never shed another Tear."[26] In spring, 1692 he was found dead in the streets after a drinking bout and was interred on May 6 in St. Clement Danes. There is no epitaph, no elegy, indeed no sign of his grave.

Whether he wrote any new plays during and after his confinement is problematical. Tom Brown quipped that Mad Nat composed a twenty-five act extravaganza while institutionalized, [27] and in 1730 William Oldys noted that "a Brother of this Nat Lees somewhere in or near the Isle of Ascholm in Lincolnshire . . . has a Trunk full of his Writing."[28] Judging from a similar remark in Oldys's letter to Edward Harley, Earl of Oxford, he first heard of these literary remains in early 1730.[29] The "Brother" would have been the Reverend John Lee, Rector of Bigby and Cadney, near the Isle of Axholme in Lincolnshire. John died in 1730, but his will makes no specific references to Nathaniel or his papers, and he bequeaths his estate to his wife Sarah. If the playwright's papers were part of this estate, they might have been passed down to John's married daughter Ann Langdon, or over to some of her cousins, perhaps to Ann Lee Pitman Holmes. They do not appear in the Harleian collection.

IV *Milieu and Dramatic Design*

Though lacking manuscripts, we still have in early printed editions a handful of Lee's poems and his thirteen known plays (including the two Dryden collaborations) together with their associated dedicatory epistles, prologues, and epilogues. They reveal a mind fashioning artistic wholes from diverse aspects of the mid-Restoration culture— no mean feat when to live in that culture as a thoughtful, sensitive man was in itself a lesson in intellectual survival. There were few verities upon which one could found a consistent set of values or programs for action. Events in the middle decades of the century had shattered or seriously crippled many of the conventional modes of thought and behavior, leaving in place of Renaissance syntheses a baffling multiplicity of intellectual and social contexts. Before 1640 the most eccentric varieties of human experience could be apprehended as parts of, or deviations from, a divinely articulated system of ideals and orders of being, and this system was "officially" interpreted and managed by a "sacred" monarch, hierarchical society, and authoritarian religion. After 1660 the monarch seemed all too human and vulnerable, his court the scene of elegant debauchery, his sovereignty the subject of legislation. Meanwhile, the societal duties of aristocrats were becoming indistinct as real political and economic power became increasingly concentrated in the hands of wealthy merchants and tradesmen, and this power began to be exercised less through the hereditary establishment than through freely associating interest groups responsive to the needs of the moment. As for religious uniformity, it was restored only nominally and legally, while pious minds struggled to reconcile it with heresies, sectarianism, materialistic philosophy, and empiricism.[30]

Several events during the cultural watershed of mid-century symbolized these directions of change. In 1649, when Charles I was beheaded, the state itself became headless. Its structure no longer reflected the conviction that a king was the divinely ordained mind and will of the body politic. The ensuing decade of civil war, dictatorship, and failure to find a sectarian equivalent to episcopal order left pre-Restoration England yearning for a more stable society. This mid-century age of experiment in religion and politics was matched by simultaneous intellectual developments. At Wadham College, Oxford, were held the early meetings of thinkers who would later form the nucleus of the Royal Society. As followers of Bacon and Descartes, they believed in expanding knowledge of the physical world through a new method of analysis which practically reversed the old deductive logic of scholastic reasoners: instead of evaluating phenomena in light of *a priori* sets of metaphysical assumptions, they first cleared their minds of all traditional perceptions, then carefully recorded and classified experience, and only then, having established the facts, generalized about form and dynamics. Moreover, such generalizations they regarded as tentative until controlled experiments verified them. At about the same time, in the realm of moral and social thought, Thomas Hobbes was using Cartesian skepticism, axiomatic logic, and a kind of thought experiment to prove that all known existence was purely material; and he insisted that like other material beings humans were basically selfish and antisocial, their behavior motivated by a natural appetite for pleasure, power, and acquisition.

Despite hopes in 1660 that the Restoration of Charles II would bring renewed order and conviction in public life, this age of experiment continued for another thirty years, the thirty years of Nathaniel Lee's youth and manhood. Charles privately hankered for his father's divinely sanctioned authority and for a religion, like continental Roman Catholicism, which premised the supernatural interdependence of God, state, and morality. But hardships in exile had taught him the empirical art of coping with rival political and moral forces, and just as he sometimes dabbled in a chemical laboratory, so he considered each parliament, and each set of privy councillors, as another experiment in disarming threats against domestic peace and his own sovereignty. Like it or not, he faced realities: the body politic was being expensively reconstructed as a legal, instead of metaphysical, entity; and a civic mentality began to flourish among subjects once content to leave state affairs to their betters.

Just as mid-century events symbolized change, so a series of disasters in the early years of the Restoration symbolized the need for reconstruction. In 1665 the Great Plague reduced London's population by some 68,000, while the Great Fire of 1666 reduced its housing and business center to rubble. The following year, as architects planned to replace the great emblems of civic vigor—St. Paul's Cathedral and the Royal Exchange—a Dutch fleet sailed up the Medway, burned several warships, and towed away the symbol of English martial prowess, the flagship *Royal Charles*.

To deal with the shattering of social and intellectual structures a brilliant generation of skeptics and builders emerged, and with them came a new kind of literary artistry to describe and assess both the damage and the reconstruction. Among the skeptics were those young courtiers whose moral nihilism has been unjustly exaggerated into a type of Restoration culture in general. It is true that Charles II revelled in the company of young blades like the Earls of Rochester, Dorset, and Mulgrave; the Duke of Buckingham, Sir George Etherege, and Sir Charles Sedley—all of whom shared an epicurean variety of Hobbes's philosophy and behaved accordingly. Agreeing that life has no compelling spiritual dimension and that reason, therefore, is made to serve animal appetites, they divided their time between the king's silken courtesans and the brothels of Covent Garden, between masquerade balls and theaters, aristocratic dinner parties and democratic tavern life. They brawled, duelled, cuckolded acquaintances, seduced young virgins, exchanged obscene lyrics, publicly performed indecent acts, and generally scandalized the citizenry.[31]

But while this merry gang burned with a gem-like flame that lasted only fifteen years, graver minds sought more permanent ways to meet the challenges to traditional thought. A new religious vision was being created piecemeal by leaders of several independent communities of devotion. Isaac Barrow, Edward Stillingfleet, Gilbert Burnet, Robert South, and John Tillotson worked at redefining Anglican theology and episcopacy and at reconnecting them to the central nervous system of public life.[32] Dissenters like John Bunyan, Richard Baxter, George Fox, William Penn, and Robert Barclay sought a fulfilling inner paradigm of convictions to provide religious certitude. Standing between these students of the invisible world and the rebuilders of social and physical order, the intellectual voyager Joseph Glanvill attempted using pseudo-empirical methods to prove the actuality of witches and devils. As outward political life was being analyzed by empiricists like the Marquis of Halifax and John Locke, a succession of pragmatic men tried to employ new sources of power to stabilize shifting national interests: the Earl of Shaftesbury tried republican maneuvers, the Earl of Danby wielded parliamentary patronage, and Laurence Hyde and Sidney Godolphin modernized governmental finance. With the king's blessing the Royal Society investigated the physical world through a curious group of theorists, projectors and inventors who were interested both in advancing knowledge and in solving practical problems. Sir William Petty collected economic facts and figures, then pioneered statistical methods. Robert Hooke improved microscopic studies, observed planets, formulated a law of gases, but also toyed with air pumps and watches. Thomas Sprat and John Wilkins defended experimental philosophy and pushed for a more precise, concrete English language. And Christopher Wren, a distinguished mathematician and astronomer, planned a new London whose wider streets, new residential squares, and tidy, pulpit-centered churches catered to a more open, sociable, discursive society.

As the pace of change quickened in so many areas of English life, London became more than ever the nation's eyes and ears, its purveyor of novel ideas, controversy, gossip, scandal. The new penny post and flocks of hackney coaches sped concepts and people to and fro between coffeehouses and townhouses, eating places and churches, theaters and chambers of parliament, pleasure gardens and law courts. And as the street pamphleteers and balladeers hawked highly perishable versions of what was happening, men of letters sought a mental and linguistic vocabulary that would possess for later generations the manifold novelty of Restoration living. Some, like Samuel Pepys, recorded experience as a staccato series of impressions whose integrity depended mainly upon the recorder's own sense of identity. Others, like John Milton and John Bunyan, created vast narrative symbols which comprehended basic human behavior as part of an eternally valid Christian myth. But most writers undertook the perhaps more agonizing, if not more difficult, task of allowing modern life its novelty, diversity, and flux, while defining its details within multiple traditional contexts.

This latter approach eventuated in literary structures whose success in shaping complicated attitudes toward experience made them widely useful to Restoration authors. If, for example, one wished to justify the beheading of a divinely ordained king and his temporary replacement by an effective republican strongman, then one might do as Dryden did in *Heroique Stanzas . . . to the . . . late Lord Protector:* show how these events make sense as parts of a larger, and ultimately incomprehensible, design of Providence. On the other hand, to account for self-contradictory or fragmentary experience without such transcendental assumptions, one might employ multiplex irony: (a) use it, like Sir George Etherege in *The Man of Mode*, to hold diverse behavioral modes in witty suspension; (b) use it, like the Earl of Rochester in *Satyr against Reason and Mankind*, to reduce possible courses of action to pairs of irreconcilable opposites; (c) or use it as Samuel Butler does in *Hudibras*, to dazzle judgment with proliferating examples of human folly and delusion. A kind of mean between these extreme structures involves creating a baroque model of experience, one that expresses diversity through diversely significant patterns of image and allusion, yet interweaves these patterns to suggest at least an aesthetic resolution of conflicts where none seems to exist philosophically or socially.[33]

In Dryden's works the use of this last structure usually leads him toward providentialism, as in *Astraea Redux* and *The Hind and the Panther*. In the works of Nathaniel Lee, it leads in the same direction, but en route it produces dramatic configurations which, without strong providential implications, combine philosophical skepticism, emotional intensity, and complexly figured beauty. Lee's early life would naturally have led a sensitive mind into skepticism. Observing his father must have taught him a good deal about inconsistencies in religious thought and ecclesiastical politics. And if, as the dedicatory epistles of *Nero* and *Sophonisba* suggest, he emulated courtly hedonism during the early London years, perhaps such behavior stimulated moral incertitude; while the sheer diversity of London life, resisting traditional classifications, might have fostered an accompanying social empiricism. Yet his mind was stocked with the Renaissance conventions of thought and literary style which he absorbed from reading in the libraries at Hatfield and Cambridge, and in the early Restoration plays and poems he could see how these conventions might be modified to express reality in an age of experiment and reconstruction. His own plays, as we shall see, reflect this dual vision. They become the crucibles in which "modern" patterns of behavior are made to react in a highly charged environment of literary and philosophical conventions, giving off great quantities of passion and spectacle, and producing suggestively unified models of experience.

In these models the interpenetration of social and supernatural reflects that unique synthesis of "modern" and Renaissance perspectives that Lee shared with Dryden and other contemporary authors. As empiricism, the idea of progress, and the sense of historical period emerged in the Restoration mind, they did not immediately displace either the classical notion of cyclical social change or the Christian conviction that all earthly phenomena ultimately acted out a providential design.[34] Accordingly, Lee's representations of royal psychology reflect at once his empirical awareness of dangerous tendencies in the Restoration court, his sense that these tendencies have parallels in earlier cycles of history, and his conviction that a creative comparison between the two can teach us how better to cooperate in the eternal dynamics of cosmic order.

Whether his subject be pagan or Christian, Lee represents moral depravity, melancholy, and madness—the sources of conflict in all his plays—as functions of man's Fall from Grace. With his Renaissance forebears, he assumes that this catastrophe is made psychologically manifest in man's tendency to yield to bestial appetites, pride, and passion, instead of conducting himself according to reason in the service of charity and social harmony. Since the Fall, this lower, animalistic nature within man has been subjected to evil influences by secondary causes, like stars and demons, which incline him toward mental and moral disturbances such as passionate love, lust after carnal and material pleasure, vain presumption, inordinate sorrow, jealousy, hatred, fear, and religious enthusiasm. Ultimately, these "perturbations of mind"[35] produce the aberrant behavior that Lee analyzes dramatically. In doing so, he uses all his resources to coordinate the changing psychological condition of each protagonist not only with the temporal condition of court and state, but also with the eternal cosmic drama involving heaven and the underworld. As we move from *Nero* to *Constantine*, we shall see him more clearly defining the metaphysics of this larger drama, until at last he envisions a messianic experience in which the entire Christian pattern—Fall, sin, and redemption—is reenacted within a single psyche.

CHAPTER 2

The Psychosis of Evil: The Tragedy of Nero, Emperour of Rome (1674)

*N*ERO is a play about the growth of moral and political evil out of its center in a deranged sovereign. It does not question how such evil first emerges or how to eradicate it. Nor does it explore any of Lee's other favorite interests—like love, heroism, social harmony, Providence—except as they may briefly appear in contrast to the diabolical activities in Nero's court. With this unvarying focus, the play almost makes up in intensity and suggestiveness what it patently lacks in plot construction, depth of portraiture, and control over dialogue. It is worth studying as a flawed but artistically wrought drama.

In order to appreciate it fully, however, we must put aside preconceptions about the way a play should develop. Lee's dense imagery and free use of sources indicate that he had in mind a somewhat unorthodox design, one that develops like a chain reaction: once Nero embarks on a career of unrestrained self-indulgence, his immorality becomes a progressive madness whose expanding energy envelops both court and country in "dark Chaos" and "Bright Ruin."[1] As the plot thus runs its course, the figurative language accompanying it carries along significance on several levels at once—spiritual, moral, psychological, political—so that we end up not exactly with a theme but rather with a multidimensional model of human conduct that has both classic and contemporary relevance.

I *Plot and Freedom from Sources*

The plot is not moved forward by convincing personal motives or by causal factors implicit in the conflicts between characters. It is driven by the persistent evil energy of the villain-protagonist. In the first scene we learn that Nero has already gained a reputation for depravity, and before Act I is over he condemns his mother (Agrippina) to death for imagined treason; imprisons Seneca for disturbing him with rational guidance; and sends Petronius, an advisor more to his liking, to lure the innocent but wanton wife of Otho, Poppea, to his bed. After Seneca's execution, reported in Act II, the emperor fatally stabs his own wife (Octavia) for refusing to murder her brother. This brother, Britannicus, is doomed because he is the legitimate successor to the late emperor, Claudius (whose throne Nero usurped), and a purveyor of civic ideals. His moralizing mistress, an angelic Parthian princess (Cyara), is the next victim after she appeals, on his behalf, to the emperor's sense of pity and mercy. Her ghost later saves Britannicus, helplessly mad with grief and frustration, from the nymphomaniacal clutches of Poppea. Meanwhile, Poppea's estranged husband, Otho, has joined her noble brother, Piso, in a conspiracy to support a coup d'etat by Galba, proconsul of Spain (aided by Vindex, propraetor of Gaul). Finally, a second ghost, that of the insane Emperor Caligula, incites Nero to burn Rome, and as it burns, the plot rushes to its gory conclusion: Britannicus dies of poison, his friend Flavius kills the assassin and is himself dispatched, Otho stabs Poppea to death, Galba lands on the Roman coast, the plebeians attack the emperor's palace, Petronius commits suicide, and Nero dies (apparently of poison as well), confident that a noble destiny awaits him. As the play ends, Otho and Piso proclaim Galba Emperor and God.

This is hardly what one would call a well-constructed plot, at least not in the conventional sense. Rather than proceeding from some probable source of motivation, Nero's diabolical acts are impulsive, almost instinctive, and while they are well connected to the two subordinate actions—the moral collapse of Poppea and the mental collapse of Britannicus—they seem unrelated to the history of Britannicus and Cyara. These two had fallen in love, the audience is informed, while Britannicus was spying incognito on Cyara's brother, the Parthian prince and general (Alamander), with whom Britannicus became fast friends in spite of their opposed allegiances. Discovered and condemned by the Parthian King, but forewarned by Alamander, Britannicus had fled to Rome, and as the play begins Cyara, disguised as Coralbo, is following him under the pretext of searching for her brother, who was lost during an intervening battle with Rome. None of this background has any real bearing on the ensuing action, and neither do two related episodes: Cyara's reporting herself dead in order to test her lover's devotion (he is unexpectedly driven mad by the revelation) and the brief entrance of Flavius in Act V, where he mutters something about France, kills his friend's assassin, and then is himself sent offstage to be executed.[2]

Still, these flaws in motivation and plot do not necessarily lead to the conclusion, espoused by both Allardyce Nicoll and Lee's latest editors, Stroup and Cooke, that the play altogether lacks a focused structure.[3] For one thing, the freedom with which Lee has handled his sources argues that he was composing very deliberately, if not with a fully conceived purpose in mind. He was no more deeply indebted to earlier historical and literary accounts of Nero's life than he might have been to previous uses of the same general themes and situations,[4] such as in *Hamlet* (c. 1602), for instance, where an amorous young prince, his father's throne usurped, sustains the usurper's hatred, becomes insane, and soliloquizes about death. Except for the unfortunate digression into the history of Cyara and Britannicus, *Nero* appears to be not a patchwork of borrowed episodes but rather an original work whose design, while emerging within the context of Lee's reading, was controlled by some ulterior idea in his mind. The design comes to light, however, only if our attention is not controlled by the notion that dramatic action must proceed from tying to untying of a knot, or from exposition to conflict to climax to denouement. What we find, instead, is a chronicle of atrocities which, as they occur in a suggestively patterned sequence, stimulate figurative commentary by witnesses (including Nero himself). Gradually but with surprising consistency, the commentary creates a symbolic paradigm for the action, conceptualizing it at a more general level.

II *Nero as Promethean Demon*

To see this happening, we must get beyond the point of being overwhelmed, as most critics have been,[5] by the improbable magnitude of Nero's depravity. Admittedly, he is the exemplar of every conceivable sin: atheism (I. ii. 31–32), boundless pride (I. ii. 28, 62), towering presumption (I. ii. 93; V. iii. 190), hedonism (I. ii. 140–41), cruel inhumanity (the murders), civic irresponsibility (V. ii. 46), and antirationality (I. i. 163–64). The point of the play, however, is not the sheer horror of Nero's viciousness, but rather what to *make* of such viciousness, or what kinds of sense *it* makes if seen within a larger framework of assumptions. An attempt to achieve this larger perspective is made right from the beginning, in the opening scene, where Otho and Agrippina define Nero's villainy within conventional contexts of belief.

When Sylvius envisions the emperor as a "Sun" ruling brightly over the "full Orb" of the Roman court (I. i. 42, 40), Otho significantly corrects the imagery:

> The darkness of his horrid vices, have
> Eclips'd the glimmering rays of his frail virtue.
> His cruelties, like birds of prey, have pick'd
> All seeds of Nobleness from his false heart. (I. i. 44–47)

Carrying forward this contrast between dark vice and bright, sun-like virtue, as well as the use of a beast metaphor, Agrippina adds vital touches to the portrait while cursing her son for condemning her to death. She no longer regards him as a natural child but rather as something sired by "Hell," a "savage Monster" whom she involuntarily "brought to light" only to watch it bred "in some dark cave." Later, to complete her "foul disgrace," she was incestuously raped by him, and "Day and Night together mingled were" (I. i. 115–46).

Two related threads of traditional imagery lead from these two early speeches: one conflates the myths of Prometheus and Phaeton, and the other draws together various occult motifs. Like Prometheus, Nero steals godly power but in the end is punished by having a vital organ (in this case the heart, for its symbolic value, rather than the liver) pecked away by his eagle-like (rather than vulture-like) cruelty. In Act IV, he is called "Traytor, worse than he that stole their [the gods'] fire" (i. 22). What he does with his "fire" recalls some versions of the myth in which Prometheus is a Faustian figure who sins against the gods not only by trickery and theft but also by learning forbidden arts and presuming to make men from clay. Nero claims this same godlike control over nature: "through every art I range," "Sexes change," command "Winds" and "floods," "Beings annihilate, and make a new" (I. ii. 33–41); "the Gods . . . / . . . see their art, by mortal wit out-done" (III. iii. 73–74). And this recalls that Agrippina, in summing up her son's villainy, focused on the basically Promethean nature of his sins: "Monster of men, who altered nature's course" (I. i. 147). By presuming to wield such divine power over nature, he does alter her course, but he finds, like Phaeton, that ultimately the results are disastrous. Determined to burn Rome, he sees himself as a "young Phaeton" (IV. iv. 57) fiercely guiding the solar chariot, but like his mythological counterpart he loses control and, as he dies, demands to know if his fate is the mythological one, destruction by a thunderbolt from the gods: "if they have any Thunder, let it come" (V. iii. 228).[6]

The occult motifs from which Lee extracts his other thread of key imagery are more complex, combining pagan and Christian demonologies. Behind Agrippina's depiction of Nero as a half-demon is the medieval and Renaissance view that what pagans called devils were the offspring of intercourse between fallen angels and human women, "the sons of God" and "the daughters of men" (Gen. 6:4). Some sort of grotesque mixture of human and bestial traits was believed to show up in these offspring, just as Agrippina indicates. For instance, there was the "monster with a wolf's head and a snake's tail" reportedly born in 1275 to a woman impregnated by the devil. Merlin and Caliban are the two most celebrated products of such relations.[7] Other characters in the play generally concur with Agrippina's account of the emperor's occult pedigree. He is a "Devil" (IV. i. 56; V. ii. 29), a king whom "Hell makes . . . great" (I. i. 65), according to Flavius and Britannicus, and the latter joins these bestial and infernal traits to the light/dark imagery by depicting him as "Cerberus" (IV. i. 25)—the monstrous dog standing defiantly at the border of earth and hell—and as "a night-Raven" whose "huge wicker wings" blot out the "Sun" and "each Star" (III. i. 122–129).[8]

III Possession, Repulsion, Holocaust: Poppea, Britannicus, and Rome

The behavior of Nero—this anti-sun, bestial half-devil, Promethean magician—generates two subplots which cross when Poppea tries to seduce Britannicus and which merge in the final holocaust of Act V: (1) the corrupting of Poppea; (2) the snuffing out of Britannicus and his allied worthies (Agrippina, Seneca, Octavia, and Cyara), each an exemplar of a specific kind of virtue.

Poppea's story chronicles the contagious nature of Nero's evil. If to Britannicus the emperor is Cerberus, to Piso he is the "Dog-star," Sirius, rising with the sun, eclipsing it, and inflaming Poppea's passion with his earthly flame (III. ii. 65).[9] An early description of Poppea, "her long black locks" flowing over white shoulders "as

thick'ning clouds o're the Sun's brightness" (I. ii. 130–31), foreshadows her symbolic role, for soon Petronius is telling her that Nero has
"a flame, whose . . . splendor drowns the Stars,/ And . . . vies with
the great eye of Day" (III. ii. 2–3). As her "pride and sensual pleasure" (III. ii. 102) are ignited by the emperor's "golden Pageantry"
(III. ii. 45), she herself partakes of his nature, almost as if possessed
by the same evil influence. Before, she was chastely cool, like
"Diana" the moon goddess, chasing "all the Savage herd" (I. ii. 125–
26); now she is herself a savage, her heart "does burn" and her blood
"boils" as she becomes the predator and tries in turn to ignite Britannicus and Piso with her "pow'rful flame" (IV. i. 110–12; V. iii. 69).

In resisting her, Piso echoes Agrippina's account of the rape by
Nero—"Who ever knew Night mingle with the Day" (V. iii. 62)—and
recalls the occult interpretation of the emperor's personality. Poppea
shares not only his fiery lust but also his diabolical evil. Just as he has
become a half-beast, half-demon, at once fiery and black, dog-star
and raven with wicker wings, so Poppea becomes "Monster . . .
Harpy" with "wings of horror" (III. ii. 81–82).[10] The idea that she
has, in a sense, become possessed by the evil radiating through Nero
is more than idly suggested by these parallel metaphors, however. It
is reinforced and extended by two important allusions to occult tradition. First, the equating of Poppea with the goddess Diana not only
underlines her formerly chaste rusticity but also implies her latent
susceptibility to diabolical influences. Among the widely employed
Christian interpretations of pagan myth still current in Lee's time
was the notion that Diana rules devil-possessed women. The author-
itative *Canon*, or *Capitulum*, *Episcopi*, a piece of twelfth-century
canon law that was still being cited in seventeenth-century witch
trials, expresses the concept thus:

. . . certain abandoned women perverted by Satan, seduced by illusions and
phantasms of demons, believe and openly profess that, in the dead of night,
they ride upon certain beasts with the pagan goddess Diana, with a countless
horde of women . . . and obey her commands. . . .[11]

Nero's mediation in transforming Poppea from Diana the chaste
huntress to Diana the devil's agent is explicated in a second traditional allusion, a development of the circle imagery posited by Sylvius and Otho in their opening discussion of the Roman court as a
darkened "Orb" (I. i. 40). In Act II Otho clarifies the figure when he
tries to dissuade Poppea from joining this court:

> . . . 'tis a fatal Circle;
> Upon whose Magick skirts, a thousand Devils,
> In Chrystal forms sit tempting innocence,
> And becken early Virtue from its Center.   (ii. 20–23)

Lee's frame of reference is the occult practice by which a "master" stands within a circle and through conjuration traps underworld spirits (i.e., fallen angels) in crystal stones. Here is Reginald Scot's account of the incantation to be used: "*O Sitrael, Malantha, Thamaor, Falaur,* and *Sitrami* . . . I doo conjure . . . you . . . by him which did cast you out of paradise. . . .*" It is as if Poppea, her "innocence" tempted by Nero's "Devils," becomes one of the "Chrystal forms" in which the evil conjurer entraps another demon; for once thus possessed, says Scot, "the christall" is turned "blacke."[12] Her belated attempt to use Britannicus as a mode of reentry into virtue's realm—"Within this circle let me ever grow" (IV. iii. 52)—is ignored.

This brings us to the second subplot, the story of Britannicus and those who share his orb of virtue. Together, they represent the key aspects of that ideal court circle envisioned by Sylvius at the beginning of the play, and as each is murdered, removing another impediment to Nero's expanding fireball, the imagery depicts an increasingly infernal landscape in the place where Rome's celestial glory once shone. The first to go are Agrippina and Seneca, the moral and philosophical spokesmen upon whom Nero has relied for guidance. "Pilot of the will . . . guide oth' mind" (II. i. 10), a Roman citizen's comment on the dead Seneca, also describes Agrippina, from whose "moral talk" (I. ii. 22) Nero joyfully liberates himself. Without their rational influence—"thou dost all reason kill," Seneca had told Nero (I. ii. 70)—the emperor finds himself in the psychological state later experienced by Poppea: "lost in Honours Labyrinth" with "no clew to guide me, but my own desire" (III. ii. 28–29). The subsequent murders of Octavia and Cyara, representing nuptial and divine virtue respectively, expand the benighting of Rome's court. Through the visionary lens of madness, Britannicus sees what is happening. To kill Octavia is to quench one of virtue's "Stars" (I. ii. 30; II. iii. 175), and to lose Cyara is to be denied the light of transcendent virtue (II. iii. 53, 61; IV. i. 55–56).

The remaining impediment to Nero's expanding field of black energy is Britannicus himself, the personification of civic virtue. Nero calls him "that bold Controller of my will" (II. iii. 82), but to the other

characters he is clearly the true "Sun" (II. iii. 110—with the implication of heir) of Rome and, thus, Nero's antithesis. If Nero is hell's
offspring, Britannicus is "the God's great Masterpiece" (II. iii. 75); if
the one is a sorcerer violating nature's laws, the other is nature's "darling" (IV. i. 124). The ultimate collision of these two spheres of influence—and of the two subplots—is marked by the appearance of two
ghosts, the one advising Britannicus from heaven, the other stoking
Nero's rage from hell. When Poppea attempts to "cure" (IV. iii. 49)
evil by giving herself to Britannicus, he is warned by Cyara's ghost to
avoid the "Sorceress" and her "Rode to Hell" (IV. iii. 59, 62). But
exactly the opposite policy is urged on Nero in the next scene, where
the ghost of Caligula, an equally licentious and deranged emperor,
demands vengeance on all Rome for conspiring to assassinate him:

> Nero, Act thou, what can't be done by me,
> Thy Genius, I, will aid thy cruelty:
> . . . I stroak thy troubled sense;
> All poyson Hell contains I do dispense. (IV. iv. 19–22)

This, together with a report that the plebians have attacked his palace, doubles the intensity of Nero's diabolical passions ("rage . . .
burns within me," IV. iv. 34), and in resonantly symbolic language
he orders the incineration of Rome itself. The "black Night" of his
evil that has already engulfed the city shall be made "into a golden
Day" by his infernal rage (IV. iv. 60).

That the burning of Rome is to be equated with the madding and
poisoning of Britannicus is indicated by two means. First, Nero's
curse on Rome at the end of Act IV—"bright Ruin, with a noise shall
swallow all" (iv. 63)—echoes the last line of a soliloquy spoken earlier
by Britannicus as he mused on insanity and death: "Time, and dark
Chaos, will devour us all" (IV. iii. 22). Second, the twin fates of Rome
and Britannicus develop simultaneously. Just as the city, whose ar-
chitectural order symbolizes the last vestiges of Roman glory, is swallowed by the "black Night" of Nero's chaotic evil, only to be consumed again by the "Bright Ruin" of his bestial passion; so the man
whose virtue is Rome's personal equivalent is first darkened by insanity ("Wrapt round with clouds," IV. i. 14) and then destroyed by the
fire of poison. As the final act opens, both Rome and Britannicus are
dying in flames: "Fire, fire, I'm all one flame . . . / . . . O my breath
is Brimstone" (V. i. 1–2).

IV   *The Madnesses of Political Reality*

Although three more scenes remain, the deaths of Britannicus and of the city end the play. It is a play about the triumph of evil, not about the reinstatement of virtue, even if the villains now expire in quick succession—Poppea, Petronius, Nero—and the rebels under Galba take control. The emphasis throughout has been on what G. Wilson Knight aptly calls "the psychology of power,"[13] in this case a diabolical power that Lee associates with moral degeneracy and progressive insanity. As Nero becomes more and more deranged, both morally and psychologically, the satellite society over which he rules becomes "darker" and more chaotic. The association of psychology with moral and political status was an established convention by Lee's time, as a cursory perusal of Christopher Marlowe, Shakespeare, the Jacobeans, and John Ford can easily demonstrate. Lee's variation on the convention lies in his charting the related developmental patterns of two forms of political insanity, both shown to be self-destructive and both interpreted using cosmic symbolism.

Thus, there are two madmen in *Nero*. One, the sovereign himself, is mad in the stock medieval sense of the term; his moral corruption is sponsored by the underworld, so that he is considered hell's offspring, a beast-man emitting dark fire and misusing nature. The other is Britannicus, the political idealist and lover, whose insanity is of a type frequently depicted in Renaissance literature: a form of divine respite for the frustrated lover and patriot, bestowing on him extrasensory perception of the tragic nature of Rome's catastrophe. Nero is descended from the demonically possessed Saul of 1 Kings 16: 14–23, from Herod the frenzied persecutor of John Lydgate's *Fall of Princes* and Chester Cycle, from the insanely vicious Nero that was "a medieval commonplace"[14]—as in *The South English Legendary* and *Festial: A Collection of Homilies*—and from such Renaissance mad sinners as D'Amville (Cyril Tourneur's *The Atheist's Tragedy*) and Ferdinand (John Webster's *The Duchess of Malfi*). Britannicus, on the other hand, combines the melancholia of an unrequited poet-lover—a Petrarch, Ronsard, or Samuel Daniel—with the moral clairvoyance of Hamlet.[15]

That Lee should include both forms of madness in the same work is remarkable, because in later plays he would confine his interest to essentially one form, the diabolical sort, showing how a character's better nature is corrupted by evil passions within his own psyche. In

The Rival Queens (1676/7), for example, Alexander the Great goes
destructively insane as he gives over martial heroism and rational
leadership in favor of selfish stimulation through sex, wine, and luxury. And the titular character of *Caesar Borgia* (1679), driven vi-
ciously mad by jealousy and power-mongering, literally sells his soul
to the devil. But the divine madness of Britannicus bears no progeny
in Lee's subsequent works (possibly excepting *Lucius Junius Brutus,*
1680), because he would never again see the need to recreate such a
negative symbol for the political realities he observed in contemporary England. If the moral depravity of a sovereign manifests itself in
an increasingly insane and contagious destructiveness, then the passive, nonvigilant virtue of influential subjects becomes a self-destructive madness in itself, for in the face of such blatant evil its inertia is
both irrational and nonempirical. While Britannicus goes pensively
mad, Nero's expanding sphere of evil envelops Rome's orb of virtue,
psychological and spiritual chaos undermines its order, and what began as a chain of private murders becomes a public disaster.

The lesson could not have been lost on a generation of spectators
who feared civil chaos above all. In a recent article, David S. Kastan
convincingly argues that "implicit parallels of situation" between
Nero's Rome and Charles II's England gave political overtones to the
play.[16] By 1674 many Englishmen had become disenchanted with
their monarch because of his moral laxness, his failure to defeat the
Dutch, his resistance to anti-Catholic and anti-French sentiments,
and his systematic attempts to free his power from parliamentary control. They tended to express their disenchantment by ascribing his
behavior to moral depravity and by comparing his court to that of
decadent Rome:

> As Nero once, with harp in hand, survey'd
> His flaming Rome and, as that burn'd, he play'd,
> So our great Prince, when the Dutch fleet arriv'd,
> Saw his ships burn'd and, as they burn'd, he swiv'd.[17]

In the context of "the correspondence that most had been condi-
tioned to see between Nero's Rome and Restoration England,"[18]
Nero himself becomes the embodiment not of Charles II but of those
negative aspects of Charles II which were being widely criticized in
the early 1670s. Britannicus embodies, in an equally exaggerated
form, the kind of blind obedience mandated by the belief that kings

are God's anointed stewards. His name, and the fact that Lee violently distorted history to place him in the play at all, suggest that his
injudicious loyalty is that of the British people in 1674, and so his
madness becomes a warning to Lee's contemporaries.

The psychological dilemma in which Britannicus finds himself is
the one felt by all Englishmen who espoused the concept of absolute
sovereignty. On the one hand, there is the impulse to pledge,

> When e're I rise against that Sacred head
> In thought, may loads of Thunder strike me dead.
> You are . . . Rome's Emperour.   (I. i. 107–09)

But on the other hand, there is the dismaying reality of the sovereign
himself, whose dark evil progressively snuffs out virtue after virtue.
Caught between the two, Britannicus becomes melancholy (II. iii.
167–76), then musingly mad (III. i. 93–132), and speaks the truths
that in a mad world only mad men know: "Honour is stabb'd, and all
the Virtues bleed" (IV. i. 16).

His death, coinciding suggestively with the burning of Rome,
warns of the consequences of national passivity towards a depraved
monarch. Yet active rebellion is not therefore offered as a viable alternative, for the attitude of Drusillus—"some noble Roman" should
be "dangerously good" and "kill this Tyrant" (II. i. 17–19)—and of
the conspirators, Piso and Otho, does not lead to a messianic kingdom
to replace the one ruled over by the powers of evil. Lee's pessimism
runs deep at this stage of his career. As Nero expires, a suicide—
consumed, as it were, by his own fire—Otho hopefully asserts that
"Rome's Sacred Genius" may "now look forth again" from her
"shroud" (V. iii. 239–40). But when Piso announces the triumphal
entry of Galba as the new emperor, he proclaims him "now made a
God" (V. iii. 247). Thus, he foreshadows not the new sovereign's
humble enactment of moral and spiritual principles but rather his
reassumption of Nero-like vanity. Rome would have to suffer new
disorders under Galba and his successors before a Vespasian would
restore organized peace.[19]

Hero as Endangered Species: Sophonisba, or Hannibal's Overthrow. A Tragedy (1675)

IN charting the modulation of high heroic drama into something resembling genuine tragedy, we can hardly afford to overlook Nathaniel Lee's first smash hit. That it usually is passed over suggests that most commentators have uncritically accepted impressionistic or satiric responses to the play—responses like those of the Earl of Rochester, Henry Fielding, and Sir Adolphus Ward, all of whom felt Lee had unforgivably distorted history into an extravaganza of ranting lovesickness. The most recent historian of Restoration drama, Robert D. Hume, continues this negative trend by reiterating the opinions of Dryden and Gerard Langbaine: Lee fails to unify his two plots and sacrifices artistry to please the ladies with emotion-freighted love scenes.[1]

Such unsympathetic reactions are not really counteracted by the enthusiasm of Lee's biographer, Roswell G. Ham, the sane pronouncements of Allardyce Nicoll, or the historical perspective of Eugene Waith, for their comments turn out to be misleading, too general, or inconclusive as they regard Lee's artistic achievement. Ham is patently wrong in classifying this play as an exemplar of the "heroic formula" that dramatizes superhuman valor and desperate love ending in "the conflict of great duties."[2] And in trying to fasten a positive judgment on Lee's expression of powerful emotions, Nicoll merely perpetuates the impressionism of Langbaine and Fielding.[3] To Waith, it is true, we owe provocative insights into Sophonisba's character as Lee interprets it—she combines Jean Mairet's death-defying lover with Pierre Corneille's (and John Marston's) stoically patriotic martyr and thus evokes both pity and admiration. But Waith unhappily confines his attention to the love affairs and mostly ignores "Hannibal's Overthrow" in the military and political sense.[4]

The result is that we so far have no firm sense of the play's controlling theme or structural design, even though Lee himself urges us to notice these aspects above all. First performed in 1675, the play seems to have been revived at Oxford in 1680/81, while the court awaited developments in the parliamentary session called there by the king. Charles had hoped to cool down exclusionist passions in the House of Commons by freeing it from influence by London's fanatical mobs.[5] Dryden's new Prologue places the play in this politically tense context—"none e're cry'd us down,/ But who dislik'd both Bishop and a Crown" (11. 27–28)—yet Lee's Epilogue scrupulously avoids political innuendo, stressing instead what he finds wanting in earlier responses to the play: its artistry. Just as Charles uses Oxford as a refuge from irrational politics, so Lee is glad to be "Free from the partial Censure of the Town,/ Where senseless Faction runs the Poet down" (11. 5–6) and to rely on "this Learn'd Audience" (1.1) who, knowing the historical and literary originals of his plot and characters, will impartially assess his witty "Copy" and "Crown the Artist with deserved Bayes" (11. 16–17). In particular, he can expect the scholars, faculty, and courtiers to note his complex adaptation of the "Loves" of Ovid and Catullus and the "Labours" of Aeneas and Achilles (11. 33–35).

In combination, the Prologue and Epilogue urge the reader to see *Sophonisba* as a work of art having sympathetic relevance to the established hierarchy of king and bishops. Specifically, we are to be sensitive to Lee's way of ringing variations on earlier versions (in history and literature) of his story and to his use of different kinds of love (Ovidian, Catullan) and valor (Homeric, Virgilian). There is no suggestion here of an heroic formula, no stress on spectacle and emotion for their own sakes, and no special appeal to a feminine audience. In fact, the female characters in the play are mentioned not as emasculating or enchanting sex objects but as inspirers of "Idea's" of different kinds of love (Epilogue, 1.23).

No scholar or critic seems to have followed up these implications. Eric Rothstein has come as close to the mark as any by noting that in *Sophonisba* "heroic self-aggrandizement" is diluted as heroic traits are divided among three leading characters. He also senses that instead of using the action to bring out the established integrity of these heroes and to reconcile private and public commitments, Lee shows his characters responding plausibly to events and learning that man's deepest desires are unrealizable in public life.[6] What Rothstein suggests here, and what a fresh examination of the play reveals, is that *Sophonisba* employs heroic conventions to study heroism itself in a context that is relevant to contemporary political life—a context of sociopolitical changes driven by Providence. Thus, Lee's artistry involves, first, selecting and recombining actions, characters, themes, and conventions, from a well-known body of history, romance, and drama and, second, representing these materials in such a way as to comment movingly on the problem of heroic leadership in "modern" life. Furthermore, if Dryden's Prologue is supposed to convey an attitude congenial to Lee, then we can expect this contemporary commentary to be pro-Establishment in some way.

I   *Plot from Sources*

William Van Lennep and Eugene Waith[7] have mentioned Lee's variations on his sources, but neither attempts to connect the variations—which both allow to be happy ones—to theme and design. A brief summary of the double plot will prepare the way for a new analysis. The first plot line involves Hannibal of Carthage, who vows to continue the war with Rome that his father trained him to prosecute. He regrets, however, the military defections, political delays and chicanery, and his own amorous procrastination, which have turned the tide of battle against him. When his spies return with glowing reports of Rome's splendid legions and when supernatural phenomena portend catastrophe, he orders his priests to consult the gods about prospects. Meanwhile, his mistress, Rosalinda, a Roman lady thought to be Scipio's captive, has persuaded the young and love-sick Massina, nephew to the Numidian king who supports Rome, to help gain her freedom. When they appear in Hannibal's tent, he misinterprets their alliance and orders the youth imprisoned, but he quickly relents when Rosalinda reconfirms her constancy. Massina, however, has been made to understand that she prefers Hannibal's veteran heroism to his youthful passion, and he stabs himself to death in despair. Hannibal regards the suicide as an ominous sign of irrational forces ranged against him and proceeds to interrogate the priestesses about the designs of fate. When they foresee an ambiguous standoff between him and Scipio, but envision Rosalinda's death, Hannibal decides to negotiate a peace, if possible, to delay a climactic battle until the signs are more propitious.

In the parallel plot, Massinissa, king of Numidia, is melancholy about losing his Carthaginian mistress, Sophonisba, to a Numidian rival, Syphax, who now moves against Rome in league with her father, the Carthaginian general Asdrubal. Scipio, Consul of Rome, persuades Massinissa to reassume an heroic posture and to attack Syphax at Cirta, capture Sophonisba, and join the Roman legions against Hannibal at Zama. After killing Syphax in personal combat, Massinissa first grimly and obediently orders Sophonisba bound, but then gives in to her charms as she convinces him she never consummated the marriage with Syphax that her father had commanded. He arranges to marry her immediately, violating both Scipio's orders and his own loyalty to Rome. Upon confronting the newlyweds, Scipio accuses Sophonisba of sorcery and places her under house arrest until he and Massinissa deal with Hannibal.

As the two plots converge, Scipio courteously rejects Hannibal's peace offering and the two armies meet in battle. A series of staccato scenes impressionistically shows that Massinissa's forces push back all but the veteran wing of Hannibal's army, while Hannibal himself nearly defeats Scipio in a duel until reinforcements beat him off. Meanwhile, Rosalinda, dressed as a soldier, is fatally wounded, and when Hannibal finds her, he curses the gods and prepares to resign himself to fate. His aides, however, persuade him to continue as the one heroic prop to a falling kingdom, and he promises a new campaign. Having been victorious on the whole, Scipio now orders Massinissa to bury his unpatriotic and unmanly passion, and Massinissa pretends to obey by having Sophonisba executed. As soon as he is alone with her, however, they pledge eternal love, drink poison, and die in a last embrace. Scipio is thunderstruck by their act and determines to stop the war, retire from public life, and hereafter bend all his waking thoughts to the subject of death.

A potent argument for the play's artistic integrity is that Lee rather deliberately constructs this action by adding his own innovations to elements carefully selected from diverse literary and historical sources. The Massinissa-Sophonisba plot seems inspired mainly by John Marston's *The Wonder of Women, or The Tragedy of Sophonisba* (c. 1606) and by Jean Mairet's (1634) and Pierre Corneille's (1663) plays, both entitled *Sophonisbe*. As in Mairet, Lee's Sophonisba pitiably and desperately loves Massinissa; Massinissa kills Syphax and thus avoids a bigamous marriage; and both Massinissa and Sophonisba commit suicide rather than compromise their love. As in Marston and Corneille, Lee's Sophonisba remains consistently true to Carthage and to her own proud freedom from Roman captivity. Additionally, there is an echo of Shakespeare's *Antony and Cleopatra* in the closing scene, where Sophonisba, disdaining Roman chains, and Massinissa, rejecting worldly acquisitions and status, give all for love. The Hannibal-Rosalinda plot owes a good deal to Roger Boyle's romance, *Parthenissa* (1654). There "The Story of Izadora and Perolla" tells of a love triangle in which Hannibal vainly attempts to woo Izadora away from her beloved Perolla. In Lee's version, it is just the other way around: Massina (Perolla) tries to win Rosalinda (Izadora) from Hannibal. To Boyle, Lee also seems to owe the scene of confrontation between Hannibal and Scipio, for the equivalent scene in Livy, the historical source for both authors, is not so clearly echoed in Lee's language.

This scene begins the convergence of the two plots, a phenomenon that distinguishes Lee's play from the work of his chief predecessors. The only earlier literary work that unites the two subplots in a meaningful whole is Thomas Nabbes's *Hannibal and Scipio* (1637, possibly revived 1671), but if Lee knew this play, he owes no apparent debt to its details. Livy, of course, recounts events involving Hannibal as well as Massinissa, Sophonisba, and Scipio, but he records Sophonisba's suicide as occurring before the battle of Zama, and he avoids the kinds of parallels between leaders, heroes, and lovers that Lee chiefly exploits. However, in using Philemon Holland's translation of Livy (1600, with many later printings), Lee may have adapted to his own uses the historian's mention of a certain beautiful and naive nephew of Massinissa (Massina in the play), and he could have transformed the historical Scipio's momentary passion for a young Spanish girl into the fictional Consul's repressed yearning for Rosalinda. Almost certainly, Lee used Livy as his source for the account of Hannibal's previous adventures and for the prodigy in which two suns appear in a blood-red sky amidst lightning and thunder.[8]

II   *Of Heroes and Statesmen*

To examine Lee's design in adapting his sources is to discover a fresh dramatic assessment of the conventional subjects of heroic drama, love and valor. The Hannibal-Rosalinda plot shows the frustration of old-style heroism in an alien sociopolitical environment. The self-indulgent confusion of purpose within Carthage, created by "Pride" (I. i. 73) and the "wicked policy" (I. i. 33) of statesmen like Hanno, has made Hannibal's fatherland unworthy of his patriotism, so that he is thrown back on three deeper motives for heroic strife against Rome: "natural hate to Rome" taught by his father (I. i. 92); "love" for the captive Rosalinda (I. i. 93); and a personal sense of honor that regards martial prowess as innately glorious (one must "perish bravely, though unfortunate," II. ii. 99). Thus, he is not a civic leader, champion of his country, as G. Wilson Knight would have it,[9] but rather an isolated powerhouse like the early Almanzor of *The Conquest of Granada*.

Throughout the play he is described as a natural force contending gloriously with other natural forces. He recalls how "Nature" was startled to see him conquer the Alps (I. i. 10) and rush "torrent like" down to "Romes proud Walls" (V. i. 5–6), and when supernatural omens intimate that fortune is against him, he sees himself as "Earth" thundering "back upon the sky" (II. ii. 106). Rosalinda sees him as "some rowling Whale" that "dashes the frighted Nations from his side" as he becomes both "the Ocean's Lord" and "Tirant of the Land" (III. i. 70–75). By the end of the play he has been deserted not only by Carthage but also, unwillingly, by Rosalinda, whose death in battle confirms the prophecy that fortune now favors Rome. Yet after a brief lament he readily accepts Maherbal's (and Bomilcar's) heroic philosophy that he must exercise, albeit to no earthly purpose, his god-given valor (V. i. 189–96), for it is the cosmically ordained, and therefore "natural," course of action: honor, says Hannibal, "shall like the Ocean in a Tempest wake./ Wee'l pass new Alpes, new Consuls overthrow" (V. i. 224–25).

The causes of "Hannibal's Overthrow" are both providential or primary—a subject to be touched upon later—and sublunar, or secondary. Among the secondary causes are his pride and his amorous weakness. The first is revealed by his boasting of godlike powers in battle (I. i. 10, 56–58 ; IV. i. 168–70) and godlike passion in love (II. ii. 21), and by his vows to force either gods or demons to foretell his destiny (III. ii. 170–79; IV. i. 122–28). The second is a recurring theme in his verbal self-recriminations: "I stood almost Immortal Man, / Till Love . . . / And pointed Beauty through my Armour ran" (III. ii. 116-18, and see I. i. 103–105). It is an important part of Lee's artistic purpose, however, to make Rosalinda oppose the "soft Contagion" (II. ii. 11) she herself has passed to Hannibal. Like the Sophonisba in Marston's play, she reproaches Hannibal for the amorous weakness that prompts jealousy (III. ii. 85–86). She subordinates the kind of transcendent, youthful passion offered by Massina, as well as loyalty to her country (see III. i. 22–23), to a more lasting commitment to "the best and bravest Man in War" and to the immortal glory conferred by such a commitment (II. i. 232–40). In Rosalinda, Hannibal finds a kindred spirit, another devotee of natural prowess and cosmic honor, and he pays her tribute "As Rocks to Seas, or stubborn Oaks to wind" (III. ii. 113). Thus, Hannibal and Rosalinda represent what happens in the world of the play when one gives all for honor in the high heroic sense. Both end by pursuing prowess and glory without the social nourishment to be derived from state or conventional love.

They are contrasted with Sophonisba and Massinissa, another non-pragmatic pair, who give all for love, rather than for honor. If Rosalinda, a Roman lady, scorns country and courtly love, in order to join her civil enemy in seeking martial glory, Sophonisba, a Carthaginian, scorns country and martial honor, in order to join her "official" enemy in seeking a transcendent passion. The effect of Rosalinda's determination is to "save" Hannibal from love in order to promote heroism. But the effect of Sophonisba's determination is to "save" Massinissa from heroism in order to promote love. Both couples, through these higher loyalties, become alienated from social commitments.

Despite her titular prominence, Sophonisba is much less visible (and audible) than Massinissa, Hannibal, or Scipio. She is, as Waith rightly observes, a clearly conceived combination of Mairet's enthusiastic lover ("all one desire," III. iv. 151) and Corneille's proud individualist ("Bondage is a load I cannot bear," IV. i. 224). Massinissa, however, is more prominent in the design and is a more complex personality than his mistress. Like Hannibal, he is torn between love and valor, but his ultimate choice is the opposite of Hannibal's . Until feeling Sophonisba's charms, he was an heroic natural force, much like Hannibal, and revelled in his prowess for its own sake. During the Battle of Zama, when he briefly recaptures this lost heroism, he fights like "a Hawke" (V. i. 83) or "as hurricans toss showers, and scatter hail" (V. i. 79). But in general he deteriorates from an heroic force to be reckoned with—"I had a Soul cou'd storms outwear," I. i. 144—to the victim of both psychological and external tempests: from the moment he held Sophonisba he felt "like a dying man" (I. i. 239), and he now begins to "sink in th' abyss of thought" (III. iv. 107; and see I. i. 156–59, 284–89; II. i. 14), "the Tempest of . . . mind" (II. i. 132), "Love's tempestuous Sea" of passion (I. i. 316). He becomes increasingly less fit to cope with "New storms of War" (I. i. 263). Throughout this degeneration he expresses his fate in nautical terms, as if Sophonisba were a siren with appeal "as powerful as Circes" (III. iii. 23, 30), and he an Odyssean mariner drowning in her charms (V. i. 413–16). Or he sees himself as a wrecked vessel's merchant-owner, who grasps the one casket of his love and "fearless, shoots himself into the Main" (IV. i. 251–56).

Massinissa's earthly failure is clearly a product of emasculating love, but, as in the case of Hannibal's overthrow, there is also a higher cause—providential design. Sophonisba's enchanting eyes are both earthly snares and "fatal fires" acting on behalf of "crosser Stars (II. i. 14–18). The adverse fate she unwittingly serves involves a larger sociopolitical change that helps account for both Massinissa's and Hannibal's failures as hero-lovers. The nature of this change is sensed by Massinissa in his first dialogue with Menander and Lelius. Under the influence of love-melancholy, he begins to question the virtue of martial heroism. Is it not merely "lust of Power," "A strong temptation, to do bravely ill" (I. i. 132–33)? And does it not result in senseless carnage that is at least as undesirable as the emasculation consequent to love (I. i. 319–22)? Menander responds that Massinissa has confused the truly "gallant souls Ambition" for "mystick Empire" (I. i. 138, 125) with the bestial and mercenary lust for power that makes empire a mere "Bawd" (I. i. 139). It is the difference, he says, between "Mirth" and "lewdness" in a bride, or between spiritualized self-denial and "Pride" in a "Vestal Virgin" (I. i. 140–41). What Menander is suggesting is that Massinissa is beginning to lose sight of "true" heroism, not only because he is love-blind, but also because there is less and less opportunity for it to emerge in a world increasingly dominated by a more pragmatic and earthly sort of ambition.

This new heroism (and the new world it implies) is fate's main operative in the play. It envelops both Massinissa and Hannibal, preventing either from achieving a vital fusion of high heroism and high love. Its personification is Scipio, the Roman Consul, just as Hannibal personifies old-style heroism and Massinissa old-style love. Scipio's values, and thus the definition of a new wave in the providential history of heroism, are most clearly enunciated in his dialogues with Massinissa. If these values seem less appealing and admirable than the superhuman courage or passion of Hannibal and Massinissa, they are at least not exactly the venal and bestial traits described by Menander. Scipio is not chiefly interested in the "Bawd of Empire"; he does not seek material self-indulgence. Yet his goals are certainly more pragmatic and mundane than those of his antagonists. What he wants to achieve is social and psychological order in the earthly kingdom, and he is not sensitive to the more transcendental aims of heroes and lovers. To conquer kingdoms as a test of personal valor is, he tells Massinissa, "to imitate great Heroes dead" (II. i. 83). Instead, he urges, conquer "for Rome, not for your sake" (IV. i. 281). And as for transcendent love, that is an illusion, mere "passion's heat" (IV. i. 332), just as Sophonisba is not a priceless jewel but rather a witch (IV. i. 367) or the carrier of some contagious mental disease (V. i. 241–42). Better to govern one's passions, "quench th'inglorious ardour of your mind" (II. i. 86–88), and seek the kind of fame that follows upon exemplary self-control, friendship, and the patriotic defense of imperial order. To the love-struck Numidian this is bland fare, and he willfully rejects and misinterprets the way of life it seems to offer:

> Let melancholy Monarchs Councel take,
> Wed by advice and sullen Nuptials make.
> But I prefer [Sophonisba] . . .
> To all the wealth that Earth or Seas can hold,
> . . . .
> Spight of proud Rome and all her haughty men.   (III. iv. 238–43)

Nevertheless, just as he has seen fate in Sophonisba's attractions, he perceives that Scipio's way is somehow the way of the gods: "O Rome! Oh Heaven: both equally my foes" (V. i. 310). Scipio, likewise, understands that he is carrying forward a providential design—"With me contending against fate you strive" (IV. i. 294)—and if Massinissa sees himself as drowning in a psychological and moral tempest, Scipio compares himself to the "Star fix'd" that commands and controls such earthly disturbances with the irresistibility of destiny (II. i. 99, and see V. i. 39–41).

If Massinissa's tragedy is most fully defined in his verbal exchanges with Scipio, Hannibal's tragedy is delineated as he interprets, with Rosalinda, the full significance of his military "dialogue" with the Roman Consul. In each case, the conclusion is the same: Scipio is heaven's new hero, and Roman order is to become fate's new steward. Of all the characters Hannibal is the most inquisitive about the providential implications of what is taking place. In his opening dialogue with Bomilcar and Maherbal he shares their feeling that time is now ripe for the "Gods" to give a decisive victory to Carthage or Rome, "As each might take up all the care of Heaven" (I. i. 86–91), and he tacitly accepts their nostalgia for "a Time . . . / When victory on Hills of Heroes sat" (I. i. 59–60). To such old-time heroism, he explicitly contrasts what he calls Scipio's "Civil brav'ry" (II. ii. 36), and he is brought to admit that while "fortune once did on our Genius shine" (V. i. 25), now she seems to have shifted her allegiance to a new kind of leadership. The dying words of Rosalinda are pitiably accurate: "The Roman glory [i.e., Scipio's star] shines too fatally bright" (V. i. 178). In his most pessimistic mood, upon witnessing the love-sick suicide of Massina, Hannibal bitterly resigns himself: "The bus'ness of our life's a senseless thing," and we are mere "Sport for the Gods" (III. ii. 146–50). But at the play's end he accepts heaven's opposition as perhaps his greatest challenge, an opportunity to display his heroism on its most cosmic and glorious level: "I could the summons meet of hell or Heaven . . . " (V. i. 204).

Appropriately, it is to Hannibal, the transcendent hero, and not to the pragmatic and temperate Scipio, that the designs of fate are revealed through supernatural omens. As usual, Lee employs his prodigies carefully, making their spectacular effects symbolize key aspects of plot or theme. In Act II Hannibal witnesses two suns, which become two gigantic warriors wearing diamond-studded armor, locked in battle while black demons drum hollow clouds and blow trumpets inlaid with sunbeams. Mountains are buried, household deities sweat, temples drop their garlands, a wolf and wild boar spread carnage through the Carthaginian army, and voices cry "Carthage is fal'n" (II. ii. 56–83 and stage directions). Perhaps the wolf and boar are Carthage's own self-destructive politicians, while the two warrior-suns symbolize the natural opposition that exists between Hannibal's heroic valor and Scipio's civil bravery. The prediction of defeat for Carthage foreshadows the actuality and drives Hannibal to seek more detailed prophecies, a determination that is intensified by what he feels is the senseless death of Massina: thus, he must "know to what good or ill this lifes design'd" and will go "for the great secret to the Gods" (III. ii. 170–79). What he learns there, through the blood-sacrificing priestesses in Bellona's temple, is that Rome will prevail over Carthage, even though Hannibal himself will survive "spight of fortune and fate: / And the Gods that oppose" (IV. i. 50–81). When this fails to satisfy him, he demands further details, this time from the underworld, and is shown a dreadful vision of Rosalinda dying. When events confirm all these predictions, Hannibal readily perceives it—"Dire Goddess of war, / Too true . . . thy presages" (V. i. 155–56)—and girds himself for the ultimate heroism in combat against fate herself.

III *"Modern" Heroism*

It should be fairly evident now that *Sophonisba* is no formulaic heroic play and that its two story-lines are both clearly conceived and well knit into a meaningful whole. Instead of using action and utterance to figure forth some admirable idea of greatness, Lee dramatizes the struggle of alternative kinds of heroism and love to survive the unfolding of a new sociopolitical order. He draws our attention to this central concern when, in the Epilogue, he asks the readers and auditors not to be surprised if he embodies various types of love (from that of Catullus to that of Ovid) and heroism (from Homeric to Virgilian). This approach to characterization was, of course, not unique to Lee, but the distinctive way in which he adapted it to his own ends is interestingly revealed by contrast to Dryden's similar technique in *The Conquest of Granada* (1670-71). There, Dryden divides heroic traits between the irregular, Herculean greatness of Almanzor and the "correct" heroic virtue of Ozmyn. As the play develops, however, the two heroic types are seen to converge as they approach—in time, place, and attitudes—their ultimate enfoldment by Ferdinand, the idealized hero-king. Thus, like most heroic plays, this one works toward a final definition of "true" heroism, and all the alternatives—including unheroic variations like Zulema, Abdalla, and Abdelmelech—sooner or later become subsumed in the controlling idea, or succumb, usually through death, to its enveloping power. Similarly, the various gradations of love/lust—from Lyndaraxa's Hobbesian desire for power (and Zulema's desire for carnal pleasure), to Almahide's agonized balance of conflicting commitments, to Benzayda's ideally constant devotion—are dramatized to show the definitive emergence of some ideal combination, in love, of Christian and pagan virtues, an ideal the lovers approach in the person of Isabella, the perfect lover-queen.

Not so in *Sophonisba*. Lee's characters are not choreographed to move symbolically toward some ideal reconciliation of opposite traits. Neither pair of lovers—Hannibal/Rosalinda or Massinissa/Sophonisba—manage to effect a relationship that can grow with the changing times. As the times change, so do the requirements for heroism and love—and with a vengeance. Isabella gains her husband's consent to the proposition that intense love will breed intensely patriotic heroism in the new Christian kingdom. In Lee's play Scipio can agree to nothing of the sort. He discourages Massinissa's amorous passion, and, when he himself once feels moved by a woman's charms (Rosalinda's), his response is to resist with all the self-control of his "yet unshaken Soul" which "No force of War, or Love cou'd ever wound" (III. i. 28–29). Like Ferdinand and his Christian state, Scipio and the Roman order he serves prevail in the world of the play, but this dominance is not achieved, in Scipio's case, by inspiring allegiance in key opponents. The Roman Empire displaces its opposition, and there is no simultaneous fusing of diverse strengths among the combatants and no purging of villainous weaknesses.

This is because *Sophonisba* is not an heroic play but rather a dramatic paradigm for the tragedy of heroism in the "modern" world. Far more significantly than it looks back to *The Conquest of Granada*, it looks forward to *All for Love* (1677); indeed, we may regard it as a source for the later play. To see *All for Love* as the heir to tendencies in *Aureng-Zebe* (1675)[10] is perhaps a less instructive exercise than to see it as an adaptation of Shakespeare along lines strongly suggested by Lee's two recent successes, *Sophonisba* and *The Rival Queens* (1676/7). As David Vieth has noted, Dryden must have been influenced by the following elements in *The Rival Queens*: its casting, blank verse, emphasis on a clash of cultures (Persia/Macedonia, Egypt/Rome), and structural focus on a flawed hero (Alexander, Antony) as related to his antithesis (Cassander, Alexas), rival lovers (Statira/Roxana, Cleopatra/Octavia), stoical counsellor (Clytus, Ventidius), and effeminate friend (Hephestion, Dolabella).[11] Yet some of these same elements were also present in the earlier Lee play, along with other aspects of theme, characterization, and structure that suggest an even stronger influence on Dryden. As in *The Rival Queens*, most of the key roles in *Sophonisba* were played by actors who took equivalent parts in *All for Love*: Charles Hart, who created both Alexander and Antony, played Massinissa; Thomas Clark, the Hephestion and Dolabella of the later plays, played Massina; Michael Mohun was Hannibal, and later Clytus and Ventidius; and Elizabeth Boutell, the Rosalinda of 1681 (the Oxford revival), was later to play

Statira and Cleopatra. Moreover, the clash of cultures is as important in *Sophonisba* as in the subsequent plays. Massinissa gives up for Sophonisba not only worldly treasures but also his short-lived attempt to manacle his instinctive self, his passionate nature, in service to the Roman virtues of rational self-control and pragmatic relationships. Hence the Africans of the play—Hannibal, Massinissa, Massina, Sophonisba—are repeatedly compared to warm or tempestuous images from physical nature (storms, powerful animals, flames), while the Romans, as represented by Scipio, are imaged as cold, emotionally distant engineers of an "artificial" empire.[12]

Though we see fewer similarities between *Sophonisba* and *All for Love* than between Dryden's play and *The Rival Queens*, there is a qualitatively more significant thematic and structural principle in the earlier Lee play that Dryden makes central to his design. This is the sense of an inexorable, not wholly sympathetic sociopolitical force pressing upon the more passionate characters. In both plays, this force is conceptualized as Rome and is personified by a Roman leader, Scipio or Octavius, whose dominance is felt to be more psychological than martial. In the process of confronting this force, the heroic lovers in both plays—Sophonisba/Massinissa, Cleopatra/Antony—reveal similar sets of attitudes (as mentioned above, p. 49) and reject worldly status and possession in order to achieve transcendent dominion in love.

But here the likenesses, and the apparent debts, cease. Dryden's focus remains fixed with Aristotelian concentration on the agonies and suicides of his two lovers, and his other characters subserve this primary interest. Lee, on the other hand, splits his attention between the heroic lovers, Sophonisba/Massinissa, and the two lover-heroes, Rosalinda/Hannibal. Furthermore, Dryden's narrow focus necessitates keeping Octavius offstage and so transforming him into a concept and a shadowy force, while Lee brings his Roman pragmatist, Scipio, before us and uses him not only to articulate the new heroics that will succeed the "Time . . . /When victory on Hills of Heroes sat" but also to provide a structural centerpiece. In *The Rival Queens*, Alexander performs the same structural function, but the dynamics of his position are radically different. Like an old star whose own spent energy collapses inward in a self-destructive catastrophe, Alexander's weakness allows his enemies, whom he has in a sense created, to destroy him. In Lee's Scipio, however, we have a strong central figure, a star on the rise, as he depicts himself (V. i. 41), and the

consequence of his confronting opposition in Hannibal and Massinissa is *their* defeat, not his own. Alexander draws opposition inward
like a vacuum; Scipio polarizes and drives away opposed forces as his
field of energy expands. Eschewing his dull, calm determination,
Rosalinda flees to the camp of Hannibal, the excitingly tempestuous
hero; and Massinissa, rejecting Scipio's stoical attitude toward love,
moves away to join passions with Sophonisba.

As we watch the concluding battle, in which these three centers of
energy come together in a tragic catastrophe, we become provocatively aware that the play offers us no villains, no winners, no losers,
no poetic justice. There is something to approve and something to
regret in each set of combatants. Rosalinda dies nobly, but we may
wish that she had sought fuller development as a lover, instead of
giving all for honor. Hannibal is admirably determined to fight on
heroically against fate itself, yet we wish pride had not blocked out
the prospect of his injecting a little Herculean energy into the new
sociopolitical order. Massina pathetically kills himself in a fit of love-
melancholy, and we regret that he could not have learned enough
Roman stoicism to get through his despair. Massinissa achieves his
ethereal palace of love, but we cannot approve his vacillation between an honorable devotion to prowess and a passionate commitment to Sophonisba, and we regret his inability to find an earthly
solution to his dilemma. Similarly, our attitude toward Sophonisba is
mixed: her self-sacrifice seems both movingly virtuous and pathetically defeatist. Finally, we cannot help but feel repelled by Scipio's
cool politics, self-righteously balanced psyche, and verbal assaults on
"great Heroes" (II. i. 83) and "storms of Passion" (II. i. 53). Yet the
kind of virtue he represents is not unseemly, and it is certainly practical. To maintain an orderly society and to orchestrate the diverse
forces of a complex body politic, a sovereign must be self-possessed
and capable of basing decisions on reasonable and practical criteria.
Such virtues—those of a strong, patriotic manager—are to be re-
spected, if not loved.

The contemporary relevance of these mixed responses, hinted at
by Dryden in his Prologue, can be no more than just that: relevance—not specific parallel, allegory, or satire. Yet we may easily
imagine that as Charles II watched this play—not only in 1675 when
his climactic troubles were brewing as he idled with his mistresses,
but also in 1680/1 when he was about to act decisively for a change—
he sensed allusions to the present state of England. The alternative

forms of heroism and love dramatized by Lee may well have seemed to imply Charles's own choices, and the results of those choices, both personal and public, would then have had their poignancy for the Merry Monarch. What of Massinissa's deadly failure to reconcile amorous passion and participation in the great public developments of his day? Can one become a Scipio without stoically subordinating his love life and his luxuries to patriotic duty? Are the high heroics of Hannibal and his dramatic predecessors merely anachronistic, unrealizable in the modern world?

Scipio's curious closing speech raises these issues to the level of tragic vision:

> These unexpected objects [the corpses of Sophonisba and Mas-
> sinissa] . . . amaze,
> My reason . . .
> . . . .
> With Carthage peace wee'l instantly conclud,
> . . . .
> To Rome our Drooping Eagles . . . shall steer,
> When after tiresome honours wee'l repair
> To some small village . . .
> And study not to live, but how to die. (V. i. 425–34)

The effect of this lament is to shift the audience's attention from the victory of Roman arms and the ascendency of a new form of heroism, to the tragic loss of old-fashioned heroic love and honor. The loss is tragic because this new episode in providential history, this new ice age of Roman imperialism, has created an environment uncongenial to the great dinosaurs of prowess and passion; its gains are matched by losses, and a kind of blandly civilized ecology takes over the once primitively exotic terrain. Rome triumphs, but *grand amour* is extinct, and the once indomitable Hannibal desperately shakes a clenched fist at fate, while Scipio, with Charles II and the rest of the audience, leaves the theater to "study" the consequences.[13]

CHAPTER 4

Journal Entries: Gloriana, or the Court of Augustus Caesar (1675/6)

EASILY the worst of Lee's known plays is his third one. It deserves the general oblivion to which its critics have assigned it.[1] For the student of Lee as dramatist, however, *Gloriana* is worth inspecting, because it shows the writer struggling to make an artistic whole out of rather promising materials, some of which would serve him well in later, more successful efforts. In this respect, it forms a kind of bridge between the effusions of his novitiate and those mature works upon which his reputation securely rests. Its plot, characters, motifs, even its rhythms and sounds, while never fully integrated, are like so many loosely connected entries in a journal of ideas for future exploitation.

I *Disjointed Plot*

He began with sources that must have seemed full of dramatic potential.[2] From La Calprenède's romance, *Cléopâtre* (1647), he took (a) a love affair between the son of Cleopatra by Julius Caesar (Caesario) and an enchanting princess (Candace, daughter of an Ethiopian king, in La Calprenède; Gloriana,[3] daughter of Pompey, in Lee) whom he rescues from an unwelcome seducer (Tyribasus in La Calprenède; Augustus in Lee); (b) the friendship between the emperor's nephew (Marcellus) and a blue-blooded hero who has incurred the Emperor's displeasure (Coriolanus, King of Juba, in the romance; Caesario again in Lee); (c) the love-triangle involving Marcellus, his flirtatious cousin Julia, who is his wife (and the emperor's daughter), and the poet-courtier Ovid. By eliminating some of the romance's characters and assigning their key traits to others (Augustus becomes the unwelcome suitor, Caesario the friend of Marcellus), Lee achieves concentration of action, if not dramatic unity. By modifying some details using historical accounts from Suetonius and Plutarch (Julia's rumored debaucheries, Augustus' agony over his maltreatment of her) and adding a good many of his own (Narcissa and her unrequited love for Caesario, love at first sight between Caesario and Gloriana, the tragic ending) he seems to be working toward some special combination of structure and theme.

But the particular configuration that results from all this juggling of sources never really jells. As the play opens, for example, Augustus worries aloud about Julia's allegedly loose behavior, yet he soon drops this concern as his sense of competition with Caesario develops; it is picked up by Marcellus, who is also able to drop it when Julia convinces him (IV. i.) that she is after all a faithful wife. To justify their continued existence, Marcellus and Julia spend the rest of Acts IV and V defending Caesario and Gloriana against Caesar while trying to cope with Narcissa's lovesickness. In the end the audience is simply informed that Marcellus has expired in the arms of Julia, who is herself verging on death. Whether they perish out of grief over Narcissa's death or out of anxiety for Caesario is left uncertain. It is equally puzzling that Narcissa's love-melancholy is in the play at all. Her unrequited passion for Caesario has no organic connection to the main plot, which chiefly involves Caesario's fatal desire to win both Gloriana and the Roman Empire from Augustus.

II *Faulty Parallels and Contrasts*

That the main plot thus fails to subsume lesser actions may be owing to the absence of control by a central theme and dominant pattern of imagery. The greatest virtue of *Sophonisba* was its organic interconnection of plot, idea, and image; but the greatest deficiency of *Gloriana* comes from Lee's apparent inability to achieve this vital fusion of elements. Such a lapse is all the more regrettable after we notice the small constellations of motifs and tropes to which he keeps returning without ever fully integrating them into a dramatic design; the effort to unify is visible, but unity eludes his grasp. The intended central theme seems to have been the emperor's battle against darker emotions that have occasionally ruled his past and still influence his present behavior. He regards Julia's self-indulgent nature as a punishment for his own youthful licentiousness; she is the "scum of boiling Youth" (I. i. 92). Caesario and Gloriana add to his torment by reminding him of earlier aberrations, such as his usurpations from

Julius Caesar and the younger Pompey. These extravagances have, in a sense, generated the "homebred jarrs" (I. i. 2; II. i. 364; V. ii. 253) about which Augustus periodically complains.

Yet the main plot and the other important motifs and image patterns are closely enough related to this central theme to suggest that with more effort Lee could have unified his play. The emperor's irrational impulses, for example, have at least an indirect bearing on the death (or impending death) of Narcissa, Marcellus, and Julia, since without Gloriana's being held captive as a sex object Narcissa would have had no rival, and if Caesario had been rewarded for his heroism and groomed for imperial responsibilities, Marcellus would have lost no friend. Likewise, if Julia had been the offspring of contractual love, instead of promiscuous lust—"loose Julia! What strong philters did unman/Augustus from whose loins thy Spirit ran! (II. i. 236–37)—she would have been bred to respect familial duties and prudent actions. As it is, however, both she and Caesario suffer from varieties of inner turmoil that Lee could have linked (but did not) suggestively to the emperor's own anxieties. Her exclamation in Act IV, "not haunting Furies . . . can rack me more,/Than Jealousies on earth" (i. 18–19), echoes her father's laments about psychological unrest, and Caesario similarly recognizes that his difficulties are at core psychological: it is easier, he says, to win "back the revolted Universe . . ./Than but our passions conquest to begin" (II. i. 110–11).

But the parallel between Julia and Caesario is not exploited, and neither is the trait they share with Augustus, a trait with great, but likewise unexploited, potential for dramatic effectiveness. This is the feeling articulated by each that he is godlike and thus above or exempt from the very worries and moral conventions that torment him. Julia feels she is a "Consort fit for Jove" and so should be "free from cares below, as Gods above" (I. i. 206–08; and see I. i. 97–98, 142), while Caesario and Augustus see themselves as Jupiter and Saturn, respectively, engaged in a kind of cosmic rivalry that soars above human pettiness (I. i. 284–87; II. i. 40–42; V. i. 39). Caesario is particularly inventive in boasting of his divine qualities: sprung "like Hercules from Jove," "in battles big as Mars" (II. i. 13–15), a "half-god" (III. i. 94). The irony of such inflated self-images is that all three characters are defeated by the human frailties from which they claim immunity—or so Lee's unrealized purpose would seem to dictate. Caesario insists he "was always more" than a man (II. i. 17), but his heroism is humanly impetuous, and his unchecked passion for Gloriana and for power renders him unequal to the tasks of empire, as the more self-conscious Augustus informs him:

> Glory than Empire is much easier won:
> Empire's like Heav'n, which who wou'd bravely win,
> Must Giant-like . . .
> . . . Project add to Plot,
> Till huge foundation for the work be wrought:
> And as he climbs, at Stars that cross him frown,
> . . . .
> Till Majesty cries out, This, This alone
> Is he who Heav'n becomes, and fits a Throne. (IV. i. 325–35)

Yet Augustus also is but a man, and his chief advantage over Caesario is that he knows it, despite his unwillingness to act consistently on the basis of that knowledge. If Caesario fails to distinguish godlike heroism from the human struggle for empire, Augustus refuses to acknowledge that human aging is beginning to disqualify him for the godlike task of ruling the empire he has won. His fear of old age and clutching for lost youth seem to motivate both his paranoia about Caesario's claims to godhead and his absurdly forced lust for Gloriana:

> . . . am I old?
> Ye Apes of fame, ye Sparks to my full day! (I. i. 271–72)

> One balmy kiss wou'd take a year away;
> But oh the rest wou'd give me Youth again. (III. ii. 33–34)

> . . . like the old Lord of Day,
> On my red cheeks the silver Tresses play.
> I shout and drive and never feel decay. (III. ii. 163–165)

> Thou mak'st me young, nay giv'st me a new birth. (V. i. 134)

Neither Augustus nor Caesario, however, finally adjusts his behavior to an earthly scale of being. In the end, Caesario opts for immortal love: "Firmer than old Atlas" (V. ii. 146) he holds the dying Gloriana and, after receiving his own mortal wound,[4] points to her, saying, Antony-like, "Give me but this, Caesar, the world is thine" (V. ii. 206). Augustus, too, feels defeated, but by fate rather than human frailty, and he compares his defeat to that of "Hercules" (V. ii. 233).

Only Julia, among those claiming divine immunity from earthly cares, actually acquires a properly human perspective on herself. In Act I she "cannot by passion check'd nice rules obey" (I. i. 98), but in Act IV she promises Marcellus that in her breast "thou shalt sway,/ And I with gentler mind thy Laws obey" (i. 75–77). Unfortunately, Lee never makes dramatic sense of her conversion, for in Act V she is reported to be almost dead of some undisclosed emotional disease.

Through Julia, Lee introduces two other themes which, like the contrasts of god/man and youth/age, offer the reader rich dramatic prospects which are not well developed as the play progresses. The first of these is the conventional idea of appearance versus reality. In Act I Julia's father insists that "she is all counterfeit" (I. i. 109), but Mecaenus urges that "her heart from common view remov'd lies deep,/As Mines of Gold in Nature's bosom sleep" (I. i. 101–02). The "real" Julia turns out to have a heart of gold, as Mecaenus said, but this discovery seems not to be significantly related to other variations on this same experience/reality theme; nor are those other variations given consistent dramatic emphasis. The bright outward appearance of Augustus, for instance, and his claims to renewed youth and to godhead, are belied by his inner turmoil, which is like "darkness at Noon-day" (I. i. 58), just as "Heav'n abroad with Conquest crowns my Wars,/But wracks my spirit with domestick jars" (V. ii. 252–53). Yet these contradictions seem unrelated to their tragic equivalent in Gloriana. Unaware of her plan to murder Augustus when his lust drives him to her bed, Caesario finds her attired for what he inter-prets to be an amorous encounter. His response is eighty lines of rhetorical variations on the theme of appearance versus reality: her weeping "hides the Crocodile," her bosom's palace conceals a black tyrant, her soul's shrine harbors "deprav'd spirits" (V. ii. 37–116). He becomes so convinced by what appears to be true that Gloriana is driven to suicide to prove her innocence. "The dreadfull Scene was so severely wrought," she fatally groans, "Except I dy'd, I must be guilty thought" (V. ii. 139–40).

Julia also becomes an agent through which Lee starts to develop, but fails to carry through, an important theme, that of the contrast between rustic simplicity and a sophisticated court life. The theme first emerges in Act II, where Narcissa's pastoral charms—"that Spring-complexion," "sweets of Nature," "Rural face" (II. i. 162–63, 206—and the worldliness of Julia and Ovid are sharply juxtaposed: "Pow'r circling Wit, and Pleasure pressing Pride" (II. i. 273). The contrast is not sustained because Julia repents of her excesses, while Narcissa personifies throughout the play an ideal of innocence, natural beauty, and instinctive virtue which even Augustus longs for at times: a "green Palace of the peacefull grove" far from "Court-witchcraft" (III. ii. 15–20) or an animal kingdom where "all the Nobler Beasts" obey the "Kingly Lion" out of necessity (II. i. 371–73). So appealing are her personal qualities that Caesario, whose fickle behavior ultimately causes her death, belatedly determines to "plant" her in his heart (V. i. 334), though by then it is too late to save her. Ignoring warnings by Marcellus and Augustus—"back to thy Country Palaces . . . / . . . tempt not Courts for which thou wert not born" (II. i. 166–67), "go to your Garden-huswifry" (V. i. 24)—she persists in trying to exorcise Gloriana, whom she regards as an infernal influence (V. i. 167–69), only to die of love-melancholy in the moment of success.

III   *Loose Ends by Violence Tied*

The trouble is, of course, that by thus dramatizing her death, Lee achieves as little as he does by starting to juxtapose her rusticity and Julia's urban sophistication. The play is full of these loose ends. What is gained, for example, by giving both Augustus and Caesario coolheaded, scheming advisors (Mecaenus and Leander) who echo one another in counselling self-control and indirect political dealings? And why is Julia's "conversion" by Marcellus followed in the next act with Caesario's "conversion" by Narcissa? That such parallels and contrasts are never well developed is as maddening to the sympathetic reader as the author's general failure to unify plot, theme, and imagery. Is the play centered on the consequences of a sovereign's lack of self-discipline? Is it mainly about ghosts out of the past haunting the present? Is it about *hubris?* about the tragedy inherent in sophisticated court life?

Failing to subsume all these ideas in one organic theme conveyed through one complex action, Lee appears to have taken the easy way out: he injects wherever possible a reference to the general tempestuousness of human life as man acts out a mysteriously fated cosmic drama. Julia attributes her sensuality to "Fate" (I. i. 205). Caesario first vows to destroy Augustus even if opposed by "Fates," "Winds," and "Seas," since his and Gloriana's "hearts were pair'd above" (III. i. 3, 11–12, ii. 278); but soon he is asking, "Can mortals help what

Heav'n sets down shall be?" (V. i. 390). And Augustus, who complains throughout of the "Storms of State, and Hurricans of Life" (III.
ii. 14; and see V. i. 87, 95), acknowledges that "Heav'n" (V. ii. 252)
has orchestrated his fall. He chooses to go down opposing the divine
decree. Finally, Mecaenus and Agrippa attempt to fix the responsibility for all the play's catastrophes on fate: "thus when th' immortals
take, they greatly give," and "we must submit to the Divine commands" (V. ii. 213, 230).

IV Rehearsal with Strings

This kind of rhetoric does not convince Augustus, and it fails to
convince us. No aspect of the plot or assembled themes can be clarified by recourse to providential design. Here, as in the disjointed
structure, patternless imagery, and ambiguous moral posture of the
play, Lee misses his mark. Yet it is worth noting that, in undertaking
this dramatic exercise, he did manage to advance toward the more
successful works of the next eight or nine years. He would never
design so poorly again. Further experiment with the notion of For-
tune-Providence would lead to its more organic use in *Caesar Borgia*,
Lucius Junius Brutus, and *Constantine*. The psychological imbalance
of a lustful but aging king, and its stormy consequences in the family,
court, and state, would find a more congenial plot in *Mithridates*.
The confusion of appearance and reality, linked with the contrast between pastoral and courtly ways of life, would be used effectively in
Theodosius.

Several less important motifs, much of the imagery, and most of
the main characters belong to a kind of matrix of dramatic conventions that were developing in Lee's mind as he worked from play to
play. The emperor's speech distinguishing glorious heroism from the
quest for imperial power recalls Scipio's attempt to show Massinissa
the difference between rash heroics and "Civil brav'ry," just as Caesario's favoring immortal love over worldly empire echoes Massinissa's similar preference. Both of these sets of alternatives would be
more complexly and meaningfully embodied in the action and language of *Theodosius*. The comparing of rival leaders to Jupiter and
Saturn was a useful part of the figurative language in *Sophonisba* (IV.
i. 167–70) and would be revived interestingly in *Mithridates* (III. ii.
185; V. ii. 387–88). Caesario's vision of Gloriana in the emperor's bed
(V. i. 224–25) anticipates more complex versions of the same vision

in *The Rival Queens* (III. i. 229–37) and *Caesar Borgia* (II. i. 73–83), and Caesario's preference for the music of war—clashing arms, neighing horses (III. ii. 249–53—is to be echoed by Clytus in *The Rival Queens* (IV. i. 386–89).

The idea of portraying an aging sovereign with a bloody past, whose desperate quest for youth and sex endangers the state, possibly derives from Racine's *Mithridate* (1673) via Dryden's *Aureng-Zebe* (1675). But Lee would later develop its implications more fully in *Mithridates* and *Constantine*. More important, the guilty self-analysis of Augustus anticipates similar traits in several of Lee's more complex protagonists, most notably Alexander *(Rival Queens)*, Mithridates, Charles IX *(Massacre of Paris)*, and Constantine. Caesario boasts like Nero, gives all for love like Massinissa, rues his infectious ill-fortune (V. i. 418–19) like Ziphares *(Mithridates)*, and like Titus *(Lucius Junius Brutus)* is killed to preserve the unity of the empire. Like Otho, Marcellus is enraged by his wife's debauchery, but Julia is the converse of Poppea, in that she regains her virtue and repute after a period of loose behavior. In her fiery strength she looks forward to Roxana *(Rival Queens)* and Marguerite *(Massacre of Paris)*. The different strength of Gloriana, a resilience and masculine resourcefulness, derives from Rosalinda and foreshadows Pulcheria *(Theodosius)* and Fausta *(Constantine)*. On the other hand, Narcissa combines Massina and Varanes *(Theodosius)* in her whining lovesickness, and looks ahead to the pastoral innocence of Semandra *(Mithridates)* and Teraminta *(Lucius Junius Brutus)*. Those calculating politicians, Mecaenus and Leander, are early prototypes of the far more interesting counsellors, Pelopidas *(Mithridates)*, Machiavel *(Borgia)*, and the Queen Mother *(Massacre of Paris)*.

Is there anything about *Gloriana* that makes it worth reading in its own right? Perhaps its music—not so much the songs in Acts I (i. 1–12), III (ii. 1–12), and V (i. 214–21) as the fluency and tonal modulation of Lee's verse throughout. No passages better illustrate his increasing control over the sounds of language, despite hackneyed metaphors and hyperbolical expressions, than the operatic duet between Gloriana and Caesario that closes Act IV:

> Why should you wish what cannot be exprest,
> But guess my flame by that which warms your breast?
> Love's magnitude is harder to declare,
> Than 'tis to tell the bigness of a Star.
> . . . .

> I linger after you, and wish your sight,
> Like Birds that languish for the morning light:
> Like Babes unkindly wean'd, that take no rest,
> But bath'd in tears lye pining for the breast;
> I seek your heart, and when I find it gone,
> I weep and sigh as I wou'd break my own (i. 437–40, 447–52)

—and Caesario's greeting to Narcissa in Act V:

> O beauteous Virgin, daughter of the Spring,
> Who to my Winter dost refreshings bring,
> Still all in tears? Like the Celestial bow,
> Bending with cares and sorrows that o'reflow;
> Though bright yet sad thy shinings all appear,
> And on thy ev'ry Glory hangs a tear. (i. 228–33)

    Gloriana is at best a literary exercise, but although Lee felt that its failure had "blasted" his "hopes" and stunted his "growth,"[5] it clearly contributed to the success of his later work.

CHAPTER 5

Shirt of Nessus: The Rival Queens, or the Death of Alexander the Great (1676/7)

L EE begins his career by dramatizing powerful evil (*Nero*, 1674) and ends it by celebrating triumphant virtue (*Constantine*, 1683). His finest works, however, emerge from his pen in the middle period, 1677-80, and concentrate on a subject of considerably greater complexity: the warping of a great man's better nature through the inner weaknesses that plague him after he attains sovereignty over an empire. This had apparently been the subject of *Gloriana*, yet there Lee had failed to embody it in a unified dramatic design. When he returns to the theme in *The Rival Queens*, the most popular and enduring of all his plays,[1] he writes with a clearer sense of artistic purpose. Derivative materials, plot, imagery, and spectacle all become defining dimensions of a clearly conceived structure. In the dynamics of this structure he succeeds in doing what he must have been attempting in *Gloriana*; instead of dividing the terms of a conflict between two or more characters—Neronian vice against Britannican virtue, the civil bravery of Scipio against the high heroism of Hannibal and Massinissa—he makes them aspects of one man's fragmented personality. The other characters then serve as projections of, or reactions to, that personality, and their interplay thus chronicles the social correlatives of psychological disease. That there are also moral and cosmic correlatives is made clear through Lee's now customary facility with figurative language and spectacle.

I *Plot and Structure*

Nothing more clearly reveals the confidence with which all this is
managed than the plot itself, which is probably Lee's most convincing
one insofar as motivation is concerned. Alexander the Great is about
to enter Babylon, the scene of contending forces that he himself has
generated by a recent series of ill-judged acts. In the first place, he
has tortured and executed some of his most competent and beloved
generals, fearing that they might try to supplant him. Secondly, he
has publicly humiliated two other prominent men—Cassander, the
aggressive son of Alexander's ambitious Macedonian governor (An-
tipater), and Polyperchon, commander of the Phalanx—because
both had criticized his claims to godhead. Thirdly, while away from
his virtuous and devoted Babylonian queen, Statira (daughter of Dar-
ius), he has once again succumbed to the fiery charms of his first wife,
Roxana (daughter of Cohortanus)—despite having promised Statira
"before he cou'd espouse her, / That he wou'd never Bed Roxana
more" (I. i. 307–08). Finally, he has chosen as his favorite the flattering and somewhat self-indulgent courtier, Hephestion, to whom he
has given the hand of Parisatis, sister of Statira, though she loves (and
is beloved by) the worthy Lysimachus. The latter is a nobly born
Macedonian general whose military prowess and outspoken loyalty
make him more deserving than Hephestion of Alexander's favor. A
great defender of Lysimachus and all he represents—as against Alexander's vanity, lust, ingratitude, and addiction to Persian luxury—is
Clytus, the crusty old soldier and stoic, now Master of the Horse,
who has loyally served both Alexander and his father Philip during
their grandest military exploits.

Ignoring omens warning him of dire consequences should he return to the center of these discontents, Alexander arrives in Babylon
with great pomp and ceremony and is immediately beset by difficulties. Lysimachus enrages him so, by refusing to accept the betrothal
of Parisatis to another, that he impetuously orders the young man fed
to a lion. Later, under the women's affectionate influence, he relents
but is too late to prevent a bloody confrontation in which Lysimachus
kills the beast with his bare hands. In a lavish gesture of recognition
and repentance he changes his mind about Parisatis, promising her
to whoever serves him best in battle, and showers Lysimachus with
gifts. Meanwhile, when Statira sees how much pleasure she gives her
rival Roxana by renouncing Alexander for his infidelity, she decides

to allow the love-sick conqueror an audience, during which, as Roxana watches with mounting fury, she relents under the pressure of his hyperbolical protestations of love. These developments enable Cassander, who has already been conspiring against the king, to complete his plans. He persuades the enraged Roxana to kill Statira as she awaits Alexander's return from the banquet he has ordered to celebrate their reunion, and to make certain Alexander does not return, Cassander arranges for his brother Philip to poison the king's wine.

Beginning in the banquet scene in Act IV (11. 283–577), Alexander completely loses control over the emotional tempest his behavior has unleashed. Goaded into drunken violence by the satiric observations of an equally intoxicated Clytus (e.g., "Philip fought men, but Alexander women," IV. i. 425), he impales the old warrior with a javelin, but his maudlin repentance is cut short by news that Roxana and her slaves have forced their way past Statira's guards and now threaten the queen's life. In Act V Statira fails in an attempt to calm her murderess, so that, as Alexander arrives on the scene, Roxana fatally stabs her, leaving her only enough life to ask his mercy on one who killed out of love. As he reluctantly complies, but only to preserve the unborn child whom Roxana carries, he learns that Sysigambis (mother of Statira and Parisatis) has perished in grief and that Hephestion, appropriately, has died of excessive drinking at the banquet. Now Cassander's poison takes full effect, and as Alexander expires in agony, amidst hallucinations of an heroic past, Lysimachus promises to discover and execute the assassins before enjoying his belatedly clear title to Parisatis.

To achieve this tightly knit, well-focused plot, Lee must have felt very much in command of his sources.[2] As in *Sophonisba* and *Gloriana*, he depends heavily on one of the popular seventeenth-century romances, in this case La Calprenède's *Cassandra* (trans. Sir Charles Cotterell, 1661, with a second edition in 1676), and draws certain details from history, this time mainly from Curtius and Plutarch. Additionally, the appearance of King Philip's ghost recalls the ghost of Hamlet's father, and the portents and soothsayer's warnings seem inspired by like events in *Julius Caesar*. Possibly the scene in which Roxana slays her rival owes something to a broadly similar section in Thomas Otway's *Alcibiades* (1675), where Timandra, forewarned in sleep by spirits, awakens as her murderess enters but fails to ward off the fatal blow until her lover returns. Yet the result of such borrowing is a set of personalities and interrelated actions that bear little resemblance to their originals in any one source. For example, in La Calprenède it is Oroondates, not Alexander, who is the object of the rival queens' affection, though Alexander does marry both of them before he dies. After his death, however, Roxana and Perdiccas (not Cassander) capture (not kill) and try to woo Oroondates and Statira; but eventually the latter two triumph as Statira forms a lasting friendship with Roxana. Moreover, in the French romance, Roxana refuses to aid in Cassander's conspiracy, Alexander marries Parasatis to Hephestion, and after Hephestion dies, Lysimachus becomes the king's favorite and undergoes further trials before wedding the beautiful widow.

Lee makes these and other changes in the interest of his own concentrated and suggestively symmetrical dramatic structure. The centrally positioned Alexander is flanked by three balanced sets of boldly distinguished personalities. First, more or less within the sphere of his domination, are the rival courtiers, Lysimachus and Hephestion, and the rival queens, Statira and Roxana. Though all of these characters accept Alexander's claims to divinity and thus indirectly contribute to his self-delusion, only one from each pair of rivals appeals strongly to the undisciplined side of his psyche. Roxana, first of all, who is a more domineering version of Poppea, has been transformed from chaste huntress to impassioned sex object (III. i. 77–127) by Alexander's earlier advances, and she has then used her newly awakened charms to seduce him by arousing his bestial desires. Hephestion, likewise, encourages his master's lower appetites for wine and luxury and is particularly fulsome in his advocacy of Alexander's divinity. That the conqueror has favored these two over their rivals indicates his irrational frame of mind. After all, Lysimachus is demonstrably the worthier man, for he disarms Hephestion as the play opens and triumphs over all odds in killing the lion, just as Statira, in her selfless devotion, is nobler than Roxana, whose love is darkened by the need to possess and control. But not only do these rivalries exacerbate Alexander's mental unrest; they symbolize it and are its by-product: they would never have come into being unless his self-discipline had already begun to disintegrate.

Coping with this disintegration is not, however, in the province of the young people who reflect it, for they are spellbound by the king's heroic reputation, beauty, eloquence, and claims to godhead. Further outside his sphere of domination, and hence better able to see him for what he has become, are the senior characters, Sysigambis, Clytus, and Cassander, each of whom handles the situation differently. Sysigambis is the pragmatist. Having seen her son's empire fall beneath Alexander's sword, she is utterly without ideals, and though she knows the conqueror is merely a fortunate man (when Statira rhapsodizes about his godlike qualities, Sysigambis responds, "Passions . . . will have their Ebbs and Flows" [I. i. 388]), she prefers to flatter his vanity and cater to his wishes rather than to suffer the consequences of his anger. On the other hand, Clytus, an heir of Shakespeare's Enobarbus (*Antony and Cleopatra*) and the prototype for Lee's (and Dryden's) later versions of the blunt, hardy old soldier (Marcian in *Theodosius*, the Admiral in *Massacre*, Dalmatius in *Constantine*; Ventidius in Dryden's *All for Love*), staunchly maintains his stoical ideals and overtly criticizes Alexander for subordinating martial heroism to women, Persian luxury, and effeminate religion. In a sense, Clytus stands to the conqueror's right, appealing to his better nature, along with Lysimachus and Statira (though her chaste, wifely affection seems to him no better than Roxana's fiery passion), and like these others he becomes a victim of the irrational violence ignited by friction with the other, less restrained half of Alexander's psyche.

Working from this other side, opposite Clytus, on the left as it were, stands the black, brooding figure of Cassander, Lee's first fully developed villain-malcontent, the forerunner of Pharnaces (*Mithridates*), Tiberius (*Lucius Junius Brutus*), and Arius (*Constantine*). He combines Nero's diabolism and love of mischief with the cool scheming of a Jacobean stage-machiavel. Like Sysigambis, he has no ideals and is willing to flatter; but his flattery disguises base intentions which are prosecuted by sinister means that are the reverse of Clytus' blunt, forthright attempts to win Alexander back to his old heroism. Seizing the opportunity offered by Roxana's estrangement, and attracted to her by what he calls their "Sympathy of Natures" (both are "jealous, bloody, and ambitious" [II. i. 62–64]), Cassander uses her fury as a weapon against the conqueror's mind and heart, while employing poison against his allegedly divine but plainly mortal body.

We cannot resist the suggestiveness of this clearly devised structure: Alexander at the center, surrounded by an inner circle of conflicting admirers who dissipate his energies, and by an outer circle of malcontents who challenge his self-image and power. Those on one side (Statira, Lysimachus, Clytus) are associated with his love, civic responsibility, and martial prowess; those on the other (Roxana,

Hephestion, Cassander) are linked with his lust, self-indulgence, and idle vanity. To David Vieth such a configuration suggests "the social psychology of assassination": the flawed greatness of a charismatic leader "creates the very forces that destroy it,"[3] those forces being what P. F. Vernon calls "parallel forms of discontent."[4] In other words, Alexander is a study in what Lee's audience would have understood as a special form of insanity, the kind that develops when a great martial hero is faced with the comparatively nonheroic task of securing political and domestic order in his newly conquered realm.[5] Energy and emotion once narrowly dedicated to the self-absorbed task of conquest now become dissipated in a quest for equally stimulating objects in the peacetime world (women, wine, enthusiastic religion). But political and domestic order require sustained, disciplined effort from the sovereign, so that irrational behavior in a leader will not only unleash mental chaos but will also create a kind of power vacuum into which the forces of disorder can expand at the expense of civil concord.

II   *Mind and Cosmos*

Although it is tempting—and in its own way satisfying—to interpret the dynamics of this structure in modern psychological terms, Lee plainly wishes us to understand it in terms of a cosmic psychology that he adapts from an older tradition of thought.[6] His first excursion into this supramundane realm is visible in *Nero*, where the tyrant has become an explosive center of evil energy that either corrupts or destroys its opposites, creating, in terms of the play's imagery, a black and fiery combustion epitomized by the burning of Rome. Clearly, it is a play about the progress of evil polarized with virtue:

> Here horrid darkness . . . there, gaudy light:
> . . . .
> . . . perfect good and evil:
> A Heav'n, a Hell, an Angel, and a Devil. (IV. i. 52–56)

The Rival Queens, on the other hand, more closely studies an alternative process through which political and domestic chaos may develop: as a powerful sovereign allows his pride and bestiality to rule him, creating psychological chaos, so in his domestic and political

realms an equivalent chaos develops, making the earthly kingdom
hospitable to forces that feed on man's lower inclinations.

This correlating of psychological status with the domestic, political, and cosmic realms is carefully managed by Lee. Alexander
briefly crosses the threshold from melancholy to insanity five times
before he is murdered, and the earliest two instances, as reported by
Alexander himself, indicate the connection between madness and
social chaos: first, when "in my Riot,/My Reason gone," Roxana "se-
duc'd me to her Bed" (II. i. 337–38) and, second, "when at Thais suit,
enrag'd with Wine,/I set the fam'd Persepolis on Fire" (II. i. 343–44).
Both the destruction of a domestic contract with Statira[7] and the destruction of a great city (symbolizing, as Rome does in *Nero*, civic
order) follow upon the loss of reason, and this is symptomatic of what
will happen on three further occasions during the action chronicled
in the play itself: (1) when Alexander sends Lysimachus to the lion's
den (" 'tis all madness," says Clytus [II. i. 405]); (2) when in a rage he
kills Clytus for denouncing his irreverence, dissolute life, and cruelty
(Alexander then blames Hephestion and Lysimachus for failing to
restrain his bestiality in order to make "Reason glitter in my dazl'd
eyes" [IV. i. 530]); and (3) when, having failed to reinvigorate the dead
Statira, and feeling the mortal effects of Philip's poison, he envisions
the sun's "Stable" of horses, with "Mains . . . of Lightning" and "red
Tails like Meteors" (V. i. 329–32), and then fantasizes the single-
handed defeat of "gaudy Persians" by a "poor tatter'd Greek" (V. i.
336–37).

Alexander does not embody the sustained madness of absolute
evil, as Nero does; but neither does he exhibit the weak-kneed melancholia of Britannicus. His madness is of a middle variety. With
Nero it shares certain qualities: it is caused partly by overweening
pride, lust for earthly pleasures, and cruel ambition; and it eventuates, directly or indirectly, in the madman's destroying virtues of
both a civic and a private nature. But the key difference between
Alexander's psyche and Nero's is that Alexander not only lusts after
carnal pleasure (with Roxana) but also loves in the transcendent sense
(Statira). Thus, his melancholia is intensified by a combination of the
sickness of an unrequited lover and the guilty anxiety of an adulterer.
Moreover, like Britannicus, but distinctly unlike Nero, Alexander is
tormented by his excesses, especially by their inconsistency with his
godlike ideal of sovereignty—though what significantly distinguishes

him from Britannicus is that this disparity exists not in something externally observed (i.e. Nero) but within himself, as Clytus infuriatingly reminds him.

One of Clytus's more telling remarks, in fact, offers perhaps the best approach to an understanding of the cosmic implications with which Lee invests the sovereign's madness. Throughout the first three acts and into the fourth, Alexander has been boasting of his divinity, calling himself a "God," "Jove," son of Jupiter, "Immortal," until finally Clytus cannot bear it any longer and rhetorically asks, "When Gods grow hot, where is the difference/ 'Twixt them and Devils?" (IV. i. 383–84, and see I. i. 222). The traditional contexts within which this remark is to be understood are, of course, multiple. To memories of mythological tales about gods who behave more like demons working against man's happiness than like man's immortal protectors, it adds the Christian assumption, prevalent in both medieval and Renaissance thought, that fallen man's proudly passionate tendencies are diabolical.[9] This dualistic vision of Alexander's personality is sustained by a paradigm of images that interpret the play's dramatic structure at a cosmic level. To Alexander's right, projecting his higher faculties and capabilities, is Clytus, the personification of civic virtue as a sovereign's highest achievement: "I'le stand upright," he says, "strait as a Spear, the Pillar of my Country,/And be by so much nearer to the Gods" (IV. i. 38–40). The opposite side of Alexander, the part nearest the devils, is embodied in Cassander, who paraphrases Milton's Satan:

'Tis nobler far to be the King of Hell,
To head Infernal Legions, Chiefs below,
To let 'em loose for earth, call 'em in
And take account of what dark deeds are done,
Then be a Subject-God in Heav'n unblest,
And without mischief have Eternal rest (IV. i. 277–82).[10]

As the satanic Nero corrupts Poppea, so Cassander draws into his sphere of evil influence the once-innocent Roxana, who is ripened for his possession by her passionate liaison with Alexander. Her fall and its consequences are conveyed through both pagan and Christian images. Once having been chaste and strong and well-disciplined, like Diana (III. i. 77–83), she sacrificed her better nature by sharing

Alexander's blasting lust, as Semele was destroyed by Zeus's fire (IV.
i. 243),[11] and thereafter she becomes, under Cassander's tutelage, a
fiery beast (I. i. 322; III. i. 51), a revengeful Medea (I. i. 315; III. i.
66), a "Fury," "Harpy," and "Queen of Devils" (V. i. 80, 124).[12] Together, Cassander and Roxana create physical havoc in the court in
direct proportion as the darker side of Alexander's personality takes
over—i.e., as he goes mad—and again the imagery charts the ascendancy of chaos, fire, and old night in cosmic terms. Before being
corrupted, Roxana was moon-like in the sense of being a chaste
Diana, but later she becomes "like the Moon" (III. i. 61) in a different
sense: "let all the Stars go out," Cassander tells her, and "wake like
the Moon" to "rule the world" (III. i. 59–61). This moon is an "Orb of
fire" (III. i. 126) whose "flame" must be quenched by "Stars" (IV. i.
200–202), and its influence on the world is not to maintain orderly
ebbs and flows but to generate storms, just as Roxana's peace of mind
has given way to madness:

> . . . make way for fire and tempest.
> My brain is burst, debate and reason quench'd,
> . . . .
> . . . while passions like the winds
> Rise up to Heav'n and put out all the Stars. (III. i. 51–55)[13]

The stars so frequently mentioned as Roxana's victims are, of
course, symbols of pristine virtue, just as they were in *Nero*, and, as
in the earlier play (where they were linked with Octavia), here they
are consistently used to symbolize the virtue of a particular character,
Statira. With Clytus and Lysimachus, she represents the bright side
of Alexander's psyche, and her death is correlated not only with the
death of an aspect of his mind but also with a kind of cosmic death. As
a "fair Star" (V. i. 236), she is a "Torch to light" Alexander "on [his]
. . . way" (II. i. 223) and a "Heavenly Beam" warming his "Brain" and
firing his "Heart" (II. i. 293–94). Her fire is transcendent, a fire of
spiritualized love that draws Alexander, as does the civic virtue of
Clytus, "nearer to the Gods." But it is "put out" (III. i. 55) by Roxana's infernal fire, the fire of lust and revenge, just as in Alexander's
mind the elevated passion of a hero gives way to the earthly desires
of a beast. That Roxana and Statira, like Cassander and Clytus, represent opposite sides of the king's psyche is underlined by a particularly suggestive use of the moon-star imagery that pervades the play.

If Roxana has become a fiery planet encased in the body of Diana, Statira is "Diana's Soul, cast in the flesh of Venus" (IV. i. 94). Their relation to Alexander's emotional state is clarified by Polyperchon, who longs "to see two Rival Queens of different humours,/ With a variety of Torments vex him" (II. i. 67–68).

Appropriately, the deaths of Clytus and Statira, embodiments of Alexander's lost heroism in war and love, immediately precede his own death. In fact, the way in which Lee structures these final events—which lead from the corpse of Clytus to that of Statira and thence to the fiery death-by-poison of Alexander himself—reinforces the notion that, in a sense, the conqueror dies in stages as the darker overwhelms the brighter side of his personality: "ha! who talks of Heav'n?/ I am all Hell, I burn, I burn again" (V. i. 324–25).

III *History and Myth*

To Lee, such cosmic and supernatural figures are more than provocatively arranged symbols; they belong to a vocabulary that, from *Nero* onward, he employs to show the interpenetrations of limited, earthly events and infinitely resonating phenomena in some larger, mythic history, a history involving the mundane with the occult and the celestial, the temporal with the timeless. In *Nero*, this multidimensional reality is rather awkwardly assumed to exist, and its representation in the symbolic collision of Nero and Britannicus is without much psychological subtlety. In *Sophonisba*, a slightly less contrived symbolism represents the larger significance of what happens as a kind of political ecology—without, however, trying to interpret its supernatural essence. Now, in *The Rival Queens*, Lee takes his first, tentative step toward depicting earthly phenomena as part of a grand, only partially comprehensible scheme that unites microcosm (man's psyche) and macrocosm (the mythical, universal drama written by the gods), and does it with a convincing flourish of spectacular omens and portents.

After all is said and done, it takes more than man's poor substitutes for divine clairvoyance, his figurative language, to establish the reality of that supramundane world toward which he imperfectly reaches. Beginning with *The Rival Queens*, Lee inevitably turns to the supernatural, not merely to evoke ambivalent fate, but to validate his characters' cosmic visions, presenting prodigies in forms that adapt traditional imagery that was familiar to his audience.

No matter who sees or articulates them, all the supernatural portents in this play connect Alexander's mental state, his black melancholy, with his impending disaster and its implications. Aristander, the soothsayer, warns that the conqueror is the equivalent of Babylon, "whose Head stands wrapt in Clouds" and must "tumble down" (II. i. 184–85). Later, in a confirming daydream, Alexander sees himself as "a pale Crown'd head" with "two dead hands, which threw a Chrystal Globe/From high," shattering it "in a thousand pieces" (IV. i. 80–82). This parallels the omen reported by Perdiccas and Meleager, a depiction of Alexander as a personality blackened by melancholy disorders that are like ravens battling, raining "black Blood" (II. i. 201–05) on the kingdom below and, finally, tumbling down like black "Clouds" that are "pondrous" as shields and crushing "Souldiers" and "Chiefs" alike (II. i. 211–15).

What Perdiccas and Meleager have seen is the central supernatural event of the play, whose appearance on stage, at the start of Act II, is even more suggestive than they infer: "a Battel of Crows, or Ravens, in the Air; an Eagle and a Dragon meet and fight; the Eagle drops down with all the rest of the Birds, and the Dragon flies away" (stage directions to II. i.). The eagle among ravens is Alexander (see II. i. 157–8), confused and enfeebled by crowding black thoughts. The dragon is Cassander. As a foreshadowing of the supernatural plan for Alexander, this imagery interestingly parallels the biblical tradition of how Providence will allow the dragon, emblem of Satan and the Antichrist (Rev. 12:7, 16:13), to triumph temporarily over sinful man (Dan. 7:25, 2 Thess. 2:4, Rev. 13:4, 13-15).[14] Before hell can triumph in the play, however, the time must be ripe. Alexander's weaknesses must have developed sufficiently. Cassander sees himself and his co-conspirators as "Silk-worms . . . hid in our own Weft," so that "when time calls" they can "come forth in a new Form: / Not Insects, to be trod, but Dragons wing'd" (II. i. 39–42). The biblical overtones of these figures remain merely overtones; they are never made explicit because the play concerns a pagan world. Yet Lee shares his Renaissance predecessors' feeling that, ultimately, all religious myths are departments of the same overarching Christian truth, so that, for instance, he expects us to read Hell for hell, Heaven for heaven, Satan for devil, God for Jove.

IV   *Herculean Tragedy . . . and Triumph?*

And it is in this context of conflated mythologies that he expects us
to understand the end of the play. Alexander has regarded himself as
the son of God (Jupiter Ammon: I. i. 256–57; II. i. 129–31), but in fact
he has become, as Cassander is informed, a "monstrous Child" weeping into the wine bowl that poisons him (II. i. 21–28). By vainly presuming to godhead, living riotously, succumbing to the lusty charms
of Roxana, he finds himself far from heaven, in "the hottest burning
Hell" (III. i. 316) of his own insanity, out of which the dragon rises to
destroy mind, body, and estate. Seeing his mistake in a last moment
of tragic recognition, he rejects the false self-image, and the "Divine
Honours" (V. i. 373) that go with it, promising that a true messiah
will come in his place:

> . . . the good Gods
> Shall send you in my stead a noble Prince,
> One that shall lead you forth with matchless conduct. (V. i. 361–63)

Whether that "nobler Prince" is Lysimachus is left open to speculation, though the events leading to his survival at the play's end
imply that he is in some respects what Alexander failed to become.
Although Lysimachus humanly fails to analyze the causes of the king's
madness and downfall—he participates in Alexander's addiction to
Persian luxury (IV. i. stage directions after 353) and calls him "sacred
Sir" (IV. i. 486)—he is certainly a better choice for sovereignty than,
say, Hephestion, whose ambition and debauchery may equal Alexander's own (as Galba resembles Nero). Moreover, his triumph over
the lion receives such emphasis that one suspects Lee intended a
symbolic interpretation of it. Traditionally, by overcoming a lion one
simultaneously gains control over his own bestial appetites and assumes such noble, lion-like qualities as courage, prowess, and gratitude. Thus, for instance, in the Middle English romance *Iwain and
Gawain* the mad Iwain regains sanity, grace, and chivalric virtue by
mastering a lion and becoming known thereafter as Knight of the
Lion: "As Adam lost the mastery of animals by sin, so did Iwain lose
even self-mastery; his control of the lion indicates his own virtuous
self-control."[15] Similarly, in one (possibly two) of his twelve labours,
Hercules kills the Nemean Lion and uses its skin as a cloak.[16]
Certainly Lee had at least Hercules in mind as he created Lysi-

machus, for both heroes destroy lions with their bare hands—Hercules strangling his, Lysimachus pulling out the beast's tongue "with Herculean force" (IV. i. 319). In recognition of this symbolic deed, Alexander presents Lysimachus with "Gold Armour" and names the "Lyon" as his coat of arms, "the Impress of thy Shield" (IV. i. 335–36). Thus, like Iwain, Lysimachus becomes "Knight of the Lion" and, like Hercules, he wears a golden outer skin symbolizing his prowess and self-mastery. And perhaps Alexander does not merely present these symbols; perhaps he transfers them, unwittingly, from himself to Lysimachus, thus making the young hero the nobler figure he once was. Such an interpretation is encouraged by the fact that Alexander himself is repeatedly compared to Hercules (III. i. 378; IV. i. 408)[17] and some of his key experiences parallel those of the Greek hero. His claim to godhead and Cassander's counterclaim that he is merely a vulnerable man (II. i. 129ff., 72) recall that Hercules was considered mortal by some and a god by others. His uncontrollable passion and fits of madness are Herculean, and so is his liaison with the Amazonian Roxana. But, most significant of all, his death parallels Hercules' death. The latter perishes in madness and flames, his body tortured by a shirt impregnated with a centaur's blood, blood poisoned by his own arrow. Moreover, the blood had been rubbed on his shirt by Deianira, a jealous ex-lover who thought she was administering an aphrodisiac. Alexander dies in a provocatively similar fashion, internally burning with a poison that, indirectly, avenges his murders and pays for his promiscuity.

Thus, if Alexander is, as Clytus with customary perception tells us, "the Lion, that had left to roar" (I. i. 49)—Hercules divested of his lion skin, insane, overwhelmed by forces of his own making—then Lysimachus emerges as a true Knight of the Lion, a champion of order and virtue. As Alexander dies, it is Lysimachus who asks to whom the empire is bequeathed, and the terse reply, heard in an intellectual and behavioral context dense with symbolic icons, lingers in multiple echoes: "to him that is most worthy" (V. i. 371).

CHAPTER 6

"famish'd Tygers . . . have us in the Wind": Mithridates King of Pontus, A Tragedy (1677/8)

MITHRIDATES is not the best of Lee's first five plays, though he himself said it was,[1] but neither is it his worst. In fact, apart from a few deficiencies that are obvious in a cursory reading—the kind of reading it seems to have received from all who have published opinions about it to date[2]—it is worthy of close attention. Structurally, it suffers from a slight blurring of the focus on Mithridates in his agony as attention is drawn to those love scenes that Lee stressed, it seems, to please the "Ladies" flattered in his dedicatory epistle.[3] One cannot but wonder, moreover, why so much is made of Pharnaces' lust for Monima if the whole affair is to be dropped before her fate is clarified. Furthermore, the play would have been better if Lee had resisted his ever-present inclination to sentimentalize inherently tragic or speculative situations—an inclination he indulges nauseatingly when the dying Semandra promises her beloved Ziphares, "we'll be wedded . . ."

> In th' other World; our Souls shall there be mixt:
> Who knows, but there our joys may be compleat?
> A happy Father, thou; and I, perhaps,
> The smiling Mother of some little Gods. (V. ii. 296–300)

This, however, is the lowest of low points in a play typified by fluent poetry and the well-integrated plot and theme of a mature writer confidently exploring a familiar subject, the mental pathology of political leadership.[4] As the last in an unbroken series of "pagan"[5] studies of this subject, *Mithridates* shows Lee reaching for a more cosmic, even transcendental, interpretation, while still holding the

80

supernatural at a mysterious distance. In *Sophonisba* several characters ascribe Hannibal's defeat and Massinissa's self-destruction to a process of sociopolitical change that is somehow fated. In *The Rival Queens* supernatural portents clearly forecast and help define Alexander's fall, implying that his tragedy satisfies an intention of the gods. But in general these earlier works emphasize sublunar phenomena and earthly causes, the human psyche amidst crosscurrents of passion and commitment during political and domestic crises. In *Mithridates* Lee gathers up the main threads of his theme and tries for a kind of *summa* whose controlling idea is nature, nature seen from several perspectives—psychological, moral, political—and nature behaving as if it were the agency of that heavenly plan which would more and more occupy the playwright's attention in future years. With the advantage of hindsight we can see in this play final preparations for the next phase of Lee's career, the era of Caesar Borgia, Theodosius, and Constantine, in whose "histories" the Christian cosmos, unfolding in time according to a providential scheme too subtle for human comprehension, comes into problematic focus.

I *From Sources to Plot*

Yet this is not to say that *Mithridates* lacks interest in its own right, for it stands up very well when regarded as a further investigation of the psychology of power—this time in an attempt to understand the dynamics of "nature" in the political activities of a royal family. Indeed, these activities alone compel interest—divested of their larger thematic dimensions—as the following plot summary indicates. Despite increasing military pressure from Roman legions led by Glabrio and Pompey, the Kingdom of Pontus survives precariously under the tyrannic rule of Mithridates, a superstitious and aging, but still miraculously virile, sovereign. The kingdom's security is defended by an army inspired and led by the ruler's heroically virtuous son, Ziphares, and his worthy old general and advisor, Archelaus; but their efforts are opposed internally by Ziphares' envious, lustful, and power-hungry half-brother, Pharnaces, whose appetites are served by a Machiavellian general, Pelopidas, aided by his priest-brother, Tryphon, and a lieutenant, Andravar. Jealous of the favor shown to Ziphares and Archelaus in honor of their recent victory over Glabrio's invading army, Pharnaces and Pelopidas plot to overthrow the monarch, liquidate their rivals, and, simultaneously, reclaim for Pharnaces the favors of Monima, a beautiful captive princess who was first apprehended as plunder by Pharnaces and later confiscated by his father. This grand plan is executed in three stages.

To start with, Tryphon creates a prodigy that seems to curse the imminent marriage of Mithridates and Monima. After the superstitious monarch cancels the wedding, Pelopidas convinces him that in revenge for her rejection Monima has been trying without success to solicit the affections of Pharnaces (who is said to be stoutly resisting). As projected by the conspirators, the king then has her confined under the close guard of Andravar, but either before or after she is raped by Pharnaces in her cell (the text is unclear about this), she manages to flee to Pompey's protection.

Meanwhile, in a second stage of the strategy, Andravar stirs the king's lust for Semandra, the spotless beauty already promised to her beloved admirer, Ziphares, who now seeks his father's blessing on their marriage. Using as an excuse the "low" extraction of her father, Archelaus, the king denies his son's suit, scolds the old general, and orders Semandra to attend at court, where she may find a more suitable marriage partner. Soon, however, he himself is wooing her with promises of power and luxury, and it is only the force of her appeal, joined with those of Archelaus and Ziphares, that wins him over again to a sense of justice, filial duty, and patriotism. At last blessing his son's betrothal, he sequesters Semandra while Ziphares and Archelaus once more battle the invading Romans. In the interim, however, Pelopidas rekindles the king's desire, and Pharnaces reports that Stratonice, mother of Ziphares, has basely purchased an easy victory for her son by surrendering to Pompey an important fortress. The two conspirators then explain that Ziphares now courts the people's favor in a grand triumphal procession (which he has been led to believe his father ordered). In a rage compounded of lust, envy, and paranoia, Mithridates forces Semandra to receive Ziphares coldly and, after the lovers part, he orders her conveyed to his chariot, thence to the temple for an enforced wedding, and finally to the royal apartment, where the marriage is consummated by rape.

The third, climactic stage of the villains' strategy involves three simultaneous efforts: Pelopidas turns the people against Archelaus by telling them the old man, coveting favor at court, has forced Semandra to marry the king; Andravar and Tryphon incite mutiny in the army by reporting that Mithridates has ravished Semandra and executed Ziphares; and Pharnaces trades a large contingent of rebel troops to Rome in return for Monima and one half of Pompey's conquests.

As these sinister plans are prosecuted by Pharnaces, his noble half-brother Ziphares dutifully attends to the defense of the realm and to the winning of Semandra. These two exemplars of virtue are, throughout the play, victims not only of the villains' plots but also of the king's irrational behavior. In the final act, Semandra's intended suicide is preempted when, mistaking her in the dark for a rebel assailant, Ziphares stabs her to death, after which he poisons himself and dies in her last embrace.

Between opposite poles of influence—the power-mongering and lustful Pharnaces, the loyal and loving Ziphares—stands Mithridates himself. His entire resource of energy is consumed in the attempt to resist temptation in order to retain sanity while encouraging his loyal son's military and nuptial campaigns. But as the conspirators succeed, he progressively loses self-control, allows his troops and people to rebel, rejects his most devoted aides, and rapes his son's mistress. Only in the final two acts, as the kingdom disintegrates, does his better nature revive; then he agonizes over his treatment of Semandra, disinherits Pharnaces, and leads the remnants of his army against the Romans. Mortally wounded by Pharnaces during battle, he lives long enough to see the traitors captured, to order that Pharnaces be thrown from the highest tower in sight of Pompey, to lament the bleakness of death, and to charge that his criminal life be blotted from history.

To say that this plot is highly derivative, while accurate, is not to characterize the play. If Lee had a great many sources in mind as he wrote, his borrowings clearly serve an artistic purpose that transcends what he could have gained from any one of them. He probably owed something not only to historians like Appian, Plutarch, and Pliny, but also to such literary forebears as Shakespeare, Fletcher, Corneille, Dryden, Racine, and Otway.[6] From the historians perhaps he learned the names of most of his characters (Mithridates, Monima, Ziphares, Pharnaces, Stratonice, Pelopidas, and Tryphon—the latter a eunuch in Appian) and the original character of Mithridates: his amorousness, cruelty, and great learning.[7] But he freely adapted the facts to suit his own purposes. The historical tyrant's victory at Triarius, for example, becomes in Lee the first victory of Ziphares. The smashing of an image of victory, which in Plutarch is said to have boded military ill to Mithridates, is in Lee part of Pharnaces' plot against the wedding of Monima to the king. In Appian, Ziphares is executed in recompense for his mother's betrayal of a castle to Pompey, but in Lee this bit of treason is a minor aspect of the case against Ziphares, who ultimately escapes his father's ire (only to commit suicide). In Appian, Mithridates has one of his captains kill him when he learns of Pharnaces' treachery, but in Lee Pharnaces himself deals the death-blow to his father. Finally, to Plutarch's account of a rather ordinary dream that troubled Mithridates just prior to Pompey's arrival, Lee adds elements reminiscent of Clarence's dream-vision of hell in Shakespeare's *Richard III*.

Insofar as literary debts are concerned, however, Lee owes much less to Shakespeare and Fletcher (Semandra modelled on the ravished Lucina in *Valentinian?*), whom he acknowledges in his dedicatory epistle,[8] than to Racine and Dryden. The former's *Mithridate* (1673) and the latter's *Aureng-Zebe* (1675) both show an aging sovereign being conspired against by one son while he competes with another, this one loyal and heroic, for the affections of a beautiful maiden. And in a different play by Racine, *Britannicus* (1669), there is a scene (probably borrowed by Dryden for *Aureng-Zebe*) in which the victorious young lover returns to claim his mistress only to find that the lustful monarch has forced her to receive him coldly. But this is about as far as Lee's debts go. Dryden seems to have owed more to Racine than Lee owed to either of these predecessors. Unlike both, he endows his aging king with almost supernatural virility and avoids having the evil son compete for the same woman desired by the virtuous half-brother. Moreover, Lee's play ends more negatively than the others. In Racine's *Mithridate* Xiphares survives and wins his mistress, while the king kills himself. In Dryden the evil son is converted to virtue, the loyal son gains both crown and mistress, and the sovereign resigns himself to contemplative retirement. In Lee's version, all the main characters, including the violated mistress, die in a variety of violent ways (possibly in imitation of Otway's *Don Carlos* [1676], where a father-son rivalry eventuates in the double suicide of lovers). Looking at the plays from a more general perspective, we note that if Lee's heroic prince is less complex than his counterparts in Racine and Dryden, his sovereign figure is compensatingly more interesting than either Mithridate or the father of Aureng-Zebe. Lee's plot is also the most organic of the three, in that the villain-sons in Racine and Dryden aggressively oppose weak fathers, while Lee's more subtle Pharnaces must manipulate the strong but unbalanced personality of a dangerously energetic patriarch.

II *The Natures of Tragedy*

Indeed, the concept of patriarchy, understood as a microcosm of nature's greater order, is central to Lee's dramatic structure and to the complex pattern of his imagery. In tracing the disintegration of a royal family—which resonates in the collapse of a kingdom—he compares psychological and political phenomena to storms, disease, and the preying of animal upon animal, implying a kind of social ecology that is ultimately non-tragic. As in *Sophonisba*, where the death of one form of heroism is compensated for by the birth of another, in *Mithridates* the fall of Pontus is defined as part of the larger process of nature. But the subject this time is a revival of the undeveloped theme of *Gloriana:* the consequences of emotional trauma within an aging monarch. To exploit this theme, Lee presents a family whose collective psyche has become unbalanced and thus erupts in a struggle between opposing tendencies. The family members and their retinue combine unique sets of motives and perceptions with traits borrowed from key figures in earlier plays. Their language sparkles with metaphors and symbols that make "natural" sense of their misfortunes.

At the pivotal point in this family stands the agonized King of Pontus, Mithridates, who must cope not only with invading Romans but, more crucially, with a "Bosom-war" (IV. i. 92) made inevitable by his own neglect of responsibility as *paterfamilias*. In some respects he is like Nero and Alexander: egocentric, cruel, promiscuously lustful, and enraged by anyone who opposes his pleasure. But in other ways he is a sort of hybrid, combining Nero's joy in licentious behavior, Alexander's guilt about having transgressed moral bounds, and Hannibal's ultrasensitivity to the supernatural. His most nearly unique quality is his sense of filial responsibility, something he shares with the emperor in *Aureng-Zebe*. Dryden's play, however, subordinates the emperor-father to the hero-prince as the latter restores order to a chaotic state, while Lee concentrates on the process through which disorder develops and so places the sovereign foremost in his design (though the attention given to his sons prevents him from dominating the action as completely as Nero and Alexander do).

What today might be called an identity crisis forms the core of disorder in the Kingdom of Pontus. Up until the time when the action begins, Mithridates has managed to keep the irrational side of his personality—lust, cruelty, superstition—from interfering markedly with the safety and order of his mind, family, and realm. When his two sons grew to manhood, for example, he assessed their aptitudes and prudently relinquished to each the appropriate military responsibilities. He invested in Pharnaces, a "rough . . . untaught Spirit" (V. i. 17), the continuing defense against barbarian incursions (IV. i. 147–51), while to Ziphares, a more conventionally disciplined leader, he entrusted the ongoing campaign against Rome. His crucial troubles begin only after he interrupts this "natural" evolution of his role by neglecting to divide his gratitude between sons as he divided military power and by failing to relinquish, along with some of his military power, some of his sexual dominion over the family. Ignoring the steady services of Pharnaces, he showers recognition upon Ziphares and Archelaus and, to add insult to injury, seizes for himself the captive princess (Monima) whom Pharnaces had already claimed as plunder. "I'm Mithridates still" (I. i. 228), he insists, and to disguise the natural course of aging "he adds such helps by Art,/That by his looks he might be thought Immortal" (I. i. 117–18).[9] But it is already clear that he has lost his identity as father, and after he rapes Semandra this title is transferred by default to Archelaus, whom Ziphares desperately addresses as "my Father,/ . . . Brother, Sister, Mistress . . . Friend" (IV. i. 369–70; and see V. ii. 69–70).

When Mithridates lapses into irrational behavior, it is as if he releases not only his own passions but also those naturally strong bestial tendencies in Pharnaces, who does precisely what Monima merely threatens to do: "disturb all Nature / With venting of my wrongs" (II. i. 155–56). He takes a certain Neronian pleasure in this mischief, but in some other respects—his complaints about the king's cruelty (V. i. 25ff.) and competition for the king's mistress—he recalls Cassander, though the latter's aptitude for cool scheming is embodied in Pelopidas, the Machiavellian advisor upon whom the animalistic Pharnaces relies. Together, these two "poyson" (I. i. 416) Mithridates as Cassander and Philip poison Alexander—except that Pharnaces' poison is psychological: he creates in his father's mind a "Tempest" (I. i. 145) of passion that corresponds to the storm released within himself by his father's neglect.

The storm is prepared for by Tryphon as he fashions a prodigy—

"An Image of Victory descends . . . but . . . the Engines break, and
. . . dash it in pieces" (stage directions after I. i. 285)—that the superstitious Mithridates interprets as a curse on his projected marriage to Monima. Then by describing Semandra in irresistibly luscious terms, the conspirators use her to trap the newly uncommitted
king in his own lust. Through his two greatest weaknesses, superstition and sexual desire, Mithridates becomes "a caught Lyon, raging
in the snare" of "his passion" (II. i. 113–14), the snare being the
"Nets" of Semandra's beauty (III. ii. 120). After a brief relapse into
virtue, he gorges his "monstrous appetite" (IV. i. 125) on her charms.
In doing so, he leaves Monima helpless to resist the equally bestial
appetite of Pharnaces, who rejects the "Romantick" rituals and values—"Honour, Courtship"—that help distinguish man from animal:
"Rather . . . / I'de be a Brute," he says, "With choice of Pasture" and
of "Mistresses" (II. i. 30, 40–47).

Only after it is too late does Mithridates perceive what is clear to
the reader almost from the start: that Pharnaces is not simply a beast
but the bestial side of the king's own unbalanced psyche or, to express it in physical terms, "an infectious limb" (IV. i. 230). Contrari-
wise, Ziphares is a good "right arm" (IV. i. 136), though by the time
his father fully apprehends this, the infection from his left side has
become fatal. Ziphares, a less complicated and intriguing character
than his black-hearted half-brother, is *la belle nature*, a well-bred,
pristinely virtuous lover-hero descended from Britannicus (though
not so weak), Caesario (but not so impetuous), and Lysimachus (yet
not so fortunate). With Archelaus, the bluntly martial successor of
Clytus, and Semandra, a Narcissa with the strength of Sophonisba,
he consistently exemplifies that natural order and rectitude above
which Mithridates soars with superstition and "art" (forced lust, cos-
metic youth) and below which Pharnaces rages in bestial heat. The
storm engendered by this interaction between two "unnatural"
forces claims Ziphares and his mistress as its chief victims.

That they are meant to symbolize "right nature," and thus the better side of Mithridates, is made clear by the way they see themselves
and are seen by others. By contrast to Pharnaces, the diseased left
arm, Ziphares is the healthy right; if Pharnaces demands that the
Romans "Plant me, like Thunder breaking from this Cloud" (V. i. 49)
during the tempest he has fomented, Ziphares falls victim to the
storm's fury, a "lovely Royal Plant,/Blown down by gusty Heav'n, in
all [his] . . . bloom" (V. ii. 352–53). When Pelopidas describes Zi-

phares' triumphal procession to the jealous Mithridates, he chooses natural metaphors: the city greeted Ziphares "like one vast Meadow,/ Set all with Flowers, as a clear Heav'n with Stars," and the crowds were like "a thousand Birds upon the boughs" preening "their feathers in his Golden Beams" (III. ii. 239–52). On the battlefield Ziphares is thought to be as inspiring "as the Air, to all the Army; / His Face . . . as the Sun, in depth of Winter" (IV. i. 138–39), but in the end "he is set, for ever set in sorrow" (IV. i. 141).

Similarly, Semandra symbolizes nature violated. She is initially described as a star (III. ii. 464), a sun (I. i. 386; III. ii. 465), "blushing Noon" (II. i. 168), a moon naturally influencing her lover's ebbs and flows (II. i. 410–11), the sea upon whose bed the sun-lover slumbers at night (III. i. 52–53), a natural "Physician" whose medications consist of "Songs," "Pity," "Tears," "sighs," "a Kiss" (I. i. 406–14). In short, Semandra is a "Master-piece of Nature" (I. i. 389), and when Pelopidas wishes to revive the king's repressed lust for her, he chooses the most sensuous natural imagery at his command:

> Behold her then upon a Flowry Bank,
> With her soft sorrows lull'd into a slumber,
> . . . .
> The Beauties of her Neck and naked breasts,
> Lifted by inward starts, did rise and fall
> . . . .
> While to my ravish'd eyes officious winds,
> Waving her Robes, display'd . . . handsom Limbs. (III. ii. 52–63)

As the king orders her carried off to temple and bedroom, Semandra curses his monstrosity—"Dragon . . . / . . . Aspic . . . Basilisks" (III. ii. 608–09)—and stresses her natural virtue: "to th' Earth, I'll grow / . . . O, root me here, some pitying God" (III. ii. 636–37). Hereafter, she is a blasted rose (IV. i. 126, 600), a "Setting-star" (IV. i. 585). To Ziphares and Archelaus, who at first misinterpret the rape, she has become part of the "Tempest" that is enveloping both family and state (IV. i. 294–309), and Archelaus feels that her "Heart-strings" have become "rank red Weeds" (IV. i. 456). But Semandra herself now raises her sights, finding in "Nature" no recompense for her destruction, and in that unfortunate speech cited in the first paragraph above, she expresses the hope that her natural role as wife and mother may be resumed transcendentally in heaven.

Unlike Nero, Mithridates does not snuff out natural virtue and de-stroy natural order without remorse. The unrepentant side of Rome's villain has been invested in Pharnaces who, using metaphors remi-niscent of Caesario's, vows even after death to displace his father's spirit, "as Saturn was by Jove" (V. ii. 387; and see III. ii. 185). Mith-ridates, on the other hand, feels keenly the psychological conse-quences of his "lawless love" (V. ii. 188). Before the rape, he had prudently cancelled the wedding with Monima, for fear that the gods deemed it unnatural: "As well the noblest Salvage of the Field / Might . . . couple with a fearful Ewe" or "Wild muddy Bores defile the cleanly Ermin" (I. i. 294–97), and in the momentary self-conquest which delays the final crime against familial order, he heeds "the soft Tongue of Nature" and "with a Father's bowels" resigns Semandra to his son (II. i. 208, 325). In Act III it is with this sense of natural ethics that he must strive in order to free himself for the violation of Seman-dra—"Down, strugling Nature; / . . . Ravisher of my Repose" (III. ii. 199–200, and see 430–31)—and with the aid of Pelopidas, he wins against "Nature" by allying himself with self-indulgent court ethics, as distinct from the natural morality of rustics: "Oh, feeble Virtue! . . . / I blow thee from the Palace, to the Cottage" (III. ii. 125–26) and will have my pleasures "tho all the Elements" oppose (III. ii. 275).

III   *The Fates of Nature*

That this is an artificial distinction, one drawn by passion-clouded judgment—a "Fence of Pleasure, fortifi'd / With reasons" (IV. i. 107–08)—is part of the stinging realization whose ramifications fill the final two acts. Mithridates now recognizes that the enforced wedding and bedding of Semandra was "monstrous Love" (IV. i. 13) promoted by wicked Pharnaces, guided by Pelopidas and his "Brother-Devils" (IV. i. 166), in order "To catch Ziphares life . . . / And ruine me . . ." (IV. i. 161–62). More significantly, he also understands that the essential culprit is his own mind, his own psychological instability. The Pharnaces within him has poisoned the Ziphares, and "strugling Virtue" has failed to "cast the Venom of . . . Passion up" (IV. i. 181–82). But by far the most important aspect of his newly clarified un-derstanding is what he learns from a dream that haunts him the very night when he consummates his "monstrous Love": "by Heav'nly Order" he is "borne by Winds" first to hell, then to heaven, where

Methought I saw the Spirits of my Sons,
Slain by my jealousie of their Ambition,
. . . .
Streight had their cries alarm'd the wounded Host
Of all those Romans, massacred in Asia:
. . . .
And tender voices cry'd, Lead, Pompey, lead.
. . . .
When I had leisure to discern their Chief,
Methought that Pompey was my Son Ziphares;
Who cast his dreadful Pile, and pierc'd my heart. (IV. i. 35, 37, 50–61)

Given his new psychological insight, Mithridates is able immediately
to interpret the dream; he is still more than a match for Rome, but
then Roman legions are not the real threat:

> . . . here . . . in my guilty Bosom,
> The fatal Foe does undermine my quiet;
> Black legions, are my thoughts; not Pompey, but
> Ziphares comes, with all his wrongs, for Arms,
> Like the Lieutenant of the Gods, against me:
> Semandra too, like bleeding Victory. (IV. i. 82–87)

The striking thing about this vision and its interpretation is that
they do more than identify the psychological core ("jealousie,"
"guilty Bosom," "Black . . . thoughts") of the play's catastrophe;
around this core they wrap other strata of plot and theme to create a
larger model of what has happened (and is about to happen). First,
they conflate into a single paradigm of revenge the various victims of
the king's previous "unnatural" behavior: the massacred Romans, the
murdered sons, and Ziphares and Pharnaces. The latter is implied
because, of course, in Act V it is he who literally "pierc'd" the "heart"
of his father. Yet the dream forces us to understand that this actual
parricide merely reiterates the psychological revenge which has already been accomplished by all of Mithridates' enemies in concert
through the final agency of Ziphares. At another level the same revenge is about to be carried out against the entire kingdom by Pompey, and again the dream, by conflating Pompey and Ziphares, informs us that these are two forms of the same catastrophe. The
disintegration of Pontus begins in the kings's psyche and resonates
through the family and thence through the kingdom itself; as Mith-

ridates the father falls to Ziphares, and as Mithridates the king falls to Pharnaces, the kingdom of Pontus falls to Pompey's Rome.

At the outermost level, the joint destruction of Mithridates, his family, and state, is shown to be part of some great natural process whose ultimate purpose is beyond human comprehension and so must be described as "Fate," "Fortune," or the decree of "Heav'n." If the reader has not already become aware of this dimension of the drama, the dream-vision reveals it to him. Mithridates says the dream is a means by which "Fate" can "foreshow a Doom in sleep" (IV. i. 5), and in the dream itself he is "doom'd" by "Heav'nly Order" (IV. i. 35) to experience the confrontation with his ghostly victims. But Lee takes care throughout the play to inform the dialogue and action with this larger perspective. The Roman captain whom Mithridates so gruesomely dispatches in Act I curses his executioners in what turns out to be the prophetic voice of destiny:

> Here what the Fates have put into my brest:
> I see my Death, by Roman Arms, reveng'd;
> And what Lucullus had so well begun,
> Pompey shall end; Pompey, thy glory's ruine.
> . . . .
> . . . swift domestick jars
> Shall overtake thee; thou shalt add more blood
> To that already shed from thy Bowels:
> . . . .
> . . . one whom thou least
> Shalt fear, long nourish'd in thy impious breast,
> Shall stab thee to the heart, and end thy days. (I. i. 265–79)

Thus Manius Aquilius puts the seal of heaven on future events which are to be explained eventually in the dream-vision of Act IV.

All the main characters share this mythic perspective, however, even before they realize the full implications of the Roman's prophecy. While on occasion both Ziphares and his father egotistically claim to be in control of destiny ("Fortune's giddy Wheel, / . . . we have fix'd with our Majestick weight," "I at last have bound her to my Chariot" [I. i. 343; III. i. 71]), Archelaus, the kingdom's only major survivor, humbly warns that "Fate yet may put a bar betwixt our hopes" (I. i. 215) and that "Destiny's uncertain; Fate, as yet, / Holds the Scale doubtful" (I. i. 511–12). In the final act, it is Archelaus who recounts the genuine prodigy (as opposed to Tryphon's earlier contrived one) whose meaning by then needs no on-stage explication: emblems of the integrity of Pontus, "sacred Oyl," "Monuments," "Tombs," behave strangely, as altars dissolve into a "yellow puddle" (of gold, recalling the molten metal poured down the Roman captain's throat) which "A flash of thirsty Lightning" (Pharnaces, "breaking from this Cloud" of Roman legions [V. i. 49]) "quite lick'd up. / While through the Streets . . . murder'd Brothers rode" (V. ii. 38–50).

Even Pharnaces, who seems to act independently and to doubt the existence of a supernatural world (III. ii. 283–84), unwittingly places his villainy within the larger design of fate. When his father's ingratitude and arbitrary seizure of Monima first move him to plot treason, he expresses his black feelings as if they were serving some mysterious purpose whose larger implications are beyond his control: "The God of Battel rages in my Breast" as "Fury / Kindles . . . the Prophetick Maid" at Delphos (I. i. 55–57), and "hopes and fears / Toss my wrack'd heart, like a poor Bark" caught "in the Tempest" (I. i. 143–45). In Act V he calls Pompey's Romans "you Race of Heav'n, you Seed of Gods" (V. i. 47), inadvertently suggesting what becomes the fatal truth: Pompey completes on the national level the catastrophe which heaven has decreed in the psyche and family of Mithridates.

Organic imagery like "Seed of Gods" is typical of the play's language, especially the language used by Ziphares and Semandra as they attempt to make sense of their "Calamaties," which both ultimately ascribe to the "just" works of heaven "and wonder at the Gods" (V. ii. 209–11; and see V. ii. 140, 291–92). Both also try to understand their misfortune as a factor in some natural progression answerable to those "Gods" in the end. Finding "in Nature" no obvious recompense for her agony, Semandra concludes that perhaps "this World be but as fire, to purge / Her dross, that she may mount, and be a Star" (IV. i. 207, 222–23). Ziphares, likewise unwilling "Monsters [to] frame where Nature never err'd" (I. i. 326), seeks some organic explanation for his problems, and among the various metaphors he employs—the fateful tempest of passion and war (I. i. 525–26; IV. i. 294–309; V. ii. 252–54), the disease of ill fortune (see I. i. 406; IV. i. 230, 373; and V. ii. 292, 336)—one is particularly telling:

> Let me alone sustain those rav'nous Fates,
> Which, like two famish'd Tygers, are gone out,
> And have us in the Wind . . . . (IV. i. 592–94)

Here Ziphares finds a metaphor that discovers to him the grand
theme of all his family's misfortunes, the central theme of this play.
When the psyche of a king is disturbed, it disturbs all the family
members through whom it projects itself, upsets the natural balance
of their interrelations, and disrupts the inner harmony of the state
over which they preside. Like a defenseless animal in the wild, this
weakened king, his weakened family and state, become prey to the
"famish'd Tygers" of passion, Pharnaces, and Rome—all of whom,
seen from a cosmic perspective, are natural agents of fate. Thus Lee,
in a further attempt to understand the psychology of power, has created a dramatic paradigm for what today might be called political
ecology, the study of natural order—and the consequences of natural
disorder—within the nuclear family of a kingdom.

CHAPTER 7

Disaster of Principles: The Massacre of Paris: A Tragedy (1678/9?)

A S a Harvard graduate student in the 1930s, William Van Lennep
mastered Nathaniel Lee's sources and wrote that of all the author's plays *"The Massacre of Paris* most faithfully follows fact."[1] For
the greater part of his plot and a good deal of his language Lee relies
on E. C. Davila's *The Historie of the Civill Warres of France* (translated in 1647, reprinted in 1678). He also borrows passages from
Francis Bacon's *Essays* and may have learned a bit more about the
court of Charles IX from Gilbert Burnet's *A Relation of the Barbarous
and Bloody Massacre* (1678), from some French pamphlets (though
he rarely used foreign-language sources), and from Christopher Marlowe's *Massacre at Paris* (though it was probably never reprinted
after c. 1594 or performed in the Restoration).[2] Possibly concluding
that such a digest of history could hardly have demanded much artistic endeavor, modern critics have avoided examining the play's design, despite the generally favorable impression it has made on those
who seem to have read it through. Lately, Robert D. Hume has been
interested only in its genre—a "lurid, bloody, and bathetic" horror
play—but Van Lennep finds it swift-moving and packed with action,
Lee's editors note its "direct" dialogue and "complex" characters,
and John Loftis admires its "tragic force."[3]

Remarks like these encourage a closer reading than the work has
hitherto been given, and so does the fact that in those few places
where Lee departs from Davila's *Historie*, he writes with a confidence obviously born of a strong sense of purpose. Such are the passages from Bacon, the repeated references to the queen mother's
villainy and to her son's guilty conscience, and the scenes which contrast the relationship between the Duke of Guise and Marguerite to
that between the Admiral of France and his wife Antramont. These

94

and other, less overt, insertions tend not to reshape the historical events themselves but rather to shade them with tragic significance. The contrasting of the queen mother and her entourage to the Admiral of France and his fellow Huguenots is elaborated in such a way as to create two effects: (1) to condemn some who use religious principles to promote selfish political ends and (2) to lament others who self-destructively espouse religious principles to the exclusion of important social priorities. When these two postures toward life converge, the result is a horrible massacre, and its tragic nature is underlined in the final speech, where the agonized Charles IX translates it into psychological terms and relays its meaning to Charles II of England.

I   *The Significance of Date*

Since I am arguing that the play has contemporary as well as longer range significance, it is important to hypothesize its date of composition. Unfortunately, the available evidence is not very revealing, for the piece was initially denied production as being too fiercely anti-Catholic and anti-French, and there are no surviving records of the banning. It was not allowed on stage until 1689, when the Protestant court of William and Mary found its biasses congenial and moving, and by then Lee had cannibalized it to provide scenes and passages for *The Princess of Cleve* (composed c. 1681/2) and *The Duke of Guise* (1682). Nevertheless, what evidence there is suggests that Lee wrote it either in 1678-79 or in 1681. Robert Hume has recently opted for the later date:

. . . following the banning of *Lucius Junius Brutus* [December 1680] Lee decided to write a propaganda piece whose 'loyalty' could not be called in question, but found . . . that the French ambassador had enough influence to get the piece stopped. Despairing of ever getting it staged, Lee then used bits of it when he set to work on *The Princess of Cleve* and *The Duke of Guise* in late 1681 or early 1682. Certainly he seems to link the composition of *The Princess* directly to *The Massacre* when he says in the Dedication that the former 'was a Revenge for the Refusal of the other.'

Hume thinks that during the period between December, 1680 *(Brutus)* and July, 1682 *(The Duke of Guise)* Lee must have been writing at his usual rate of one or two plays per year, and since *The Princess of Cleve* seems to fall in that period, so must the source of some of

its scenes and passages. Moreover, says Hume, it is unlikely that the
banning of *Massacre* would have occurred before June, 1680, since at
that time Elkanah Settle's "violently anti-Catholic" play, *The Female
Prelate*, was holding the stage, while in the eighteen months after
Brutus was forbidden "excisions and bannings are numerous."[4]

On the other hand, the design of *Massacre* seems more fully accounted for if we suppose it was composed in late 1678 or 1679, for
this was when the English translation of Davila's *Historie* suddenly
reappeared after thirty years, along with a number of stongly phrased
pamphlets, all apparently exploiting the obvious parallel between
the St. Bartholomew's Day massacre of French Huguenots in 1572
and the projected massacre of English Protestants, the so-called Popish Plot "discovered" by Titus Oates in fall, 1678. One of the pamphlets, Burnet's *Relation* (mentioned in the first paragraph above),
covers the characters and events used by Lee, and it is possible that
some of Lee's departures from Davila were suggested by Burnet,
rather than by Burnet's French and Italian sources. For example, in
negotiating a Papal dispensation for the marriage of the Catholic Marguerite to the Protestant Prince of Navarre, Lee's Charles IX sends
the Pope a diamond ring inscribed with his vow of continuing religious zeal (I. ii. 120–24). In Davila the king's gift (which is refused) is
described as a precious jewel, whereas Burnet's version of the trans-
action, derived from Catena's *Vita del . . . Pio Quinto* (1586), more
clearly anticipates Lee: Charles is said to have offered the Papal leg-
ate "a Ring of great value" as "a pledge of his Faith."[5] Two other ways
in which Lee's play differs from Davila's narrative, the stress on
Charles IX's feelings of guilt and the presumption that he was being
slowly poisoned by his mother, may also derive from Burnet, since,
if Lee continued his usual practice, he would not have read Burnet's
source, Mezeray, until the English translation appeared, and this did
not occur until after *Massacre* had been written (1683).[6]

A further argument for placing the composition of *Massacre* in the
middle of anti-Catholic hysteria associated with the Popish Plot is
that this would help explain why "it is perfectly in tone with *Caesar
Borgia*" (1679), another "excursion into the byways of papal intrigue
and English terror."[7] Both plays accentuate Roman Catholic villainy;
both employ the imagery of the sea, tempests, beasts, devils, and the
Garden of Eden; and both depend to some extent on Davila. Interestingly, the poisoned gloves that Davila says were used to kill la
Reine de Navarre are transformed into poisoned *sweets* in *Massacre*

(IV. i. 31), only to reappear in their original form as a murder technique in *Borgia* (IV. i. 300–20). If the two plays were composed back-to-back, then it would seem that Lee borrowed this detail to use in *Borgia* after *Massacre* was banned, so that when *Massacre* was finally performed in 1689, he changed the account of the queen's death to keep from repeating a device already used and committed to print.[8]

Finally, if *Massacre* were composed, say, in fall or winter 1678—when Dryden and Lee were having *Oedipus* (c. September 1678) produced—the banning would make more sense in terms of theater history. As a collaborative effort, *Oedipus* was both authors' first play since, in spring, 1678, they had abandoned the squabbling King's Company for the more stable Duke's. Because both were apparently under contract to the King's, however, their desertion must have rankled both the old manager of the Theatre Royal, Thomas Killigrew, and his son Charles, who had become manager in 1676/7.[9] Perhaps, therefore, these two used Charles's position as Master of Revels to promote the prohibition of Lee's first independent venture for the rival company. Such a scenario would, in turn, help clarify Lee's 1689 dedication of *The Princess of Cleve*, where he calls this play a "revenge" against those who banned *Massacre*, for *Cleve* patently satirizes the court circle of which both Killigrews (in fact, all three, including Charles's half-brother Henry) were at least tangential members.[10]

Although none of this evidence is conclusive—Hume rightly cautions that "we shall probably never be certain" when the play was written[11]—it finally "works" better to read *The Massacre of Paris* as a generalized commentary on the Popish Plot of 1678–79 than as a document from the era of the Exclusion Crisis of 1681. It does not examine the Shaftesbury-Monmouth relationship, as *Absalom and Achitophel* (1681) does, or dramatize a king's response to republican threats against his sovereignty, as in *The Duke of Guise* (1682). Instead, at the height of apprehension that an actual massacre of Protestants could occur in London, and so ignite another civil war, it reminds the public (1) that such horrid plots can originate in the Catholic branch of a royal household, (2) that influential persons who get wind of the plot might be murdered to silence them (in a digressive episode of *Massacre* one Lignoroles, an associate of the Duke of Anjou, is killed after he learns of the plot [III. ii. 226–77; IV. i. 1–21]), (3) that the marriage of a royal princess (Marguerite) to a Protestant noble (the Prince of Navarre) could be used to lull fears of a Roman

Catholic stratagem, and (4) that a key target of such a stratagem might be militant Protestants headed by an estranged royal advisor (the Admiral of France) who advocates unifying the country by making war against a Roman Catholic neighboring nation (Spain).

The allusions to contemporary London would have been too obvious to ignore. First, Charles II, like Charles IX of France, was widely believed to be unduly influenced by foreign, Roman Catholic women—such as the Portuguese queen, whom Titus Oates accused of poisoning her husband; Hortense Mancini, whom Oates accused of consulting enemy agents; and Louise de Kéroualle, who in 1680 would be indicted "as a common whore."[12] Second, when Sir Edmund Berry Godfrey, a London magistrate, was found dead in October, 1678, many believed he (like Lee's Lignoroles) had been murdered by Jesuits to stop him from publicizing what Oates had told him about the Plot. Third, less than a year before reports of the Plot began circulating, the king had allowed his niece, Princess Mary (as Charles IX allows his sister in the play), to marry a Protestant Prince, William of Orange, in an apparent effort to placate those who feared Roman Catholic tendencies in the royal court. Finally, the Protestant militancy of the king's sometime counsellor, the Earl of Shaftesbury, together with the Earl's advocacy of war with France, found suggestive embodiment in Lee's Huguenot Admiral.[13]

II The Structure of Plot

Within this context of political implication, the vacillation of Charles IX between Roman Catholic Machiavellianism and Calvinist idealism becomes pointedly relevant to the situation in which Charles II, popularly thought of as a weak-willed monarch, found himself in 1678–79. Yet if *The Massacre of Paris* thus becomes another of Lee's advisories to the crown (like virtually all of his noncollaborative plays), it is not doctrinaire propaganda but rather a moving dramatization of the fruits of extremism in religion and politics. Through the agonized mind of Charles IX Lee encourages his own troubled king to seek some working synthesis of opposed religious and political forces, before England acts out its own tragedy as envisioned by Titus Oates. That the message also transcends the moment is what Tom D'Urfey means in his 1690 Epilogue:

> His [Lee's] Tale is somewhat bloody, but 'tis true,
> A Tragick Truth shown to an Honest end,
> And can the Good or Wise of neither Sect offend.[14]

To understand how Lee conveys this truth, one must begin with a closer look at the plot than most readers take time for.

Ostensibly to end civil strife between Catholics and Protestants (Huguenots), but actually to consolidate her family's power, the unscrupulous Queen Mother of France (Catherine de Medici) develops a twofold scheme: join Catholic and Protestant sympathies by marrying her daughter, the fiery Marguerite de Valois, to the Huguenot Prince, Henri III de Navarre; murder the Huguenot leaders—the Queen of Navarre (Jeanne d'Albret) and the Admiral of France (Gaspard de Coligny)—along with as many of their adherents as possible. Before she can execute the scheme, however, three impediments must be removed, two of which are more or less internal. First, she must persuade her melancholy son, King Charles IX (former protégé of the admiral), that her ends justify the diabolical means, and this is managed by invoking the Church's approval as enunciated by the wily Cardinal of Lorrain. Second, she must dissolve her daughter's engagement to the cardinal's powerful brother, the Duke of Guise (Henri I de Lorraine), and this she accomplishes in two stages. Knowing how deeply the duke hates the admiral, whom he suspects of having murdered his father (Francis, le Duc de Guise), she allows him to participate in the projected massacre only if he agrees to relinquish Marguerite and marry Catherine Cleve. Then, to overcome Marguerite's passionate resistance to the plan, she has the king force Guise to tear up his engagement contract.

The third impediment, the most difficult to remove, is the admiral's rooted distrust of the queen mother—a distrust which keeps him, with the Huguenot court, at a safe distance from Paris. To get past this hurdle, she must appeal to his respect for the Queen of Navarre and to his latent sense of loyalty to Charles. She persuades the Queen of Navarre, once again using the Cardinal of Lorrain, that Charles now intends to rule a unified France without his mother's interference, that to symbolize this new unity the Queen of Navarre must witness her son's Parisian wedding to Marguerite, and that to demonstrate his sincerity the king names Coligny chief advisor to the crown and general of the combined French-Dutch campaign against

Spain. The admiral represses a feeling of impending doom (shared by his wife, Antramont), orders an immediate attack on Spain to test the king's resolve, and follows the Queen of Navarre to Paris.

There she is promptly poisoned, but a mock autopsy convinces her family she died of natural causes while the admiral's reviving suspicions are quieted by lavish displays of the king's "affection" for him. Such displays make him feel honor-bound to remain at the king's side, even after he is warned of the king's complicity in an assassination attempt that cripples him. Now, having the Huguenots well within her grasp, the queen mother releases Guise to carry out the massacre, and the play rushes to its gory conclusion in a series of brief scenes. Windows light up as the palace bell rings in unison with the sounds of firing guns and groaning men. Two soldiers, led by one of Guise's lieutenants (Besnie), burst in upon the wounded admiral and his friend (and ambassador) Cavagnes. After a respectful hesitation, the intruders bludgeon both of their captives and, following Guise's orders, throw the admiral's body from the window to the mob below. The duke now commands that the admiral's children and estate be destroyed, and that his posterity be forbidden to hold titles or public offices, while the queen mother orders a firing squad to execute the surviving rebel leaders. When Charles IX hears about these events, including Guise's account of how the furious rabble decapitated the admiral's corpse and hung it burning from the scaffold, he writhes in psychological pain and moans a command to end the slaughter.

There is something refreshingly uncomplicated, yet highly suggestive, about the way this action is constructed around a basic set of contrasts. Perhaps remembering the effort required to achieve such resonant simplicity, Lee would later say that the "Play cost me much pains."[15] The framing contrast—that between the Roman Catholic court of Catherine de Medici and Charles IX, on the one hand, and the Protestant court of Jeanne d'Albret and Henri de Navarre on the other—is deepened by subsidiary contrasts of character, philosophical stance, and symbolism. The juxtaposition of queen mother to Queen of Navarre is, of course, only implicit, since we see little of the latter. Nevertheless, her passive, trusting, and gentle nature, as revealed in a few short speeches (II. i. 84–94, 96–100, 154–57), lingers in the mind as a foil to the diabolical Catherine de Medici. Much more telling is the contrast between the Duke of Guise and the Admiral of France—the one willing to sacrifice his mistress to political expediency and revenge, the other protecting his wife from political evil while he pursues moral and religious ideals.

III *Faction as World View*

This philosophical division between bestial pragmatism and a kind of piously rational idealism extends well beyond personality differences between Guise and the admiral. It informs much of what happens in the play and leads toward a general idea that raises the action above the level of propaganda. Gradually, the audience begins to see the two behavioral patterns—that of the queen mother and her intimates and that of the Huguenots—as manifesting two fundamentally opposed world views, two conflicting attitudes toward life whose eventual collision seems inevitable and tragic.

The queen mother and her cohorts are motivated by the desire for power, earthly glory, and revenge (III. i. 9, ii. 35–36). Their priorities are entirely political and mundane, and this applies even to their religious views, for they regard "Conscience, and Heav'ns Fear, Religion's Rules" as "State-Bells, to toll in pious Fools" (II. i. 267–68; and see I. i. 86; V. i. 90). One by one, the three characters within the queen mother's circle of influence who do not initially share her infernal nature are corrupted by it. In this respect she operates like Lee's Nero, spreading contagious evil all around, though in her aggressive scheming she is more like Petronius, Cassander, Pharnaces, and Machiavel *(Caesar Borgia)*. Although the Duke of Guise falls into her satanic ways without much resistance, because he is dominated by a passion for revenge against the admiral (I. i. 120–128), Marguerite gives way only under great pressure and sees herself as a sacrificial victim in some pagan political ritual (IV. i. 186). And while the king is persuaded to lend his authority to his mother's plot, he never fully accepts her system of values. Inside, even in the last moments before the massacre begins, his "Conscience" threatens to "drown the Voice of Policy" (V. i. 89).

If "Policy" dictates the behavior of the Roman Catholics, "Conscience" guides the Huguenots (II. i. 267–68; V. ii. 58–59). As their exemplar, the admiral conscientiously tries to combine martial heroism with a strong belief in predestination, regarding himself as the leader of a kind of Calvinist Church Militant. Admitting that he "blew the coals of Calvin's kindled Doctrine" into civil war (II. i. 34–36), he

now promotes a foreign war to reunify France into a latter-day version of the Roman Empire—an ambition which differs markedly from
that of the queen mother, since it emerges not out of a self-interested
desire for worldly power but rather from an inner conviction that God
wills the Huguenot ascendance as part of His grand plan. Nothing
more clearly distinguishes the admiral from his antagonists than this
predestinarian assumption. At the door of Providence he lays the
ultimate responsibility not only for his key decisions and acts—loyalty to the Queen of Navarre (II. i. 113), blindly persistent allegiance
to Charles IX (V. ii. 36), determination not to accompany Antramont
to a safe retreat (V. ii. 41–42)—but also for the bloody tempest that
finally engulfs the entire Huguenot enterprise: "There is a Providence that over-rules: / Therefore submit . . ." (V. ii. 21–22).

The imagery used to reinforce this vision of God's plan also underlines the dramatic contrast between the queen mother's pragmatic
and self-serving court (she "thinks there is no God above Ambition"
[II. i. 20]) and the admiral's realm of service to higher ideals. Catherine
de Medici and her disciples are seen as furies, devils, or the devil-
possessed, savage beasts, a badger or predatory lion, and the creators
of a political storm whose thunderbolts, lightning, and turbulent seas
overwhelm the Huguenots. The admiral, on the other hand, is regarded as being made of better stuff; he is the king's "better Angel,"
an eagle, a majestic lion, a great whale, or ocean-going vessel plowing
grandly through increasingly tempestuous waters.[16] By repetition
such images influence the audience to see Roman Catholics on stage
as bestial and diabolical, and to see Huguenots as exercising man's
highest qualities of courage, idealism, and spirituality. But to the
admiral it is not enough merely to observe this contrast; as a Calvinist
he must understand it as part of the cosmic drama whose meaning
has already been fixed by God and articulated to man in the Scrip-
tures. Lee uses the admiral's interpretive efforts to help convey the
"Tragick Truth" of his play.

IV   A Destiny for Predestination

From a Calvinist perspective the queen mother exemplifies what
has happened to the Church that was to have functioned on earth as
a second Garden of Eden for devout souls. In the admiral's mind she
is both the serpentine devil and an iron-age Eve whose proud lust for
power turns the civil Eden into a wilderness:

I see the forked Tongue betwixt her Teeth,
Hissing us from the Stage of Life and Honour:
O, she's a Serpent equal to the first,
And has the will to damn another World. (II. i. 9–12)

Imagin then the King, like Adam laid
Among the Sweets of Paradise to rest,
While to his listning Soul this Second Eve,
Full of the Devil, and design'd to damn us,
Thus breathes her Counsels fatal to the World. (II. i. 257–61)

Because he sees both Church and state as a wilderness, the admiral
has attempted to sow "those glowing grains" (II. i. 34–36) of the re-
formed religion, hoping thereby to foster the growth of a new garden.
When it becomes clear that the "Second Eve" has triumphed for the
moment, he modifies the vision only slightly, imagining that the new
faith will sprout from his own blood (V. ii. 10–12) until its "Root shall
reach the Center" and its "top touch Heav'n" (V. iv. 21–22). His imagery conflates the Eden myth with the biblical symbolism of vines
and vineyards. France under the queen mother, like ancient Israel,
is a vineyard gone to weeds, and the admiral regards himself as a
messianic figure, the vine of true faith whose blood/wine proves his
love and provides nourishment for new growth of branches, forming
a new vineyard/Eden/Church (Jer. 2:21; 8:13; Matt. 21:28—46; 15:13;
Mark 12:1–9; S. John 15:1–16).

Yet the admiral's vision is only partial, for it leaves out perhaps the
most important point of the Eden myth, that man is a fallen creature
and must therefore work out his salvation in earthly terms. Through
the admiral's wife, Antramont, Lee expresses the tragic nature of this
oversight:

I see the Vine that spreads his Arms to Heav'n
With all his Clusters rotting on the ground,
Blasted with Lightning from a clouded Council
By her that is the Juno of your Fate,
That Murd'ring Sorceress, that dry Hag of Florence,
That Midnight Hecate of ten thousand forms,
That varies with all Shapes, that tryes all Spirits,
Selling her Soul to each, and all together,
To make your Fate inevitable sure. (II. i. 218–26)

To Antramont the admiral is no Christ-like saint but rather a human being whose ethereal ideals have led him to neglect critical matters in his own proper estate. Before the vineyard can bear spiritually nourishing fruit, it must be cared for and allowed to ripen on the earth. In so exclusively following the lead of what he takes to be conscience—a sense of honor plus faith in Providence—the admiral overlooks the continuing need for action, for the vigilant cultivation and weeding of the postlapsarian garden. His Calvinism cancels out his heroism, and he becomes passively idealistic just when the queen mother's amoral pragmatism exfoliates in violent activity.

Thus, the resulting massacre is more than horribly pathetic; it is tragic. The admiral and Antramont repeatedly compare their circumstances to those of Cato Uticensis and his wife, Marcia (see II. i. 116–19, 182–84; V. ii. 15–16, 20–24), the Roman couple who were separated when Cato refused to compromise his ideals and fled to the stronghold of Utica. He later committed suicide as Caesar besieged the fortress,[17] just as the admiral, in effect, commits suicide by coming to Paris. Like Cato, the admiral dies confident that he is serving a cosmic purpose, so that, in his own mind, his death is not tragic. But from the audience's point of view it is tragic because it is made possible by his belief, virtuous in itself, that all is predestined. Empirically, he knows that the queen mother is bent on his destruction, but he remains the passive victim of her scheming because he is committed to the notion that God has already arranged matters for the best.

V   Ineptitude as a "Tragick Truth"

The one character who is free enough from both ambition and religious enthusiasm to assess the earthly kingdom with any degree of objectivity is the king himself, Charles IX. Once the admiral's devotee, he is now dominated by his mother, even though he knows that her "Garden" is so overgrown with "Weeds" that "she will turn a City to a Wild" (I. ii. 69–75). He alone struggles inwardly to reconcile the demands of conscience with those of political expediency, and while he is too weak to implement his wisdom, he does manage to express it in the play's closing lines. "O Mother," he exclaims, "Stop the vast Murder," for

> . . . all Churches by Decree and doctrine,
> Kings by their Sword and Balance of their Justice,
> All Learning, Christian, Moral, and Prophane,
> Shall by the virtue of their Mercury Rod
> For ever damn to Hell those curs'd Designs
> That with Religion's Face to ruin tend,
> And go by Heav'n to reach the blackest end. (V. v. 20–29)

This is the last of several speeches in the play that borrow heavily from Francis Bacon's *Essays*—in this case a passage from "Of Unity in Religion." Like Bacon, who uses the "Massacre in France" as a case in point, Charles IX urges that there are better ways of unifying factions than "by Warres, or by Sanguinary Persecution."[18] Instead, he implies, a king must try to handle political realities in ways amenable to those classic ideals inculcated by intellectual tradition, a sense of communal justice, and Christian doctrine. Within the context of this play, Charles is saying that neither Machiavellian maneuvering nor otherworldly enthusiasm (nor the one disguised as the other) can substitute for a difficult, precarious, and evolving compromise between perishable, mundane issues and timeless, suprarational values.

To achieve and maintain such a balance, however, requires just that initiative and resourceful strength that Charles IX patently lacks, and that Lee's own sovereign, Charles II, was widely believed to lack as well. Thus, it must have pleased the playwright, who so often had represented monarchs as weaklings, to observe the courageous behavior of his king during the coming crises of 1681–82. In these years of resisting threats to his own sovereignty and to his brother's lawful succession to the throne, Charles II was, according to his latest biographer, "at once tough and resilient. He exerted himself to destroy the Whig leadership . . . and in the end he won through. No one could accuse him either of laziness or lack of will power at this time of supreme political testing."[19] Predictably, during this period of Charles's resurgent strength Lee chose to leave behind his degenerate stage monarchs—his Alexanders and Charles IX's—and began to celebrate triumphant royalty in *The Duke of Guise* and *Constantine the Great*.

CHAPTER 8

Providence and the Fallen Psyche: Caesar Borgia; Son of Pope Alexander the Sixth: A Tragedy (1679)

TO the informed reader, *Caesar Borgia* is one of Lee's most rewarding compositions, though it is commonly thought little more than a terror-filled, verbose affair hastily thrown together to compensate for the prohibition of *The Massacre of Paris*. Some critics, indeed, have praised it for occasional passages of powerful verse and for success in making Borgia and Machiavel compelling characters, and William Van Lennep has instructively noted its indebtedness to specific historical sources and to Elizabethan and Jacobean dramatists.[1] But such observations do little to highlight distinctive qualities of the play or to elucidate its artistic design.

More to the point would be a series of questions, based on just such critical notations, but leading to a fuller understanding of theme and form. If the banning of *The Massacre of Paris* necessitated the creation of a politically tame play, what can a comparison of the two works reveal? How and to what end does Lee fictionalize history? What is the artistic intent of his most obvious borrowings from earlier literature: the Machiavellian villain, the Iago-Othello relation between the two central characters, and the motif of Columbus's discovery of the New World? Dealing with these and related issues suggests that in this play Lee continues to comment on contemporary affairs but that he does so chiefly through psychology and symbol rather than through historically parallel actions and political ideologies as in *The Massacre of Paris*. In *Caesar Borgia* he explores psychological relationships that are fundamentally relevant to the era of the Popish Plot and Exclusion Crisis. He shows these relationships and the actions they generate developing within an aesthetic environment of highly charged traditional symbols that connect psychology and behavior to political theory, morality, and religion. Ultimately, then, he urges his audience to see the play not as specific political editorial but as symbolic paradigm showing how Providence unfolds implications inherent in minds and hearts of the sorts that flourish in all eras of intense political intrigue.

I *Redesigning Sources*

Caesar Borgia could hardly have been composed in haste. Careful design was required if Lee was to avoid creating another overt commentary on current events like *The Massacre of Paris*. He faced essentially two alternatives: either to ignore current politics altogether and write a play with no apparent contemporary relevance—another variation on eternal themes, like *Oedipus*, another study of tyrannic love, like *Mithridates*—or to avoid only the specific parallels while exploring the underlying moral and psychological dimensions of the present scene. In typical fashion, he undertook the latter.

What he carried over from *The Massacre of Paris* is as revealing as what he avoided. The sheer horror of the earlier piece, for example, is not materially reduced. If a stage strewn with corpses formed a morbid background for the stabbing, mutilation, and burning of the Protestant leader in *Massacre*, in *Caesar Borgia* the audience witnesses the bludgeoning of Gandia in view of his beloved Bellamira (Borgia: "here, dip her Handkerchief,/ . . . in his blood, and bid her dry her eyes" [V. i. 112–13]), the subsequent strangling of Bellamira as she gazes, horror-struck, at the corpses of her murdered family, and the presentation to the dying Borgia of his maimed and blinded son, Seraphino. In both plays these atrocities serve essentially the same purpose, to show that vicious politics, supported by a corrupt church, inevitably lead to cruelly inhumane consequences. As he wrote the second play, however, Lee apparently wished to emphasize the vices of Machiavellianism more than those of Roman Catholicism. Thus, when he replaced the Paris of Charles IX, the Guises, and Catherine de Medici with one less patently mirroring the contemporary scene—the Rome of Pope Alexander VI and his bastard son Caesar Borgia—he gave a more central role to the unscrupulous political advisor (Catherine de Medici in the earlier play) and embod-

ied it in "Machiavel" himself. The anti-Papist bias remains in the
offstage presence of Alexander VI and in the minor character, Cardinal Ascanio Sforza, but the emphasis now falls on "Machiavellian
Magick" (III. i. 454).

In this respect the play would have been more aptly entitled "Machiavel *and* Caesar Borgia," for it deals primarily with the interaction
between these two figures. Machiavel's scheme to promote Borgia
initiates a chain of gory murders that unexpectedly ends with Borgia's own. Machiavel is directly responsible only for the first of these,
that of Bellamira's confidante, Adorna, who is disposed of through
the use of poisoned gloves, once she is no longer useful as a source of
chamber keys and fraudulent letters exposing her mistress's infidelities. The remaining homicides, except his own, are accomplished by
Borgia after he becomes obsessed with the notion, implanted by Machiavel, that Bellamira prefers and, indeed, carries on an affair with,
his brother the Duke of Gandia. Once this conviction gets possession
of him he is driven far beyond Machiavel's immediate purpose in
inciting him, which was to have him reject the unheroic role of pu-
sillanimous lover by doing away with the unfaithful Bellamira and her
"incestuous" devotee, Gandia. So the tragic action of the play
emerges from Machiavel's powerful mind operating on Borgia's passionate nature. They are two parts, as it were, of a single personality.
When Machiavel calls Borgia "my second self" (I. i. 84) he does not
mean "another me" but rather "a complementary side, that part of
me which feels and acts out my grand designs."

This is a stylized version of the Iago-Othello relationship, but the
accent on what we now call the fragmented personality makes it distinctive, and Lee's way of endowing it with larger implications is, on
the whole, new and ingenious. This can best be demonstrated by
examining the extent to which he borrowed and modified historical
facts and literary traditions. Van Lennep has identified the chief historical sources as Tomaso Tomasi's *Vita del Duca Valentino* (1671),
Francesco Guicciardini's *Historie* (trans. Geoffrey Fenton, 1561,
going into many later editions), and Machiavelli's *The Prince* and so-
called "Sinigallia Tract" (entitled "A Relation of the course taken by
Duke Valentine [Borgia], in the murdering of . . . the Family of the
Orsini"), published together in a 1640 translation by Edmund Dacres, with several later editions.[2]

That Lee employed dozens of details from these sources is not so
striking, however, as his way of fictionalizing the facts. His major

changes were designed to draw together separate historical episodes into a unified whole where their different kinds of significance—political, moral, religious—would interpenetrate and develop as a single pattern of meaning. First, he altered the love triangle—which Tomasi and Guicciardini define as an incestuous one involving Borgia, Gandia, and their sister Lucrezia—by replacing Lucrezia with the wholly fictitious Bellamira, supposed daughter of Paul Orsino, one of the leading enemies whom the historical Borgia liquidated at Sinigallia. Bellamira becomes a pivotal character around whom Lee can make historically separate murders revolve in one time and place. Envisioning her as having an illicit love affair with Gandia, Borgia first murders his own brother, an incident which Guicciardini and Tomasi ascribe mainly to sibling rivalry for temporal power and popularity. Using as a lure the temporary conciliation which Bellamira has effected between himself and her father, Borgia next draws the Orsini and Vitelli into his murderous clutches, a development which the historians locate in Sinigallia, not Rome, and which they connect not to Borgia's love life but to his political machinations. Finally, he murders Bellamira herself, an entirely fictional event, and his resultant insanity prefaces his own accidental death (and that of his father, the Pope) by drinking the poisoned wine he had intended for others—another historically based occurrence with a changed set, slightly altered cast, and modified outcome (the historical Borgia lives to laugh at Fortune).

II *Machiavel's Fortunes*

If the invention of Bellamira provides a means of achieving unity of time and place and of fusing the central political episodes to the love plot, Lee's second key innovation, the injecting of Machiavel into this boiling cauldron of tensions, adds psychological and moral ingredients. Despite his use of Borgia as the exemplary "Prince" in his own writings, the historical Machiavelli seems never to have served for long as Borgia's confidential advisor, though he tells us that at the time of the Sinigallia massacre he was on the scene, having been sent as Florence's ambassador to aid Borgia against his enemies.[3] Possibly this is where Lee derived the notion of giving Machiavel a central role in the whole chain of events dramatized in the play. It is more likely, however, that he took his cue from the long English literary tradition of creating Machiavellian villains, and it is by examining his belated employment of the type that we can best appreciate this aspect of his artistry.

In the earlier seventeenth century Machiavelli had become an established figure in philosophy, religion, political thought, and drama. Usually when he was invoked it was to represent his realpolitik in a negative light, though a few republican or disinterested writers could see him as a practical student of classical history who founded a kind of political science. More often, however, he appeared as the embodiment of Satan (or, at the very least, as a pagan or atheist) intriguing against the moral order to acquire wealth and power. Cruelty, cynicism, and an "aesthetic appreciation of his own villainies"[4] were his most prominent personal traits. This mythical Machiavel shared few characteristics with his original, the sane political observer, statesman, and classicist, who wrote *The Prince* and *The Discourses*.

Lee's Machiavel owes something to both the imaginative tradition and the historical figure. With many of his literary predecessors he shares a keen pleasure in the aesthetics of his own schemes (III. i. 60–63), and his frank egotism (III. i. 244) and scorn for the dictates of conscience (III. i. 251–52) recall similar attitudes in previous villains like Thomas Kyd's Lorenzo and Shakespeare's Richard III. His apparent atheism and penchant for using poisons are also typical of earlier stage Machiavels. But he seems to inherit at least two traits from the historical figure as well, though Lee avoids featuring the latter's republican ideals (perhaps to avoid the censure that greeted the republican admiral in *Massacre*). Unlike his original, Lee's Machiavel is a monarchist interested only in promoting his "Italian Tyrant" (I. i. 206), and he is motivated not by a political philosophy that sees Borgia as a necessary evil in corrupt times but rather by an obsession to mold another's destiny—an obsession that springs primarily from a visionary desire to recreate the ancient Roman Empire. This last notion links him to the author of *The Prince*, for both are students of classical history and wish to raise Borgia "to the old height of Roman Tyrants" (I. i. 86). Lee's Machiavel wants to do this personally, by snatching Borgia away from Bellamira, who melts his passion for "Arms and Glory" (I. i. 151), and by removing the impediments of Gandia, the Orsini, and the Vitelli.[5]

The second trait that Lee's Machiavel shares with the political writer is his concern for the relation between individual will and Fortune. Though, as Aubrey Williams has been reminding us, this whole issue of the role of Fortune (or Providence if seen from a Christian viewpoint) was "of crucial importance" to many Restoration authors,[6] Lee seems to have derived his interest in it in this case less from the "climate of opinion" than from *The Prince*, *The Discourses*, and the Fenton translation of Guicciardini. In all three works Fortune is taken very seriously and is conceived of in essentially the same way— the only great discrepancy being that to Fenton's Guicciardini she is God's handmaiden, while to Machiavelli she is a symbol for the constellation of social forces that share with individual will the responsibility for specific events in history. Both authors regard Fortune as being partially comprehensible by human judgment. Perceptive men may discern the direction toward which she tends and adjust their own designs so as to reap benefits derived from assisting her. Machiavelli adds that since men are bound by the limitations of their individual natures—their particular configurations of passion and intellect—they are not always able to change their tactics as Fortune changes hers, so that the drift of affairs will sometimes operate against them. Moreover, even when man manages to predict Fortune's course accurately, his most prudent decisions may not be able entirely to prevent her from acting against his interests.[7] This is what Machiavel's overzealous protégé in Lee's play means when, in a paraphrase of *The Prince*, he resolves to "dam . . . up" Fortune's torrent, so that "if she does ore-flow, she may . . . /Bring but half Ruine to our great designs" (V. iii. 68, 71–72).

Lee's Machiavel shares his original's respect for Fortune, but in his drive to define her inclinations he leaves out of consideration what Lee, like the translator of Guicciardini, senses to be her ultimate characteristic: her subservience to God's cosmic design. Machiavel cannot see that Fortune is, in fact, Providence, and his blindness leads toward a tragedy so fundamental that it shakes the foundations of his confidence and sanity. In the beginning he regards Borgia as Fortune's choice of the perfect raw material out of which he can "finish forth a greatness," for Borgia, like Dryden's Absalom, is "a Bastard, got in a fit of Nature!" (I. i. 93–94). His father, a priest, "stampt the Bullion in a heat, " possibly while "in the Embraces of a Nun" (I. i. 96, 102). Like his brother and sister, therefore, Borgia is "a start of Nature" formed by a chance collision of "wandering Atoms" and measuring up to one of "Lucian's Gods" (I. i. 108, 272, 276). Thus, he has all the raw traits any Machiavel could wish for in a protégé: powerful natural parts, politically useful religious connections, and the apparent approval of Fortune. It remains to disburden him of

Bellamira's softening charms and of his bugbear conscience, in order
to show him that "Self-love's the Universal Beam of Nature,/The
Axle-tree that darts through all its Frame" (III. i. 246–47). Only then
will it be possible to make his "Golden Fortune" (V. iii. 9) by "another's ruine" (III. i. 250) and by carefully husbanding "the Pope . . .
that rich source" (V. iii. 10).

Lee's Machiavel, then, like the author of *The Prince*, thinks in pre-
Christian terms. He wishes to make Borgia into a fine Roman tyrant
who is guided by Machiavel's own philosophy of opportunism combined with egotism, Lucretian materialism, and a love of diabolical
machination. The trouble with this ambition, as the events of the play
make clear, is that it ignores the nature of the Christian cosmos, that
Augustinian universe which still held fascination for Lee and his contemporaries, even though it was being reinterpreted to account for
the findings of science and realignments in the political and economic
order. To Lee's Machiavel the whole conception of a fallen world,
where only a precariously maintained social and moral organization
prevents the Devil from capitalizing on human pride and passion, is
a fiction whose chief manifestation in the human mind is Christian
conscience, which he regards as a childish superstition. The universe
consists, he believes, of mind, matter, power, passion, and Fortune,
and whoever orchestrates these to his own advantage can count on
success. Passion, in particular, is ignoble only when it expends itself
purposelessly, on women or mere pleasure. Such "Gothick Fury" (I.
i. 563) Machiavel condemns in Borgia's feeling for Bellamira, feelings
which he presumes were generated by "the Vandals" (III. i. 336)
when they overran old Rome and put out the flames of "manly Confidence and Roman Vertue" (I. i. 562). Equally ignoble is Christian
passivity, the gutless absence of passion, the otherworldly "meekness
of an Anchorite" (II. i. 287) which insults manhood. In its place he
would inspire a "dazling Passion, and becoming Fury" (II. i. 376) to
drive Borgia forward to greatness. He envisions an invincible partnership between his own omniscient intellect and Borgia's fortunate
combination of natural strength, passion, and prestige.

He is defeated because this vision, based soundly enough on a pagan conception of the universe, is erroneous. In the world of this play
at least, an Augustinian order prevails, Fortune is Providence, and
egotism and earthly desire are the Devil's tools. Interestingly
enough, Lee does not make Machiavel himself an embodiment of
Satan, though this was a common practice on the Tudor and Caroline

stage. Instead, he is shown to be an unwitting agent of Hell who, by misinterpreting the universe, enables Satan to possess the soul of Borgia. On various occasions Machiavel defines his strategies by using metaphors drawn from the imagery of demonism, but he is not serious about them. To his mind they are merely metaphors, aids to expression which he peppers among others of a less occult nature. He regards himself, for example, as a sculptor whose brass or marble is Borgia (I. i. 81–93), as a physician mixing the ingredients of "the potion Death" (I. i. 215–16), as a shipwright whose vessel is designed to brave the tempests of Fortune (III. i. 60–63), the holder of a key to victory over Borgia's enemies (V. i. 40–44), the trainer of a champion greyhound about to run his most triumphant race (V. i. 76–77). Amidst such rhetorical images appears the telling one: thus far his evil influence is merely an "Infant Fury," but he intends to "nurse this Brood of Hell to such perfection/As shall e're long become the Devil's Manhood" (III. i. 452, 455–56). He knows not how truly, how nonmetaphorically, he speaks in this case. The infant mischief brought into Borgia's personality by his midwifery, and nursed by his continuing strategies, is more than the simple jealousy which he expects to result in the expedient deaths of Bellamira and Gandia. It is, in fact, "the Devil's Manhood," whose gory acts ensanguine the stage of Act V, presenting a spectacle that temporarily destroys Machiavel's rational self-control: in an hallucination he sees ghost-like forms of Borgia and the Pope, and he confesses that his "mind" is "deeply shockt, even from her own Foundation" (V. iii. 35–43, 242–44) by the extravagance of suffering his schemes have caused.

III *Borgia's New World, the Flesh and the Devil*

But if Machiavel's confrontation with the true nature of Fortune results in a shock, for Borgia such knowledge is to be had only at the expense of his humanity, sanity, and salvation. From the moment he comes on stage Borgia carries with him an ugly reputation for cruelty, lust, and incest, and it is only the flicker of a higher, redeeming sort of relationship with Bellamira that alerts him to the radical disjunction between her humane, Christian world and Machiavel's world of ego, power politics, and the passion for conquest. As Machiavel gains more and more control over his will, Borgia becomes progressively less capable of distinguishing the two worlds, of differentiating love from lust, humane justice from bestial revenge, the establishing of a relationship from the exploitation of others. Three, interrelated strands of imagery helps us to follow Borgia's degeneration. All three are significantly woven into his conception of Bellamira, whom he sees less frequently as a "Cherubim" (II. i. 373), "bright Augusta" (V. i. 345), and "pattern of the Gods" (IV. i. 371)—or in moments of fury as sorceress and serpent (IV. i. 96; V. i. 74)—than as an Edenic New World which he must seek through perilous seas. What emerges most noticeably as we examine different uses of this cluster of images is that the three central metaphors—Columbus's New World to describe Bellamira, Eden to express the ideal state of loving her, and tempestuous seas to represent the psychological and social impediments to Borgia's ambitions—grow and change in significance as the play develops.

The ambivalent symbolism of New World imagery was well established by the time Lee chose to employ it. In England the literary response to America began in the 1550s with Richard Eden's translation of Peter Martyr's *Decades* and with John Ponet's *Short Treatise of Politicke Power*. By the early seventeenth century the New World had made its way into all the major branches of imaginative writing—lyric poetry, drama, essay, chronicle—where it began to be seen in certain conventional perspectives. Later seventeenth-century writers like Lee could, therefore, presume that allusions to Columbus, the New World, and Indians would automatically convey a variety of connotations simultaneously: on the positive side, the spirit of adventurous discovery, a virgin resource of riches and medicinal cures, an Arcadia, Utopia, New Eden or earthly paradise, where the Golden Age still existed. Negatively, such references carried connotations of natural terrors—jungles, strange and deadly plants and animals—and of aboriginal cannibals who served the Devil, sacrificed humans to an insatiable sun god, and originated that scourge of the accomplished rake, syphilis. Moreover, almost any allusion to America conjured up the popular myth of Spanish atrocities against the Indians.[8]

Lee's references to the New World—which are made not only through Borgia but also in the remarks of Cardinal Ascanio—emphasize five of these conventional connotations: the spirit of exploration and discovery, the rediscovery of the Golden Age or New Eden, the aura of Devil worship, the "pox," and the cruel exploitation of America's land and inhabitants. He selects these because they can be logically connected in order to bring out part of his theme. Briefly, the point he makes with this set of images is that Machiavellian poli-

tics and Roman Catholicism deal with human beings in essentially
the same way, from the same motives, as the Spaniards were thought
to have dealt with the New World. Finding it a pristine paradise,
they barbarously exploited it in order to possess its gold and Indian
slaves. Such behavior not only betokened bestiality and depravity; it
also resulted in increased corruption, for the exploited Indians who
were brought to Europe carried with them the influence of Satan and
the "pox." As with the Spaniards, so, in Lee's version, with the Roman Church (headed during the era of Columbus's discoveries by the
Spanish Pope, Alexander VI, Borgia's father) and so with Machiavellian politics as acted out by Borgia.

Before demonstrating this in respect to politics, Borgia, and the
play's overarching meaning, let us briefly turn to the most interesting
minor character, Cardinal Ascanio Sforza, and the satire of *ecclesia*.
He personifies the secularized, unscrupulous, materialistic, and lustful Roman Churchman. That by his past actions he had already sealed
his pact with the Devil is clear from the beginning, for, unlike Borgia,
he is incapable even of perceiving human relations on a level higher
than the material and sensual. He drools over Bellamira's "skin full
of alluring flesh" (I. i. 29), and it is to avenge himself on Borgia for
possessing her first that he causes Seraphino's eyes to be gouged out
and his face mangled. While admiring Machiavel's earthly wisdom
("Brain, all brain" [I. i. 104]), Ascanio is realistic about his own grosser
merits ("stuff to him—/Meer . . . Guts of Government" [I. i. 105–
06]). In essence, if not in spirit, he agrees with Machiavel and Paul
Orsino, who consider him a "dull . . . walking lump of Lust" with an
"ungorg'd appetite" for whores to whom he has given "the Neapolitan
Pox" (I. i. 203-04, 357)—presumably having picked it up in Naples
to which, according to Guicciardini, it had come from Spain after
Spanish adventurers brought it from America. Ascanio is a caricature
of the venal prelate (of the same name) described by Guicciardini,
and it may well be that Lee decided to connect him with images of
the New World by reading in that same source brief discussions of
the origins of the "pox," of Columbus, and of the Spanish practice of
exploiting riches in America instead of propagating Christianity.[9]

At any rate, it is Ascanio who has brought to the Papal Chamber of
State the "little American Boys with Boxes of Jewels in their hands"
(stage directions to Act I), and it is implied that they were part of his
payment to the Pope for raising him to the Cardinalate (Guicciardini
says Ascanio was among the first to buy Papal patronage). As the play

opens, he has Alonzo introduce these "Children of the new-found World" (I. i. 155) to Machiavel and offer their jewels as an earnest of further compensation should Machiavel agree to sever Borgia from Bellamira. To back his own program for promoting Borgia, Machiavel has already decided to accept "Ascanio's new golden World" (I. i. 110), implicitly including the Pope's favor, and later he reminds Borgia that such support is a kind of "Golden Fortune" (V. iii. 9) that always favors their designs. Here, Machiavel is of one mind with Ascanio, who explains to Alonzo that for "twenty thousand Crowns" many "Monks, Fryers, Jesuits . . . would kill their Fathers,/Ravish their Mothers, eat their Brothers and Sisters" (III. i. 24-27). We are not surprised, then, when the dying Ascanio begins to babble with seeming incoherence about a corrupt Church, the New World, and the Devil: the Church is "like Babels Whore"; the Pope is "a very leud/And wicked Head"; it is time to "drink Columbus's health," for these dancing Indians "are pretty Children, very fine Boys"; his "Guts" are on fire, and "Devils are quarter'd in my Bowels" (V. iii. 153, 156–57, 170, 173, 214, 221).

Ascanio and his Church have become diabolical exploiters of nature, rather than ministers to the human spirit. Whether their object be America or Bellamira, they are chiefly interested in material gain, in Devil-worshipping slaves, in riches, and in carnal pleasure.[10]

A common seventeenth-century notion was that, without the Spaniards and their Church, America *could* have been a New Eden, a paradise where the Golden Age might begin anew.[11] Sir Thomas More located his *Utopia* in the New World, and Sir William Davenant in his play, *The Cruelty of the Spaniards in Peru* (1658), shows the Indians enjoying a Golden Age before the Spanish arrive. But the Spanish did arrive, and in Lee's play this is tantamount to saying that Ascanio and the Pope are rank weeds that spoil "the Churches Corn" (I. i. 368) and that Borgia, through Machiavel's instigation, exploits and destroys, instead of loving and protecting, the woman who could have been his New World, his Eve in Paradise. We might wonder if Lee had somehow got hold of a copy of Samuel Butler's little-known Character, "A Modern Politician," which defines a Machiavellian type as one who "makes new Discoveries in Politics . . . like those that *Columbus* made of the new World, very rich but barbarous. He endeavours to restore Mankind to the original Condition, it fell from, by forgetting to discern between Good and Evil; and reduce all Prudence back again to its first Author the Serpent, that taught *Adam*

Wisdome. . . . "[12] Such, indeed, would appear to be Machiavel's way of dealing with Borgia. While the latter may never have had much in common with Adam, Machiavel does, in effect, teach him the Devil's wisdom that prevents him from achieving with Bellamira a relationship akin to that of Adam and Eve in Paradise.

The change in Borgia's attitude toward her and, at the same time, in his entire personality, is underlined by his use of the three kinds of images noted above. In his least corrupt frame of mind he sees her as the New Eden that he can reclaim by heroically navigating the fallen world (and his own psyche):

> Thus, to a glorious Coast, through Tempests hurl'd,
> We sail like him who sought the Indian world.
> 'Tis more; 'tis Paradise I go to prove,
> And Bellamira is the Land of Love;
> . . . .
> . . . like the first Maid she walks:
> Fair as the Day when first the World began;
> And I am doom'd to be the happy man. (II. i. 377-84)

But we can perceive a difference when he speaks under the direct influence of Machiavel, whom he regards as "my Heav'n, my . . . / . . . God" (I. i. 575–76). In this context she becomes not an Edenic New World but a "White World" to "travel o're, to feast my Love," and to become "gorg'd with Revels" and "all the Liberties of loose desire" (III. i. 207–12). She is now an "Indian Treasure" (II. i. 203) open to exploitation. Borgia's love has turned to lust, and his state of mind begins to resemble that of Seagull in George Chapman's *The Middle Temple and Lincoln's Inn Mask* (1613), when he says in reference to America, "Come, boys, Virginia longs till we share the rest of her maidenhead."[13] Borgia is now in the position of John Donne's rake who calls his mistress "my America! my new-found land" and "My Myne of precious stones."[14].

IV   *Tempests of Mind and Soul*

Whenever this attitude takes over inside Borgia's mind, not only does the New World become a gold mine and Eden a bed in a brothel, but also the associated imagery of tempestuous seas assumes new significance. That ocean which, in the quest for Bellamira/Eve

in her paradisiacal New World, provided a glorious trial of his devotion, now becomes a "dismal Gulph"—specifically referring here to
marriage—"which like the Hellespont do'st rore between/Me and
my Joys" (I. i. 582–84). Thus, he'll "plunge, or perish, or enjoy her"
(I. i. 588). As this lust becomes transformed by jealousy into what
even Machiavel regretfully sees as "blind, ungovern'd rage" (IV. i.
223), Borgia begins to give way to violent, self-destructive passion, so
that he is ready to submit his Indian treasure to his own fate, just as
"the weeping Merchant," to "gorge" the sea's "ravenous Jaws,"

> . . . hurls all his Wealth,
> And stands himself upon the splitting Deck,
> For the last plunge. . . . (IV. i. 217–20)

Machiavel's "start of Nature" has become a natural disaster, and the
way to Bellamira's New World has become the tempestuous sea of
Borgia's own insanity and depravity. He has learned, as he says, "to
follow Nature;/For so do Flames that burn, and Seas that drown" (II.
i. 324–25).

This connection between insanity and depravity, and the relation
of both to Providence, is insisted upon in the play. As Machiavel's
blasting rhetoric convinces Borgia of Bellamira's infidelity, it is as if
"two Furies leap" from the counselor's "red Eyes" and Borgia is no
longer "Master of [his] Passion" (III. i. 364, 372). Hereafter he is
tortured by "ghastly fears and cloven jealousies,/ . . . Monsters"
that, like "sullen Fiends" make "sick" his "Brain" (III. i. 557–60). By
Act V he sees himself as a "poor Lunatick" (V. i. 262) who in his quest
for paradise has been overwhelmed by "this Torrent of the world,/
Fortune" (V. iii. 67); " 'Tis all the work of Chance," he laments, "and
trick of Fortune" (V. iii. 249). Like Machiavel, he is ignoring what
Lee has made clear all along: Fortune is really Providence, the handmaiden of God, which has consigned Borgia to the underworld of his
father and Ascanio. Just before her death, Bellamira discerns what
has happened. The human lover has become a "Monster," "Beast"
(IV. i. 412–413), "Hellhound," "Devil," "Son of that old cursed Serpent,/Who daubs the holy Chair with blood," "Hells Vicar, and his
first begotten Devil" (V. i. 108, 110, 127–28, 131). And as Borgia
insanely struggles against the effects of the poisoned wine he had
intended for his enemies, his delirium reveals what Providence has
in store: a sea of fire, emerging from which "the Master Devil" (V. iii.

305) offers full pardon in exchange for gold. "Gold for my pardon, hey—'tis seal'd and given!/And for a Ducat thus I purchase Heav'n—" (V. iii. 358–59).

V *The Divided Self and Restoration Depravity*

Curiously, Borgia's "second self," Machiavel, does not perish along with the other main characters—even though he has claimed that when Borgia, "a very Limb of me," dies, "thou'lt see me halt" (V. i. 13–14). The psychological pressure which Machiavel exerts on Borgia has not materially changed his own personality, though it does seem to have altered one tenet of his philosophy. Unlike his historical original, he is at this point not so much a student of the classics as he is the vile empiric, for at the play's end he is prepared to regard the whole previous chain of tragic events as so much mere data from which to generate a political maxim. Momentarily "shockt" by the proceedings, he can now coolly conclude, "No Power is safe, nor no Religion good,/Whose Principles of growth are laid in Blood" (V. iii. 371–72). This sounds a good deal like Shakespeare's King John telling Hubert, "There is no sure foundation set on blood,/No certain life achiev'd by others' death,"[15] but it is the direct opposite of Machiavel's philosophy earlier in the play, where he would have agreed with his namesake in the "Prologue" to Marlowe's *The Jew of Malta*: "Might first made kings, and laws were then most sure/When, like the Draco's, they were writ in blood."[16] Perhaps there is a clue here to the ultimate contemporary significance Lee meant for his play to convey.

In the first place, even if Machiavel's second doctrine is more appealing than the first, we cannot expect much from a man who induces generalizations from such gory "experiments." At the end of the play he continues to hold in our esteem a place alongside that of the Nazi medical teams who did research on human guinea pigs. Moreover, we are apprehensive about the lone survival of a cruel philosopher who instigated horrors that overtook all the other main characters. It is as if Lee had read Marlowe's "Prologue" rather attentively:

> Albeit the world think Machiavel is dead,
> Yet was his soul but flown beyond the Alps,

> And, now the Guise is dead, is come from France
> To view this land and frolic with his friends.[17]

In Marlowe's time the Duke of Guise had recently been murdered.
Lee's Duke, along with his Machiavellian accomplice, Catherine de
Medici, had been "assassinated" a century later when *The Massacre
of Paris* was denied the stage. So Lee decided to send Machiavel
again "beyond the Alps," only this time in the other direction, and to
inject him into a scene with fewer obvious parallels to contemporary
London. But he retained almost the same symbolic and moral dimensions, for both plays convey their themes through the imagery of seas
and tempests, beasts and devils, the Eden myth and Providence.
Both warn against the importation of diabolical influences connected
with Machiavellian politics and the Roman Church. And both imply
that the "soul" of Machiavel and, indeed, the souls of Borgia and
Ascanio, are reincarnated whenever the time and circumstances allow.

Since in *Caesar Borgia* this warning could not be expressed
through events parallel to the Popish Plot, it is made more than implicit in Borgia's final speech: "I'll live," he says, to "create new
wicked Popes" and

> Murder successively two Kings of France;
> Brittain attempt, though her most watchful Angel
> Saves the Lov'd Monarch of that happy Isle,
> And turns upon our selves the plotted Wound,
> . . . yet still wee'll on,
> And hatch new deeds of darkness; O Hell, and Furies!
> Why should we not, since the great Head himself
> Will back my Plots, joyn me in blood and horror,
> And after give me Bond for my Salvation. (V. iii. 340–52)

Clearly, Borgia becomes more than Borgia here, just as in Marlowe's
"Prologue" Machiavel expands into a symbol for all satanic politicians. The sense of this passage is that we Borgias, we fraudulent
priests of the Romish Church (Borgia had been, as Bellamira informs
us, "Priest," "Archbishop," and "Cardinal" before being made Duke
[V. i. 124]), possessed by the Devil, will appear in this fallen world in
all eras to do mischief—just as the demented friar, Jaques Clement,
and the fanatical monk, Ravaillac, stabbed to death "successively two
Kings of France," Henri III and Henri IV (Lee could have learned

this partly from Davila's *Historie*, his source for *The Massacre of Paris*).[18] In his "Epilogue" Lee asks the audience to "damn those Rogues" who "act" out terrible schemes such as those in the play "o're again" on the stage of mid-Restoration London (1. 22).

But Lee has not created an historical parallel or political prophecy.[19] Each of the more active characters represents a different aspect of the same corrupt element of society or, to use a psychological analogy, of the same kind of mind. If Borgia and Machiavel are two parts of the same "self," Ascanio is a third part. Together and separately they represent the fallen psyche, its corrupt tendencies exaggerated, divided from the beneficent influence of the rest, and subjected to Satan's dictates—the kind of personality that exploited rather than cultivated the American garden. Machiavel is the sterile, inhumane intellect; Ascanio the sensual priest; and Borgia the fanatical and destructive man of action. Lee's message, therefore, is political only in the sense that its significance pertains equally to politics, morality, and psychology, within the cosmic framework of religion. The kind of Roman Catholic plot that presently threatened England was not so much a consequence of particular actions by specific individuals as a sign of periodic degeneration in the human spirit. In the long run what England, with her "watchful Angel," must guard against is the "Machiavellian Magick" of powerful minds bent on creating tyranny at the expense of humanity (possibly the Jesuits, who were sometimes connected to Machiavelli?),[20] sensual indulgence that ignores moral duty (the Stuart court?), and fanatical violence for the sake of distorted principles (on the part of both Roman Catholics and Radical Whigs?). Such extravagancies both invite and manifest the Devil's work in fallen man, and, Lee seems to say, if Providence acts against us while we harbor such criminal psyches, let us not say we were not forewarned.

CHAPTER 9

Christian Heroism: Theodosius: or, The Force of Love, A Tragedy (1680)

IN *Theodosius* Lee returns not to the "soft" heroic play, as some critics have insisted,[1] but to the problem of heroism in modern life, the problem raised in *Sophonisba*. In this later play, as we might expect after the intervening works, the nature of the problem is rather more complicated, though the central question remains: what actually constitutes heroism when it is removed from a highly stylized setting, like that of Dryden's Almanzor (*The Conquest of Granada*, 1670–71), and placed in a more realistic environment of social, political, and psychological forces? Yet if this question is more complexly defined in *Theodosius*, its dramatized answer is less ambivalent than in *Sophonisba*, for by now Lee was interested not only in the human struggle of an Alexander or Mithridates to achieve control over self and state but also in the wisdom of Providence as it organizes such struggles for the long-range benefit of man. Against the melancholy and despair of characters like Varanes and Theodosius (the Massinissa and Scipio of the piece) he poses the progressive vigor of others, Marcian and Pulcheria, who resolve their religious, psychological, and political problems. They do so through a providential fusion of sanity and faith which is a corrective to the admiral's obsessive and irresponsible providentialism in *Massacre*, and which bears a surprising relevance to sociopolitical developments in the England of 1680.

I *The Design in the Past*

That the story of Theodosius was relatively familiar to Lee's audience is assured by its availability not only in historical works but also in fictional forms—especially in Massinger's *The Emperour of the East* (1631), La Calprenède's *Pharamond* (1661), and Corneille's *Pulchérie* (1672).[2] To approach this kind of familiarity the modern reader would need to turn to the lucid account by Charles Diehl, a distinguished historian of Byzantium.[3] With the historian's sense of factual accuracy and the literary man's eye for the arresting detail, Diehl tells us that in the early fifth century, A. D., the pious and virginal Pulcheria, Regent Empress of Byzantium, chose a somewhat unlikely bride for her younger brother, Theodosius, the comparatively passive emperor. The bride-to-be was Athenais, the stunningly beautiful and highly educated daughter of a pagan Athenian professor of philosophy, Leontius, who had recently died and left his estate to his sons. Paupered by their greed, Athenais had sought refuge in the court at Constantinople, and her beauty and eloquence had brought her to the empress's attention. The marriage was consummated after Athenais agreed to be baptized and to assume the name Eudocia (or Eudosia), which embodied traditionally Christian connotations in the Eastern Empire. Despite the pressures of religious controversy and court intrigue, the marriage survived more or less intact until Theodosius died, when Pulcheria made good her claim to the throne by insuring that Eudosia, now in genteel exile for alleged religious heresy, remained out of touch with court affairs. For her consort, Pulcheria wisely chose the distinguished but aging general and senator, Marcian, and their subsequent joint management of imperial affairs gained for both lasting reputations as competent and pious heads of state.

Lee's variations on this historical episode are both less and more factual than those of his three main literary forebears, Massinger, La Calprenède, and Corneille. He is less factual, in that he fabricates a good deal more than the others—the boyhood friendship of Theodosius and Varanes in Persia, for example, where each supposedly met Athenais without his friend's knowledge; the subsequent love triangle and resultant suicides of Varanes and Athenais, followed by the morbid withdrawal of Theodosius. More important, Lee departs from history and from his main source, La Calprenède, by centering all key events in Constantinople during the hours preceding the emperor's marriage. This enables him to infuse the action with moral and political significance by juxtaposing in one time and place the tragic love triangle and the exemplary union of Pulcheria and Marcian—a union which, historically and in earlier literature, is represented as occurring after the death of Theodosius. In one outstanding way, however, Lee has written not less but more historically than his predecessors, for he alone reclaims from history the milieu of tension between pagan and Christian systems of value that characterized fifth-century Constantinople. This tension, in the play heightened by the lure of pastoral retreat as almost a third value system, is felt by all the main characters. As it is worked out in contrasting fashions by the two sets of lovers, it becomes the vehicle for Lee's moral, psychological, and political meanings.[4]

II *Providence and Identity*

The action of *Theodosius* is presided over by Providence in the form of destiny, fate, the stars, and even pagan gods. Before Varanes realizes that he and his emperor-friend, Theodosius, are fatally opposed in their love for Athenais, the poor philosopher's daughter, he urges Theodosius to join in running "the Race which Fate has set before us" (I. i. 300). Theodosius responds by lamenting the "Cruel Destiny" (I. i. 301) that makes him love-sick. Later, torn not only between natural love for Athenais and social conventions that dictate against his marrying one of her low station, but also between love for her and for his friend, Varanes blames his melancholy situation on the stars (II. i. 344; III. ii. 228), Fortune (III. ii. 310), Fate (III. ii. 320; V. ii. 57), and "cruel Gods" (IV. ii. 351). His consequent suicide is attributed by Theodosius to the "Eternal Pow'rs / That guid the World" (V. iv. 16–17).

If to Theodosius those powers are controlled by the Christian God and to Varanes they are at the behest of Persian deities, to Athenais it is unclear whence their force derives. Just as she is divided between her love for Varanes and her oath to Theodosius, she is also uncertain as to her religious convictions: whether she is the pagan lover, Athenais, or the Christian convert, Eudosia; whether she is to become a star in the pagan paradise of Varanes (V. iv. 69) or a star of virgin piety in the Christian heaven of Theodosius (III. ii. 4). He and his sister, Pulcheria, are themselves unsure of her status in the providential scheme, for each hails her using ambivalent symbols. To the emperor she is the "morning Star" (III. ii. 120) that is both the Venus to his earthly love and the messiah to his imperial authority ("this bright Star directs us," III. ii. 176). And to Pulcheria she is both the Astraea that one identifies with the return of pagan Justice in a renewed Golden Age and the Astraea-Mary who is expected to descend with the second coming of Christ and the new Eden.[5] In taking her own life she seems to deny both sets of identity, but in reality her tragedy, by effectively removing both Varanes and Theodosius from active life, does make way for a kind of reincarnation of justice and order in the marriage and joint rule of Pulcheria and Marcian. In their contract "the Roman-Gods" (II. i. 108) to which he is most loyal unite with Pulcheria's Christian "Innovations" (II. i. 107) to act providentially for the future benefit of the earthly kingdom.

III *Identity and Heroism*

The psychological equivalent, or correlative, of this integration of pagan and Christian forms of fate is the central dramatic issue of the play. Marcian strikes to the heart of the matter when he denounces the apathetic emperor as "a pretty Player, one that can act a Heroe,/ And never be one" (IV. ii. 98–99). It is precisely this challenge to *be* oneself—which in the later seventeenth century meant being in rational control of oneself—while struggling to reconcile contradictory elements in one's experience, that confronts all the characters in the play. Their respective failures or successes to achieve this complex synthesis of psychological forces seem to determine the way Providence disposes of their lives.

The failure of Theodosius to maintain self-possession while experiencing love's enchantment incapacitates him for resolving the venerable conflict between pastoral *otium*[6] and responsible, heroic action. Theodosius begins ignoring the imperial obligation to *be* heroic when he and Varanes, students together in Persia, play the heroic roles of Alcides and Theseus, comrades in Seneca's tragedy, *Hercules Furens* (I. i. 244–63). This exchanging of self for a false role symbolically foreshadows for both men, as does the changing of names for Athenais, their subsequent tragedies. When the pastoral enchantment of Athenais truly dispossesses Theodosius of "self" (I. i. 170), he is rendered vulnerable to the equally potent enchantment of "Christian Enthusiasm . . . / . . . work'd by Melancholly" (I. i. 267–8). Unlike his sisters, Marina and Flavilla, whose commitment to Christian devotion is a carefully deliberated choice of heavenly faith over all "humane Charms" (I. i. 354), Theodosius surrenders to the exterior attractions of a religious way of life, of a role that eschews heroic duty as it fixes his resolve to lay down the "golden Reins of Empire" (I. i. 269).

As with Theodosius, so with his friend. Having similarly fallen victim to the "Charms" (I. i. 137) of Athenais, Varanes loses his grip on reality, and determines either to "lose my self" (I. i. 100) in a vision of pastoral love, free of all obligation to act heroically in the mundane world, or to undertake an equally false role: not that of melancholy Christian but that of melancholy pagan. Soon, he becomes "distracted with this world of passion" (IV. ii. 500) and, fulfilling the intention of Seneca's protagonist, commits suicide. He erroneously interprets this to be an act of heroic Roman Stoicism (V. ii. 60), just as Theodosius confuses his final withdrawal with Christian piety.

IV   *Heroism and Faith*

Only at the very end of the play does Theodosius show a glimmer of more mature awareness when, having seen in Athenais and Varanes the deadly consequences of failing to compromise between contradictory schemes of value, he charges Marcian and Pulcheria to "attone for all the present Crimes" by combining "Roman Spirit" with "true honour" (V. iv. 91–94). Throughout the play, these two are points of psychological reference between which the central plot follows its path. As heir to Clytus, Marcian dramatizes the height of excellence to which pagan values, properly managed, can motivate a man. He personifies the Old Rome of military prowess and proper subordination of personal and romantic inclinations to public and martial duties. Yet his pompous representation of himself as "this Roman-healer" (IV. ii. 55), who can brave Jupiter's wrath to cure Theodosius of his passivity, suggests his vital deficiency (which Pulcheria, and Lee's religiously sensitive audience, would immediately have apprehended). Without the therapy of *Christ* the physician, Marcian's exemplary ideals and conduct are no more fully adequate to Byzantine rule than is the spineless resignation of Theodosius. Wisely perceiving this, Pulcheria maneuvers him into the marriage that guarantees a vigorous hybridization of two value systems, the paganism of the Old Rome and the Christianity of the New.

Without this fusion Pulcheria is no more complete than Marcian. Despite her reputation for wisdom (I. i. 156; IV ii. 230), courage (II. i. 129), and martial spirit (V. iii. 45), she has in the process of ruling, during the minority and *weltschmerz* of Theodosius, allowed a swarm of foppish courtiers and "luxurious Bawds" (II. i. 28ff, 89) to drain the strength of the empire. Sequestered Christian values alone will not do for one intent on living effectively in a complex world, and because Pulcheria knows this, much as she feigns scorn for Marcian's condemnation of escapist "Devotions" and "Female Councils" (II. i. 95, 158), she arranges the wedding of her own strong piety and his strong commitment to Roman honor and empire. The combination promises to transcend the sorts of dilemmas that prove so fatal to Athenais, Varanes, and Theodosius. Historically, its success is symbolized by the fact that Marcian becomes the first emperor to be crowned in a Christian religious ceremony.[7]

V *The Design in the Present*

Such a world was Byzantium in the early fifth century, and such also, as Lee must have been keenly aware, was England in 1680. While *Theodosius* is far from being a political allegory, even in the ambiguous way that *Venice Preserv'd* is, it does bear interpretation as a politically relevant drama, and we may speculate that its political relevance was calculated by Lee as part of his didactic intention. Like fifth-century Constantinople, London in 1680 was beset by a crisis involving dangerous crosscurrents in religion, court behavior, and royal duty, and Lee appears to have designed his play partly as a study of the implications inherent in the general parallels between these two scenes of crisis. The politico-religious orientation of both the "Prologue" and the dedicatory epistle, together with a few contemporary allusions in the play itself, suggest that Lee wished to point up the contemporary relevance of the play without insisting on a specific equivalence between dramatic details and current events.

That he dedicated it to Frances Stuart, Duchess of Richmond, suggests not only that he was seeking the popular approval which her patronage would inevitably bring, but also that he was aware of her restraining influence on an otherwise licentious court, a court whose counterpart in the play had become dissolute for lack of such restraint. Frances Stuart, like Athenais, had gained repute as a chaste beauty—the only one of Charles' mistresses, it was said, who had preserved her virtue against his advances—and, like Athenais, she is hailed by Lee as a reminder in "the present malicious times" of "the Golden Age."[8] Again like Athenais, she was once wooed by her unrequited lover (Charles himself) through the medium of pastoral

fantasizing. Perhaps Lee knew that after the queen had recovered
from illness in 1663, Charles had curiously celebrated his relief by
writing a song to express his passion for Frances: "I pass all my hours
in a shady old grove, / But I live not the day when I see not my love; /
I survey every walk now my Phillis is gone, / And sigh when I think
we were there all alone."[9] While the correspondence between the
Duchess and Athenais ends here, it may not be too far-fetched to
suppose that Lee wished his readers to be instructed by both differences and similarities between the two love objects. If Frances Stuart
did not commit suicide out of confused frustration, she did possess
qualities which could, if properly credited by Charles, strengthen his
management of conflicting forces that were challenging his effectiveness as a ruler.

These forces are alluded to in the "Prologue" and at certain points
in the play itself: the "Prologue" ridicules religious fanatics who mistake sensual passion for divine inspiration, anticipating the falsely
pious pose of Theodosius that permits women and venal courtiers to
"act their wicked Wills and lawless pleasures" (IV. ii. 156); the "Prologue" also scathingly refers to "modern" armchair "Hero's" (1.3),
foreshadowing Marcian's representation of Theodosius as a mere
stage hero, whose actual lethargy dangerously ignores "the growing
French" under "Pharamond" (II. i. 133–34, 116). Few members of
Lee's audience—which had become highly politicized—would have
missed the general parallel with English state affairs of summer and
fall, 1680.[10] Religious fanaticism, whether personified by noncon-
forming divines or by the Papist Duke of York, was regarded as a
serious threat to civil order. Parliamentary leaders were planning to
reignite the Popish Plot. Williamites and Monmouthites pressed for
a second Exclusion Bill, as Monmouth himself campaigned for popular support in the West country. And France seemed a strong
enough menace for Charles to give Sunderland permission to form a
European coalition against Louis XIV. Yet if such problems seemed
to demand immediate, decisive action, Charles appeared to prefer
the armchair (and bedtime) heroics, and the sedentary pastoral pleasures, to which he devoted himself at Windsor for most of the summer of 1680.

Thus, faced with the need to avert possible national disaster by
reconciling the competing persuasions of religious enthusiasts, military strategists, female councillors, and his own self-indulgent nature, Charles seemed irresponsibly to withdraw, partly like Varanes

but more like Theodosius, into an unreal, pastoral world, there perhaps to indulge not only his passions but, far worse, his rumored
inclination to espouse the papistry of his sibling. Clearly, a much
better alternative would be swift action to create some sort of working
synthesis of priorities, something like what Lee was representing in
the hopeful marriage of Marcian and Pulcheria—and disturbingly
like what many projectors in 1680 foresaw in planning to exclude the
Catholic Duke of York from the throne and, on Charles's death,
crown a martial hero (William of Orange) and a pious Protestant
churchwoman (Mary).

CHAPTER 10

Providential Surgery: Lucius Junius Brutus; Father of his Country. A Tragedy (1680)

I F *The Rival Queens* and *Mithridates* are twin peaks of Nathaniel Lee's attempt to understand the tragic psychology of monarchic power, *Lucius Junius Brutus* is his highest achievement in dramatizing the tragic dimension of republicanism. He had hinted at this second kind of tragedy in *Nero*, where the leader of a coup d'état, Galba, is shown to be potentially as vain and self-indulgent as the emperor he supersedes. And if *The Massacre of Paris* was written before Brutus, then it too leads toward a fuller comprehension of republican *hamartia:* the Huguenot admiral, for all his impressively trumpeted political principles, is shown to be incapable of closing the inevitable distance between ideals and sinister political realities. In *Brutus* it is as if Lee brings the lens closer to Galba and the admiral in order to find in a strong republican personality the same tragic resources of human imperfection that he had found in Alexander and Mithridates.

The result, however, is not so much tragic as tragicomic. While the most virtuous and attractive characters—the Romeo and Juliet of the piece—are tragically destroyed by political forces beyond their control, the deeply flawed protagonist, Brutus himself, ousts a diabolically corrupt monarch and establishes a commonwealth. It is nevertheless a mistake to conclude, as so many have done, that Brutus therefore embodies Whig propaganda,[1] for he is far from being the paragon of virtue that Constantine would become in Lee's most blatantly monarchist play (1683) or that Aureng-Zebe had been in Dryden's dramatic essay on the traits of a great leader (1675). Instead, as

130

he himself knows, he is merely the man of the hour, one whose weaknesses as well as strengths qualify him to ride the latest wave of history. Although his ascendancy is dramatized within the context of republican convictions, Lee is more interested in the psychology of those convictions than in their long-range political efficacy. The latter he leaves, as does Brutus, in the hands of Providence.

I *Plot and Structure*

Even a bare plot summary suggests that the play chiefly involves something other than what Robert Hume has recently called "a celebration of the establishment of a republic."[2] Lucius Junius is "Brutus" (i.e., the foolish one) because, like Hamlet and Webster's Flaminio *(The White Devil)*, he feigns madness to avoid detection as a political malcontent. In this respect, he is the converse of Britannicus, who is driven mad by the very forces that Brutus eludes and studies by assuming an antic disposition. The Nero in this later play is Tarquin, the Roman king whose lustful cruelty spills over into court and religion, infecting even Brutus' eldest son, Tiberius. When Tarquin's son adds to the long family history of evil deeds by raping Lucrece, prominent daughter of Lucretius and wife of Collatinus, Brutus feels fatefully moved to throw off his mask and use her dishonor (and subsequent suicide) to inspire a political rebellion against the Tarquinians. His second son, Titus, however, is drawn by love for Teraminta, daughter of Tarquin, into complicity with the evil older brother, who now plots to restore the monarchy. When the mindless republican, Vinditius, discovers and reports the plot, Brutus is torn between paternal love for Titus, who was blackmailed into a treason that he recanted before criminal acts occurred, and devotion to the republic, whose endurance depends, he thinks, on strict, impersonal enforcement of democratically established laws. His final determination to execute both sons is decisively motivated by a now-obsessive conviction that this is part of a cosmic plan, that he is Fortune's earthly agent.

The best index to Lee's guiding purpose lies in the way he carves this plot out of a few major sources, discarding the irrelevant and giving a different emphasis and design to what remains. He depends mainly on Madame de Scudéry's *Clélie* (1655–61) and Livy's *Roman History* (trans. 1600), inserting in appropriate places situations and passages from Plutarch's "Life of Valerius Publicola," Machiavelli's *Discourses* (trans. 1663), and Otway's *Caius Marius* (1679). There are also echoes of Dionysius Halicarnassus, Fletcher's *Thierry and Theodoret* (c. 1617), Bacon's essay "Of Death," and various plays of Shakespeare.[3] In surveying these materials, one is especially struck by five of Lee's adaptations: (1) Brutus is divested of the amorous inclinations toward Lucrece that Scudéry gives him, and his patriotism is strengthened into an obsession; (2) the competition between this obsession and his fatherly affection for Titus is intensified; (3) Titus is sharply contrasted to Tiberius (in the romance they were much alike), whose hurt pride (Brutus denies him public office) and royalist sympathies drive him to satanic counter-rebellion; (4) Teraminta is taken from Tiberius (whom she loves in Scudéry) and given to Titus, and their relationship, uniting feuding families in Romeo-Juliet fashion, is contrasted in warmth and naturalness to Brutus' "cold" political zeal; (5) the obscurely historical figures, Vinditius and Fabritius, are made into contrasting caricatures of republican and royalist points of view, respectively, and by his mindless bias each discounts the value of the political philosophy he supports.

The framing technique that emerges out of these—and other, less important—changes, is one Lee had employed more or less successfully before. It is the deceptively simple contrasting of extreme personalities or philosophical stances in order to lament the absence of an attractive compromise between them. In *Nero* there is only Galba between the infernally active emperor and the irritatingly passive Britannicus. In *Sophonisba,* Scipio makes "civil bravery" seem a bland substitute for martial heroism (Hannibal) and transcendentally passionate love (Massinissa). In *The Massacre of Paris* only the weak, hypochondriacal Charles IX understands the need for a working synthesis of Machiavellian intrigue (the queen mother) and star-gazing idealism (the admiral). And in *Theodosius,* Lee gives in to an inspired optimism that celebrates through the marriage of Marcian (pagan prowess) and Pulcheria (Christian beauty) a promising union of those traits which, in their extreme forms (Varanes and Theodosius), are so self-defeating. As the play immediately following *Theodosius, Lucius Junius Brutus* takes up similar contrasts but emphasizes politics and "nature" instead of religion and romance and, rather than celebrate a practical synthesis of priorities, suggests that hybrid moral vigor is not a real possibility in the tragic world of imperfect man.

II *Innocence and Experience*

Using this technique of elaborated contrasts, Lee fashions a dramatic structure that is a variation on the one used in *Mithridates* and in Dryden's *Aureng-Zebe*—with the love rivalries removed, the father-son conflicts stressed, and the basic political stances reversed: i.e., the father is the rebel, the evil son the royalist. As in *Mithridates*, the loyal son and his mistress are victims of the clash between factions, but if in the earlier play the rebel's victory is considered evil, here it is cause for some celebration, though of a highly qualified sort. It is highly qualified because, unlike Dryden, Lee does not show the ultimate resolution of personal and public values, of the natural and the political, humanity and law, mercy and justice. Instead, there is the bittersweet victory of Brutus over Tarquin and Tiberius, superhuman law over savage prerogative. The desirable middle term, represented partially in the wedding of Titus and Teraminta, is lost in the tempestuous meeting of extremes.

Herein lies the tragic dimension of Lee's tragicomedy. Titus and Teraminta are in every way attractive and natural. In their wedding the best aspects of Brutus and the Tarquinians unite. They are a variation on Marcian and Pulcheria—and on Aureng-Zebe, who manages to combine the potentially conflicting roles of general, lover, and son. Titus is "most like" his father, yet "not so quite severe" (IV. i. 335–36), and Teraminta, though illicitly sired by the vicious King, blooms from his lust into a "Saint-like . . . Roman Wife" (IV. i. 366). Together they are (to use their own terminology) natural order personified, a microcosm of the Great Chain of Being, a well-tuned instrument (I. i. 26–33; II. i. 429–32). But when they are separated, it is to Teraminta as if death had snatched an infant from its mother (II. i. 523–28), and to Titus as if "th' eternal Chain" is broken and the "World . . . is Chaos" (I. i. 26–27). After recognizing his dilemma, Titus decides that the time is out of joint and nature is inverted (II. i. 439–50; III. iii. 33–47, 127–29; IV. i. 138–41), and on his wedding night this melancholy state of affairs is aptly symbolized by his being unable to consummate the marriage (IV. i. 170–73).

He is unable to perform this naturally virtuous function because of the unnatural forces ranged against him. In the metaphoric vocabulary of the play, he is swallowed up in the disorder of a tempest, which is both a natural and an unnatural (i.e., extraordinary) phenomenon, literally a natural disaster (e.g., IV. i. 445–48). It is, of course, easy to see Tiberius as one of the purveyors of the unnatural and disorderly. Not only does he participate in a cannibalistic ritual, which moves Vinditius to call him a hellhound (IV. i. 120–21), but once his hatred for Brutus becomes intense enough, he explicitly rejects his natural role as son—"I look on Brutus as a Traytor, / No more my Father" (III. i. 78–79)—and becomes a predatory beast:

> Like a grown Savage on the Common wild,
> That runs at all, and cares not who begot him,
> I'll meet my Lion Sire, and roar defiance,
> As if he ne're had nurs'd me in his Den. (III. i. 169–72)

It is no accident that what Tiberius deliberately puts off—"Blood . . . Reverence, Fondness"—is what Titus finally clings to at the expense of his and Teraminta's lives (see III. iii. 139–41; IV. i. 404–07; V. ii. 184–6). The two sons are sharply contrasted in order to define their father's position in the scheme of things. Titus is humane, devoted to traditional domestic values and to the distinctly human capability for love. But he is apolitical. He does not recognize the unpleasant fact that man cannot simply live Adam-like in a harmoniously arranged social garden. When he gives in to Teraminta's reluctant temptings to commit treason, the scene is set in the Fecialian Garden, a garden of false priests, and there he falls into the tragic world of postlapsarian man, where religion becomes cannibalism and politics is either bestial (Tiberius) or dangerously zealous (Brutus).

Tiberius is man gone savage, gone to weed (III. i. 134), and as a monarchist he dramatizes the corruption that is latent in any system based entirely on human prerogative: the system is only as virtuous and orderly as the man who runs it. Tiberius's notion of monarchy is not unappealing in itself:

> . . . A King is one
> To whom you may complain when you are wrong'd;
> The Throne lies open in your way for Justice:
> You may be angry, and may be forgiven.
> There's room for favor, and for benefit,
> Where Friends and Enemies may come together,
> Have present hearing, present composition,
> Without recourse to the Litigous Laws. (II. i. 9–16)

But all these advantages depend on there being a worthy king, and Tarquin is rather far below the mark. Although we never see Tarquin, we hear of his son's criminal lust and we watch his courtier, the low-born Fabritius, make a mockery of the noble patronage to lower classes which Tiberius imagines as an ideal: "the Multitude," says Fabritius, "is a mad thing; a strange blunder-headed Monster" (II. i. 31–32). By association with him, and with the other wenching, self-indulgent courtiers and princes, Tiberius further indicts his own behavior—which is already enslaved to envy and pride (in IV. i. 32, he calls the people "Beasts for Sacrifice")—and becomes a dramatic contradiction of the monarchical ideas he espouses.

III *Brutus and Civic Brutality*

It is, perhaps, not so well understood that Brutus, too, represents an extreme personal and political position, that his behavior also belies his philosophy. Like Tiberius, he is contrasted to Titus and Teraminta. If Tiberius is the courtier-savage, one who sacrifices humanity to satisfy bestial passions, Brutus is a constitutional enthusiast, one who sacrifices humanity to satisfy law. Tiberius eschews his natural role as son to participate in the corruption of monarchy, and both forms of abnormality tend toward disorder, toward natural disaster. Likewise, Brutus, who is tugged between the natural inclinations of flesh and blood and the abstract commitment of civil law (II. i. 351–53), ultimately gives over fatherhood in favor of the artificial role as chief executive. In Act I he is "not Roman Brutus, but a Father" (I. i. 243); but by Act IV the merciful and loving "Father" has been overruled by "Rome's Consul," who condemns his sons to death for treason (IV. i. 305–11). Moreover, just as Tiberius signifies his own deviation from nature (as normatively embodied in Titus) by undertaking a diabolical blood ritual, so Brutus begins and ends his absolute commitment to the republic by parallel rituals. In Act I he forces his colleagues to kiss Lucrece's bloody dagger, join hands, and swear to drive Tarquin from Rome (I. i. 435–50). In Act V he sacrifices his own sons to the same cause and, according to Sempronia, Teraminta, and Valerius, thereby becomes as inhuman as Tiberius: "barbarous," "inhuman Judge," "monstrous" (V. i. 70, ii. 75, 155).

The political side of this inhumanity is interestingly brought to light in a way that continues the parallel between Brutus and his elder

son. Tiberius is implicitly criticized for pride, injustice, and association with those who abuse the royal prerogative. Similarly, Brutus
cooperates with grosser forms of republicanism (Vinditius), unjustly
treats Teraminta, and has too high an opinion of himself. Yet, just as
monarchy in the abstract seems appealing when enunciated by Tiberius, so Brutus' ideas of republican government are unexception-
able when divorced from the context of human imperfections. He
envisions a Utopia where the people elect worthy leaders (III. ii. 33–
49), where religion, learning, and moral virtue remain inviolate (III.
ii. 52–54; V. ii. 48–49) and factions do not exist (V. ii. 50),

> . . . A Balanc'd Trade,
> Patriots incourag'd, Manufactors cherish'd,
> Vagabonds, Walkers, Drones, and Swarming Braves,
> The Froth of States, scum'd from the Common-wealth:
> Idleness banish'd all excess repress'd;
> And Riots check'd by Sumptuary Laws. (V. ii. 54–59)

> Where Rancor and Ambition are extinguish'd,
> Where Universal peace extends her wings,
> As if the Golden Age return'd, where all
> The People do agree, and live secure,
> The Nobles and the Princes lov'd and Reverenc'd,
> The World in Triumph, and the Gods Ador'd. (III. ii. 62–67)

In concept, all this sounds very appealing, but it hardly allows for
the basic flaws in human nature. The social aims would, of course,
not offend either faction, royalist or republican, but that such aims
would actually be achieved rests on two assumptions that no royalist
could accept: first, that the people will elect leaders who are morally
upright and capable of administering an orderly and prosperous state;
and second, that the law, rather than a sovereign's flexible judgment,
can insure justice within the body politic. The play casts serious
doubt on the validity of both assumptions. One of the people's chosen
leaders is the upstart demagogue, Vinditius, hardly a worthy guard-
ian of the commonwealth, and by reposing confidence in him Brutus
undercuts republican ideals, just as the royalism of Tiberius suffers
by association with Fabritius. Vinditius is driven by personal ambition, not by the quest to implement political principles (see IV. i.
217–22), and he has not even a rudimentary understanding of what a
commonwealth is or why it is better than a monarchy:

. . . I am a true Commonwealths-man, and do not naturally love Kings, tho
they be good; for why should any man have more power than the People?
. . . Can he make Corn grow . . . give us rain . . . or make our Pots boil, tho
the Devil piss in the Fire? (II. i. 41–48)

Furthermore, not only does Vinditius have little respect for those
whom he leads—he calls the rabble "my Mirmydons" (II. i. 190)—
but he abuses the very concept of legality that Brutus values above
all. In Act II he summarily condemns to death his opposite number,
the foolish courtier Fabritius, without giving him benefit of counsel
or jury:

Hang 'em, Rogues, Pimps; hang 'em I say. Why, look you Neighbours, this
is Law, Right, and Justice: this is the People's Law; and I think that's better
than the Arbitrary power of Kings. Why, here is Trial, Condemnation, and
Execution, without more ado. (II. i. 122–26)

Obviously, Brutus does not have this kind of mob violence in mind
when he says that law is to insure justice and prescribe "Bounds . . .
for raging Kings, / Like Banks and Bulwarks for the Mother Seas"
(III. ii. 11–12). Yet, in actuality, he himself demonstrates the fundamental drawback in transferring the burden of justice from human
judgment to written rules: such a procedure ignores the fact that men
are feeble creatures, subject not only to their own perversions, passions, and illusions, but also to the unpredictable phenomena of the
physical universe. They require law tempered by judgment, justice
with mercy and understanding. Brutus seems incapable of taking this
more empirical attitude toward justice. He remains unmoved by the
human frailty that causes both Titus and Teraminta to buckle under
pressure and support the conspiracy. Titus is condemned to the same
ignoble death as the most hardened criminals among the other conspirators. And although Brutus promises to protect Teraminta from
reprisals by Vinditius' mob, she is left vulnerable. Brutus, she
charges, "Let me be whooted like a common strumpet, / Toss'd . . .
and drag'd about the streets" (V. i. 78–9). Like Vinditius, then, Brutus administers republican justice in a way that proves the royalist
argument of Tiberius, who abhors

Laws that are cruel, deaf, inexorable,
That cast the Vile and Noble altogether;

Where, if you should exceed the bounds of Order,
There is no pardon: O, 'tis dangerous,
To have all Actions judg'd by rigorous Law.
What, to depend on Innocence alone,
Among so many Accidents and Errors
That wait on human life? (II. i. 17–24)

Thus, Brutus and Vinditius enact the deficiencies of republicanism—its unrealistic confidence in ordinary men, its inhumane adher-
ence to legal rigor—and Tiberius and Fabritius show what is wrong
with absolute sovereignty: it empowers bestiality. Yet in Titus and
Teraminta there is no viable alternative, for man is no longer capable
of living in the natural harmony they embody. Some contrived,
earthly authority is necessary, whether it be vested in law or in royal
prerogative. That Lee offers no workable compromise between these
two badly wrought devices for social order indicates his own assessment of human nature and his own tragic vision of English political
life.[4]

IV *Heaven's Hero*

Why, then, does he distinguish so elaborately between the savage
pride of Tiberius, which is clearly connected to defeated monar-
chism, and the triumphant self-puffery of Brutus when the republic
is in the ascendant? How can this comedic dimension of the play be
accounted for? Does Brutus rise, despite his inhumanity, because
Lee had decided, with Machiavelli and Hobbes, that among fallen
men order can be maintained only by a republican leviathan? Should
the play therefore be regarded as the purging eruption of anti-mo-
narchic passions that had been boiling up in *Nero, The Rival Queens,*
and *Mithridates?*[5]

Surely not. After all, if earlier plays criticize monarchy, they offer
no viable alternatives, and *Sophonisba* and *Theodosius* are, if anything, pro-monarchy, on the condition that the current sovereign is
worthy. It would be more accurate to say that something in the Exclusion Crisis of 1680–81 convinced Lee that the current monarch
was, in fact, not worthy, that he was irresponsibly indecisive and self-
indulgent, so that Providence was once again nudging England toward commonwealth. That he soon found himself able to reaffirm the
king's integrity (through *The Duke of Guise* and *Constantine*) therefore represents not a radical turnabout but rather a return to basic
principles. Seen in this light, *Lucius Junius Brutus* becomes a dra-

matic equivalent to Marvell's *Horatian Ode* (1650) and Dryden's
Heroique Stanzas (1659), where Cromwell the republican strongman
is seen not as the initiator of a continuing political tradition but as a
unique, temporary operative of Providence. While he performs a
necessary reinstitution of social order and a reconsolidation of Britain's collective strength, his place in the cosmic scheme cannot be
wholly understood, imitated, or resisted.[6] The crucial difference between *Lucius Junius Brutus,* on the one hand, *Theodosius* and *Constantine* on the other, lies not so much in political principle as in the
distinctive ways in which Providence distributes her favors. In these
other plays time is ripe for reform, and Providence prescribes therapy, a changing of the guard. But in Brutus the fruit festers on the
bough and radical surgery is in order: the palace must be stormed to
preserve the State. Thus, by favoring Rome through Brutus, with all
his deficiencies intact, Providence compensates for the tragic deaths
of Titus and Teraminta and gives the piece a comedic shading—but
does so without drastically reducing its meaningful ambiguity.

Brutus, of course, revels in the conviction that he is Fortune's
earthly agent—"the force of angry Heavens flame," as Marvell describes Cromwell in the *Horatian Ode*[7]—which suggests that he
tends toward the kind of presumption that led to the destruction of
Nero, Alexander, and Mithridates (and we wonder if Lee also had in
mind the fate of Cromwell's protectorate). His vanity is made plain
in the early speech where he congratulates himself for demonstrating
"Virtue . . . . / Which never any Age could parallel" (I. i. 131–32),
and he readily ascribes his long endurance as pseudo-madman to the
support of "Fate" (I. i. 112). Having decided to cast aside his "Vizor
of . . . madness" (I. i. 111), he publicly attributes what he knows is
merely an earthly stratagem to the miraculous intervention of the
"Gods," who have chosen him, he says (as Miltonians in the audience
knew God had chosen the Archangel Michael), to drive Tarquin
"from the Earth with Sword and Fire" (II. i. 143, 158; and see I. i.
447). Brutus now sees himself as a divinely ordained avenger, a social
and moral surgeon who, in the words of Titus, comes "like an Aescu-
lapius / Sent by the Gods" to cure the ailing body politic (II. i. 445–
46). Echoing Cardinal Ascanio in *Caesar Borgia*, Vinditius declares
that the people of Rome, "the Guts of Government" (I. i. 298), find
their head and their healer in Brutus. Since this is precisely the way
in which Ascanio describes Machiavel, the "brain" to everyone else's
"guts" (I. i. 104–06), it casts further doubt on the integrity of Brutus.
So does his godlike claim to be vested with the power to "mould" and

"fashion" the personality of Titus (II. i. 303–12) and his later rationale
for ordering the boy's execution: "Methinks I see the very hand of
Jove / Moving the dreadful wheels of this affair" (IV. i. 509–10). By
Act V even his best friend and supporter, Valerius (who begins to
sound like Clytus of *The Rival Queens*), wonders whether he has not
carried matters too far:

> . . . he's no more a man;
> ....
> He looks and talks, as if that Jove had sent him
> To be the Judge of all the under World;
> Tells me, this Palace of the Universe
> ....
> With all that Circulation of Heav'ns Orbs,
> Were so establish'd from before all Ages
> To be the Dowry of Majestick Rome:
> Then looks, as if he has a Patent for it. (V. i. 8–19)

In despairing over her husband's unnatural cruelty and pride,
Sempronia asks about Brutus the same question that one might ask
about Hamlet: has his madness been wholly feigned or, in fact, "Is he
not mad?" (V. i. 93). Our answer must be no, though he clearly shares
the mental infirmities of all Adam's sons: for Lee lets it be known,
through intuitions of Titus, supernatural signs, and symbolic actions
and allusions, that Providence has actually ordered these affairs, just
as Brutus supposes. Throughout his ordeal Titus attributes his suffer-
ings not to his father but to heavenly will, variously defined as "Fortune" (II. i. 437; III. iii. 39; V. i. 179), "the Gods" (II. i. 491), "Fate"
(III. iii. 38), and "Stars" (III. iii. 62). Appropriately, it is Titus to
whom the most telling prodigy appears in order to confirm his father's
divine ordination. He sees a fiery heaven pouring blood "like a Torrent down," then a "Flaming Sword" destroying "three Romans"
(perhaps representing the three sons of Tarquin, whom Brutus had
vowed to drive off "with Sword and Fire"), and finally a "Fleeting
head" that cries,

> Treason and Tyranny shall not prevail:
> Kingdom shall be no more . . .
> And that vast turn Imperial Fate design'd
> I saw, O Titus, on th' eternal Loom. (IV. i. 146–61)

This divine sponsorship of Brutus is further confirmed by the symbolism in the blood ritual performed by Tiberius with Tarquin's priests. As they crucify and burn two commonwealth men, then cannibalize them, Vinditius secretly watches and tells the audience how to react: "Eat one man, and drink another! . . . if a man can't go to Heaven, unless . . . Priests eat him, and drink him, and roast him alive; I'll be for the broad way, and the Devil shall have me . . ." (IV. i. 121–28). Here Roman Catholic transubstantiation is hideously parodied as a black eucharist, forming in the audience's mind a symbolic background against which Tiberius becomes a servant of the underworld, while Brutus emerges as heaven's hero combatting "the Devil's Cooks" (IV. i. 42).

To readers of Lee's other plays the imagery is by now familiar. Like Alexander, Mithridates, and the Admiral of France, Brutus struggles against diabolical forces and is weakened by inner flaws,[8] but unlike these others, he can rely on the full support of heaven. If in *The Rival Queens* Alexander's defeat by Cassander is providentially foretold in the prodigy of an eagle being destroyed by a dragon, in this play a similar prodigy, possibly invented by the fertile mind of Brutus, symbolizes the opposite determination of heaven: "a monstrous Dragon" (I. i. 319) is struck down by thunder, and Vinditius concludes, "Tarquin's the Dragon, and the Gods shall swinge him" (I. i. 332). In the biblical tradition dragons represent Satan and the Antichrist (Rev. 12:7, 16:13), both of whom are said to be resisted, as decreed by Providence, with fire and sword (Dan. 11:33; Rev. 19:11–21)—just as Brutus intends to combat Tarquin. Thus Milton's Michael, sending forth Adam from paradise beneath a flaming sword, is conflated with images of God's final victory over the Antichrist (in Revelation 12:7, Michael again appears as God's agent, this time fighting against the dragon), in a complex symbol for what Providence has in store for Brutus.[9]

V *The Price of Divine Madness*

Possibly Sempronia justly calls her spouse's sanity into question, for Lee seems convinced that when a leader seeks to pilot mankind amidst the grand crosscurrents of body politic, body corporeal, and soul, he risks both his own mental health and that of society. Perhaps Brutus *has* moved from feigned madness (which he acknowledges to

himself and the audience) to actual insanity (which he refuses to acknowledge). But if so, it is a distinctly sublunar insanity, unnatural
by earthly, domestic standards alone: "Instead of tears," Brutus must
"weep blood" (IV. i. 493) to perform his ordained role in history. As
the physician violating social nature by surgery in order to heal its
corruption, he finds himself in an abnormal psychological position: to
sire a body politic he must destroy his own corporeal offspring. Yet
he is steeled to the task by certain knowledge that, from a cosmic
perspective, this amounts to true sanity. The time is out of joint, but
unlike Britannicus—and paradoxically like both Dryden's Cromwell
and his later King David—Brutus understands how a series of new
time is to be initiated. With uncharacteristic humility he subordinates his own analysis of earthly affairs to the higher understanding
of heaven; yet at the same time, unlike the Admiral of France, he
continues to act aggressively on the best information his own judgment can supply. In his speech on this theme he articulates more
clearly than any of Lee's other heroes the psychological nature of that
tragic gap between man and the divine:

> Behold the Game that laughing Fortune playes;
> Fate, or the will of Heav'n, call't what you please,
> That marrs the best designs that Prudence layes,
> . . . .
> Yet after all I justifie the Gods,
> And will conclude Ther's Reason supernatural
> That guides us through the World with vast discretion,
> Altho we have not Souls to comprehend it:
> Which makes by wondrous methods the same Causes
> Produce effects tho of a different nature,
> . . . for Man's Instruction, and the Glory
> Of the Immortal Gods . . . . (IV. i. 280–82, 293–300)

Here is Lee's final understanding of true sanity. His practical politics may have changed temporarily but not his conception of the
conditions necessary for societal and individual peace and order. If in
his first play Britannicus, emblem of Britain herself, is driven mad by
a Machiavellian world, in this later creation the hero, taking stock of
the evil odds against him, sanely dons a mask of madness, thereby
classifying himself as harmlessly apolitical, and bides his time. What
he awaits, the necessary condition for his conquest of self and society,
is not merely an opportunity to launch his own rational stratagem but

rather some propitious sign from heaven that his aspirations make sense to the "Reason supernatural." As in *Constantine* such sanction and the personal prowess it bequeaths are not to be had without an ordeal. Two years hence, Lee will show the first of Rome's Christian emperors reliving Christ's passion and death, in that his near-insanity and subsequent recovery are described in a dream as his "Cross and Triumph" (I. i. 6). But for the time being, Brutus brings the exemplum of Abraham and Isaac to its potentially tragic conclusion as he sacrifices his own son in order to become "Father of his Country." Perhaps Lee's choice of Old Testament allusions—in this father-son relationship, as in the imagery of Adam's being driven from paradise—implies that his overarching political ideals have not markedly changed, though indeed his analysis of England's political condition has. Seen from the vantage point of Providence, perhaps the sinful Britain of 1680 needs purging and disciplining by a Cromwellian strongman—a Moses, a Solomon, a Brutus—in order to prepare for the restoration of a truly Christian kingdom. In Roman history, as in the canon of Lee's plays and as in his political beliefs, the messianic victory of Constantine is yet to come.[10]

CHAPTER 11

A Playwright's Revenge:
The Princess of Cleve (1682/3)[1]

O F all Lee's plays, *The Princess of Cleve* is perhaps richest in significance, yet it is often condemned as a clumsily constructed
hodgepodge of sentiment, grossness, and farce.[2] Even its first audience, out of tune with the playwright's intentions, probably took "no
notice" of its design and granted it only a brief run.[3] When it was
revived in 1689, however, Lee insisted that he had worked hard to
compose it out of "all the Variety that Arts can give," and he defied
the mindless formalists by labeling it "Farce, Comedy, Tragedy or
meer Play."[4] Recently, critics have shown that it makes sense to read
the piece as a satire operating on several levels at once,[5] though no
one thus far has unravelled the various contexts within which the
satire achieves what Lee said he aimed at: "revenge" for the "refusal"
of *The Massacre of Paris*.[6] That he has had to wait three hundred
years for his revenge may serve as a commentary on his own tragic
failure to communicate some of his best ideas.

I   Plot

Some encouragement to undertake a more thorough study of the
play is offered by the bare bones of its plot. Its dimensions, when
seen in overview, are surprisingly symmetrical, considering the established opinion that it is badly constructed. Its lack of closure, seen
in relation to this overall symmetry, becomes more suggestive than
disappointing. The action is overtly two-sided, with the basic conflicts in both halves fueled by the expansive energy of the amorous
and witty Duke Nemours. The whole is set in motion by what could
have been a third subplot, had it been further developed. Offstage,

outside Nemours' energy field, stands the shadowy figure of Queen Catherine de Medici, who wishes to dissolve his presumed betrothal to Marguerite, Princess of Jainville, so that Marguerite can be married to the Dauphin, soon to become King Francis II. In pursuit of this end, she orders one of her ladies in waiting, Tournon, to become Nemours' whore and to get him interested in other women as well, so that Marguerite will become jealous and redirect her passion toward the Dauphin. Tournon, for her part, resolves to prosecute her charge in three ways. First, she suspects that a certain revealing letter from a bawd to her anonymous lover, which was found on the tennis court and subsequently read for amusement at court, belongs to Nemours; and she therefore sends her confidante, La March, to convey these suspicions to Marguerite. Meanwhile, an effort is made to interest Nemours (who is always game for a novel challenge) in Celia and Elianor, lusty wives of two foppish courtiers, St. Andre and Poltrot; and arrangements are made for Marguerite, by now convinced of Nemours' duplicity, to witness his assignation with the wayward wives. The third prong of Tournon's attack develops later in the play, when she learns from the Vidam of Chartres that his newly married niece, the Princess of Cleve, feels an adulterous passion in response to intense wooing by the indefatigable Nemours. This bit of information Tournon immediately spreads as gossip at court, hoping further to alienate Marguerite.

In the end it is unclear whether the queen's scheme, as developed by Tournon, has more than a temporary effect, since both women have underestimated Nemours' ability to sustain and manage conflicting intrigues. The more relationships he has to juggle, the greater his opportunity for multiple rhetorical and sexual conquests and, hence, for satisfying his highest aims.

The subplot involving the Prince and Princess of Cleve, partly a by-product of Nemours' gallantry, has its own dynamics as well. To assuage her guilt about returning an adulterous passion, the Princess confesses to her husband that she loves another, and he later manages to identify the rival by observing her emotional reaction as he pretends to include Nemours in their party for a projected trip to Spain. Increasingly tortured thereafter by the knowledge that his wife and his best friend are lovers, the Prince literally consumes his own life in grief and despair, leaving the widowed Princess to make one last stand against the advances of Nemours. This she does, vowing to spend her remaining years in retirement, although, before the final interview is over, she relents so far as to suggest that time may work in his favor at last. After she departs, Nemours throws aside his mask of sincerity, along with his promise never to think of other women, and prepares to renew the "Battle" (V. iii. 264) for Marguerite, but he tells the Vidam that he still plans to "Bed" (V. iii. 254) the Princess as well.

The second subplot also has its own inner logic, once it is set in motion by Tournon, through Nemours. Because they worship contemporary modes of dress, expression, and behavior, St. Andre and Poltrot are easily persuaded by Bellamore (acting for Nemours) that it is fashionable to ridicule one's wife and seek a mistress. Similarly, their wives (Elianor and Celia), after sustaining verbal abuse from their spouses, greedily follow Tournon's prompting to take lovers à la mode while youth and high spirits permit. First, they flirt incognito with their unsuspecting husbands and incite them to revile marriage; then they let themselves be led off by Nemours and the Vidam, who have made a timely entrance according to Tournon's plan. Knowing that after the masked ball Poltrot plans to slip into Elianor's bed while St. Andre sleepwalks, Nemours now arranges to occupy Poltrot's place with Celia. Meanwhile Tournon, to compensate the Vidam for revealing his niece's moral frailty, hides him in Elianor's closet so that he can join her when St. Andre starts walking in his sleep. During the ball itself, St. Andre and Poltrot, masquerading as a mute Scottish fortune-teller and his interpreter, get revenge by leading their wives to admit infidelities. That night all goes as planned, except that Bellamore substitutes for Nemours, who is drawn away by the more challenging prospect of seducing the Princess in her bower. St. Andre begins to sleepwalk, but as Poltrot goes for Elianor, he discovers that someone (the Vidam) has beat him to the starting line, and when he returns to Celia he finds that she, too, is being enjoyed by another (Bellamore). As Poltrot awakens St. Andre on the pretense that they are being burgled and cuckolded, the Vidam shoots a pistol and escapes with Bellamore and Tournon, leaving the husbands with the impression that, indeed, their house (and wives) have been penetrated by thieves. Later, considering that he might have been killed with all his sins upon his head, Poltrot forgives his wife, and when St. Andre reports how jealousy and infidelity have caused the death of the Prince of Cleve, both witwouds and their wives prudently elect to remain faithful spouses hereafter.

II   *Satire Through Literary Context*

Three dramatic traditions are drawn together in this multilayered plot: split-action comedy, heroic tragedy, and libertine comedy. The first is suggested by the overall structure of the play, which is divided between high and low episodes, heroic love and sexy farce—somewhat like Etherege's *The Comical Revenge* (1664) or Wycherley's *Love in a Wood* (1671). At the low end are Poltrot and St. Andre (with their wives), who are coarser versions of Estridge and Modish in Sir Charles Sedley's *The Mulberry Garden* (1668). They sing smutty songs and awkwardly emulate the elegant wenching made fashionable by worthier blades. The scene in the Luxembourg Garden (III. i. 148–286) where the two fops, mistaking their masked wives for willing sluts, boast of sexual conquests ("we never miss hitting between Wind and Water"), recalls the similar scene in *The Mulberry Garden* where Estridge and Modish are tricked into affecting rakishness while Olivia and Victoria overhear them from an adjacent arbor.[7] The high end of the split plot is drawn from the central story of Madame de Lafayette's short prose romance, *La Princesse de Clèves* (1678), which Lee probably read in a 1679 translation.[8] By omitting several characters and lines of action, exaggerating the love-honor dilemma,[9] and freighting the originally measured prose with intense emotion, Lee transforms it into a stereotypical heroic tragedy: "Take one last kiss, e'er I to Death retire" (II. iii. 208); "Oh my Heart! in spite of my resolves,/Spite of those matchless Virtues of my Husband,/I love the Man my reason bids me hate" (IV. iii. 42–44).

In some split-plot plays (e.g., *Marriage A-la-Mode*, 1671) a resolution of comic and romantic modes of behavior is sought, while in others (e.g., *The Spanish Fryar*, 1680) the comic underplot may actually support the more serious level of action. In *The Princess of Cleve*, however, as Robert Hume has instructively shown, the comic action degrades the heroic:

The husbands' wenching schemes mirror and travesty Nemours' upper-class love-intrigues. . . . St. Andre's "sleepwalking" speeches and Poltrot's description of catching his wife *in flagrante delicto* (concluding, "I feel something trickle, trickle in my Breeches") are bluntly and joylessly obscene. . . . This rancid smut is followed instantly by Nemours' announcement that the Prince is dying of a fever brought on by the violence of his love for his chaste but unloving wife. This juxtaposition is no accident. The report of the

Prince's death comes . . . at the end of a page on which Celia justifies her
adultery by saying that her "ravisher" had threatened to "rip open" her husband's body. To this Poltrot replies, ". . . I must praise thy Discretion in
Sacrificing thy Body, for 'o my Conscience, if they had seen this Smock-face
of mine, I had gone to pot too before my Execution". . . . This excremental
reference from a cowardly cuckold makes a weird prelude to the announcement of the Prince of Cleve's romantic love-death.[10]

Helped along by their experience in watching earlier split-plot plays,
the audience would not have missed Lee's double-edged satire here.
Not only is the "heroic ethos" punctured by comic parody, but also
the Hobbesian/Epicurean values affected by St. Andre and Poltrot
are made to seem grossly ridiculous in contrast to the Prince's social
ideals and his wife's genuinely painful moral confusion. The mutual
cancelling works against the two traditions in drama as well as against
the two value systems.

But a more powerful and general satire on libertine comedy *per se*,
and on its rake-heroes, is managed through Nemours, for if Poltrot
and St. Andre are bungling and scabrous, Nemours is vicious and
predatory. In the 1689 dedication Lee makes it clear how we are to
understand his "Ruffian" hero: "The fourth and fifth Acts of the
Chances, where Don John is pulling down; Marriage Alamode,
where they are bare to the Waste; the Libertine, and Epsom-Wells,
are but Copies of his Villany."[11] The point is that Nemours is a kind
of archetype for sexual misconduct as portrayed in comedies like
Buckingham's revision of Fletcher's *The Chances* (1667), Dryden's
Marriage A-la-Mode, and Shadwell's *Epsom-Wells*, (1672) and *The
Libertine* (1675). Especially like Don John in the last of these,[12] he
inspires not admiration but contempt for selfish sensuality. He is, as
James Sutherland has pointed out, the darker side of Etherege's Dorimant *(The Man of Mode)*.[13] Like Dorimant, he sees himself as "a
winning Gamester" (I. ii. 12) who knows "the Souls of / Women bet-
ter than they know themselves" (V. iii. 258–59) and dictates "to more
Whores at once than . . . [Caesar] did to Knaves" (II. iii. 21–22).

But unlike Etherege's glamorous wit, Nemours seriously disorders
the lives of others and mixes very little civility with his savagery. His
plan for dealing with an attractive vizard (Tournon), for instance—
"slipping out of the crowd into a corner, breathing short an Ejacula-
tion, and returning as if we came from Church" (IV. i. 31–3)—sounds
less like Dorimant's assignation with Bellinda than like Lady Gim-
crack's back-room copulation with Longvil and Bruce during the masquerade in Shadwell's *The Virtuoso* (1676).[14] Hume's observation is

well taken: "Dorimant and Nemours represent opposite poles of opinion about . . . the libertine heroes of contemporary comedy. . . . Lee tears away the tinsel and false glamor with icy distaste. . . . Nemours emerges powerful, glamorous, and successful—and all the more horrible for that. The audience ought to feel his attractiveness just enough to be revolted by its own readiness to tolerate this slippery, goatish scoundrel."[15]

Nevertheless, he dominates the action far more completely than his counterpart in Madame de Lafayette's romance does. There is, for example, no duel in the romance; by inventing one, in which Nemours disarms the prince, Lee symbolizes the duke's dominance as warrior over the otherwise more heroic figure. His equivalent sexual dominance is stressed by other changes. Whereas in the romance the letter dropped on the tennis court belongs to the Vidam, Lee attributes it to one of the duke's whores, thereby underlining his flourishing promiscuity. And even more revealing is the way Lee changes Madame de Lafayette's ending. In her version, the widowed princess resists Nemours and, dividing the rest of her life between service in a convent and austere retirement in her own country home, becomes an example of hard-won virtue. Lee's ending is quite different. Like her original, his widowed princess vows to seek "Sunless Caves . . . Dungeons of Despair" where she can keep the duke's "Form at distance," but then she offers him a parting hope: "have patience, / Expect what time, with such a love as mine, / May work in your behalf" (V. iii. 119, 199, 231–33). Encouraged by these remarks, the irrepressible Nemours makes the following promise as he turns for diversion to Marguerite. "I'll Wager my State, I Bed her [the princess] eighteen months three weeks hence, at half an hour past two in the Morning" (V. iii. 254–56).

Lee's manipulation of language reinforces our sense of Nemours' triumph: his mastery of withering rhetoric overwhelms the Prince's garden of verse-order. Guileless, forthright, sensitive to threats against reason and morality, the Prince and Princess speak in elegant blank verse. On the other hand, Poltrot, St. Andre, Celia, and Elianor, are social empiricists who match their conduct to what they observe to be in vogue; they consistently speak prose. But the amoral Nemours, the dissimulating Vidam, the cynical Tournon, all speak verse or prose as it suits their moods or purposes. For them language is a rhetorical tool rather than an outward sign of inner truth. Yet the fact that this triumphant rhetoric, in both language and action, does not gain our sympathy or admiration is Lee's way of leading us toward a larger rhetoric, his own rhetoric of allusion and imagery representing a "reality" that finally overwhelms even Nemours.

III *Satire through Historical Context*

Through his use of history, Lee helps us to see beyond the relatively explicit satire on weak-kneed romantic idealism, rake heroes, and knockabout sex farce. Behind the collision of such extreme forms of behavior, we can discern, with the aid of historical background, the selfish political initiative of Catherine de Medici, the shadowy queen never seen by the audience. By juxtaposing other well-known historical characters onstage, Lee makes us realize that all their actions emerge from the queen's offstage effort to gain power over warring Huguenot and Roman Catholic factions, and the implications of this realization are devastating.[16]

Several of his characters belong historically to the Huguenot camp. François de Vendôme, le Vidame de Chartres, was a prominent land baron (owing fealty to the Bishop of Chartres) who was thrown into prison for allegedly authoring the Huguenot insurrection at Lyons (1560). Later, just before the Massacre of Paris (1572), he tried to persuade the Admiral, Gaspard II de Coligny, to withdraw from the city to avoid assassination. He had a reputation for inconstancy and for *affaires d'amour*. La March, confidant of Tournon, was the younger daughter of Henri II's notorious mistress, Diane de Poitiers, la Duchesse de Valentinois. She married Robert IV de La Marck, le Duc de Bouillon, and their son Henri became a Huguenot cohort of le Prince de Porcien. While there is no historical counterpart to the Princess of Cleve, her husband the Prince was a son (probably the third) of Francis I de Cleves, le Duc de Nevers (1516–62), a pro-Huguenot killed in the Battle of Dreux. Nothing is known of the son's having an unfaithful wife, but one of his sisters, Marie, married a Huguenot, le Prince de Condé the year before he was killed in the Massacre (1572), and another sister, Catherine, married the gallant Huguenot soldier, Antoine de Crog, le Prince de Porcien.

In a provocative twisting of history, this Catherine becomes Lee's Marguerite, "the Princess of Jainville" (I. i. 52). The title alludes to Catherine's childhood, which she spent at the castle of Joinville, seat of the Guises, under the tutelage of Antoinette de Bourbon, grandmother of Henri de Guise. After Porcien's death, she married Henri, now le Duc de Guise, in 1570—an affair which forms part of the scaffolding for Lee's treatment of subsequent history in *The Massacre of Paris*. Thus, as Catherine de Cleves, la Princesse de Porcien and child of castle Joinville, becomes Marguerite, Princess of Jainville, she assumes as Huguenot the political role assigned in *The Massacre of Paris* to Marguerite de Valois, Roman Catholic daughter of Henri II and Catherine de Medici (Lee's "Queen" in both plays). In *Massacre*, the Queen schemes to distract Guise from Marguerite, so that she can unite Roman Catholic to Huguenot interests by marrying Marguerite to the Prince of Navarre. In this play, the situation is the same though the allegiances are reversed: now the queen schemes to distract another duke, Nemours, from another Marguerite, this time a Huguenot princess, so that she can unite Huguenot and Roman Catholic interests in a marriage between Marguerite and "the Dauphin" (I. i. 54), Prince Francis.

Lee's point, here as in so many other plays, is that such political chicanery creates a moral vacuum into which the likes of Nemours, St. Andre, and Poltrot are bound to expand. Just how dangerous this development can be is implied through the historical traits of these three figures. Finding Madame de Lafayette's Duke too refined and prudent for his purpose, Lee gives us a "Ruffian" who closely resembles the historical Nemours, Jacque de Savoie (1531–85), a clever, unscrupulous, and sexually attractive courtier (he was once caught "in the act" with a maid of honor to the Queen). He promoted his fortunes by abandoning Huguenot leanings to marry Anne d'Este, widow of Francis, le Duc de Guise. Thereafter, feigning fanatical devotion to the Catholic cause, he became Governor of Lyons and a renowned commander of Roman Catholic forces. Historically, St. Andre was le Maréchal Saint André, a powerful, dazzlingly rich, and militant Roman Catholic. With le Duc de Montmorency (1530–79) and le Duc de Guise (Francis, 1519–63) he formed in 1561 a triumvirate of military and political power leagued against the Huguenots, and he was killed while leading Roman Catholics in battle. Curiously, he was anything but a friend of Poltrot—historically Jean de Poltrot, le seigneur de Méré, an excitable and melancholy Huguenot fanatic, who imagined that God had chosen him to avenge his country and creed against the House of Guise. As a double agent in the Roman Catholic camp, actually serving the Huguenot Admiral, Poltrot gained the confidence of le Duc de Guise, then assassinated him in 1563.

When two such able political foes, the perpetrators of momentous and bloody events that shape a nation, can privately become friends and collaborators in self-indulgent folly, then something is rotten in the state. When two such conscientious men can become associated with an unprincipled pleasure-seeker like Nemours, it implies an absurd and ominous disharmony between politico-religious and sociomoral allegiances. The humor in *The Princess of Cleve* darkens as we become aware of these discontinuities. Comedy becomes black comedy.

IV   *Satire through Imagery and Biblical Allusion*

If plot structure, literary tradition, and historical background tell us a good deal about how Lee's satire shades into assessment, both the most general and most specific implications of this assessment are revealed by a closer look at his use of imagery and allusion. What we find is that in this play, as in the others, Lee assumes that psychology, behavior, and philosophy ultimately become part of some suprarational cosmic design.

In the world of the Prince and Princess of Cleve, as in the traditional stage world of romantic heroism, all specific behavior is analyzed for its cosmic meaning. From start to finish the Prince regards his ill fortune as "Martyrdom" and ascribes it to some incomprehensible purpose of heaven (III. ii. 50, 144–45). Like Dryden's Morat (*Aureng-Zebe*) or Absalom (*Absalom and Achitophel*), he wishes God had "cast" him in a lesser "Mould" (I. iii. 61), so that he would not have aspired to match his "fire" (II. iii. 209) with that of the Princess. Similarly, the Princess interprets her divided affections as fate's mode of testing her virtue: "Fate set two Bowls before me, / Poyson and Health, a Husband and Nemours" (I. iii. 195–96). She dreams of avoiding this dilemma by escaping to an undersea world where Christian moral paradigms are irrelevant, where she can enjoy Nemours in "Green Courts" among "naked Nymphs" (II. iii. 88–99). But in Act V, after she knows of her husband's end, she returns from dreams to a mournful awareness of "Men below, and Gods above": "Mortals, Mortals, try your skill, / Seeking Good or shunning Ill, / Fate will be the burden still" (V. iii. 26, 31–33).

This confidence that life is ultimately to be understood by intuition of a supernatural purpose is not shared by the other characters in the play. They organize their behavior according to those earthbound criteria of appetite and expedience which the Princess regards as threats to virtue. If the Prince and Princess see each other as corpse-enslaved souls battling for heavenly blessings, the other characters see each other as animals competing for the blessings of sexual fulfill-ment, as hunted game, predatory birds or beasts, livestock and household pets.[17] Yet where this bestial love-chase might have be-come carefree bedroom farce, Lee informs the dialogue with biblical and occult references that implicitly denouce the proceedings. While revelling in their own depravity, the Calvinist Poltrot and his wife anathemetize each other in Old Testament language. She is "Lot's Wife," "Goody Bathsheba," a second Eve, and so on (II. ii. 30–32, 101–02; III, i. 286; IV. i. 104–05; V. i. 46–57), and he is an Adam choosing damnation out of "meer Generosity" (V. i. 42–43).[18] More-over, he and St. Andre are called devils (II. ii. 3; IV. i. 68–69), while their wives are described in authentic language as witches who an-noint themselves, ride broomsticks, nourish familiars from unnatural teats, and form sexual covenants (III. i. 177–78, 195–211).[19] Though Poltrot, St. Andre, and their wives behave as if unconcerned about Christian ethics, their frequent recourse to biblical analogies and de-monology shows a subconscious awareness of where their debauch-ery places them on the postlapsarian scale of values.

Like them, Nemours also has an arsenal of Christian allusions and a sense of the Christian cosmos. But he uses these as part of his rhet-oric to advance purposes more in line with a materialistic, hedonistic philosophy (see I. i. 16–17, ii. 65–69; V. iii. 258–62). At the masquer-ade in Act IV, for instance, when confronted by Tournon and Mar-guerite dressed and speaking as Huguenots, he woos them in the appropriate idiom: to Marguerite's "I love a Man that keeps the Com-mandment of his word" Nemours replies, "and I a Woman that breaks hers with her Husband, yet loves her Neighbour as her self" (IV. i. 53–55). He can use such phraseology without the slightest hint of sharing Poltrot's repressed faith in its transcendental potency (see also I. ii. 47–50; II. iii. 281; IV. i. 226). For his more "sober design" (I. i. 41) on the Princess, however, a different rhetoric is required, "the Heroick Vein," "Hypocrisie and Softness" (IV. i. 260, 272–73). Thus, when she accuses him of having no soul, therefore no divine sanction for his advances, he fluently responds that, in fact, both na-ture and God conspire to unite passionate lovers such as they (IV. iii. 175–76, 191, 206–11).

If this sounds like Achitophel's persuasion of Absalom or Satan's argument to Eve in Milton, it may be no accident. Like these archdissimulators, Nemours is a consummate role-player. He finds aesthetic pleasure in "all sort of acting" (III. i. 77), and when it serves his appetite for other pleasures, he can employ a variety of idioms and adjust tone of voice and mannerisms to suit the occasion. He revels in this protean nature (with its hints of bisexuality: see II. iii. 1; IV. i. 280–82), comparing himself to Zeus when the god became an eagle to capture the beautiful youth, Ganymede, and when he became a bull to seduce the lovely Europa (II. iii. 1, 26). A more apt comparison, one more closely connected to a major vein of imagery, is drawn when Marguerite calls him "a Fiend, Devil, Devil, Devil" (III. i. 105) whose "Monstrous, Diabolical Arts . . . seduce Young Virgins . . . to set 'em on the High-way to Hell and Damnation" (IV. i. 186–87).

The vehemence with which she repeatedly applies this label to Nemours (see also II. iii. 253) is disturbingly convincing. It partakes of the undercurrent of seriousness which runs through Poltrot's employment of witch lore, and reminds us that, like Poltrot, Marguerite is probably meant to be a Huguenot. Like the devil, Nemours assumes many disguises to further his schemes, and St. Andre says he is "black" and keeps a "Black airy shape" as a servant (I. i. 89, 114). Tournon says he specializes in "Damning of Souls" (I. ii. 2–3), and Nemours admits he would trade "Body, State and Spirit" (I. ii. 23–24) so that "the Devil and I" could be "as great as ever" (II. iii. 273). In Marguerite, "such a ranting Devil" (I. iii. 23), he sees an opportunity, for she has told him that to discover the contents of the tennis-court letter, "I'll sell my Soul to Hell" (II. i. 24). Later, Nemours confides to himself: "Well, if she be a Devil, Hell by her shou'd be a merry place" (III. i. 119–20). In a dialogue preceding this soliloquy, such generalized name-calling gets down to occult jargon that is as specific and authentic as that used by Poltrot and St. Andre:

MARG. But . . . cou'd you find in your heart to ingender with a damn'd Spirit?
NEM. Yes Marry cou'd I, for all you ask the question so seriously: . . . I have long'd . . . this seven years to be the Father of a Succubus—
MARG. Fiend, and no Man—
NEM. Besides, Madam, don't you think a feat Devil of yours and my begetting, wou'd be a prettier sight in a House, than a Monkey[20] or a Squirrel? (III. i. 58–66)

The popular witch lore with which Lee's audience would have been familiar is full of covenants involving sexual union with the devil—or with his succubi and incubi—and involving the monstrous offspring of such unions.[21]

In effect, what this serious undercurrent of demonism does to the already deeply flawed character of Nemours is to make it seem dangerous, more dangerous than the clumsy amorality of Poltrot and company is made to seem by a parallel use of similar imagery. If Nemours' insatiable whoremongering and blatant deception of his best friend makes his roguery less glamorous than revolting, his diabolism gives this roguery a status in the Christian world picture that he rejects. To him, the rhetoric of devils and witches is merely another verbal weapon, part of the rake's arsenal, to be used at will alongside biblical maxims and the language of romantic heroism. But to Marguerite and Tournon, he is devil-possessed, and in light of Tournon's mission for the queen, this becomes a symbolic gloss to the overall form and theme of the play: the forces of evil, ever prepared to seize an opportunity, will invade a society driven by political ambition and fouled by carnal desire.

V Satire through Contemporary Allusion

That Lee meant the audience's discomfort about this state of affairs to be instructive is made clear when Poltrot unwittingly equates his own behavior with what his English wife calls her "filthy Country way" (II. ii. 177):

O there's not such another Drinking, Scowring, Roaring, Whoreing Nation in the World[22]—And for little London, to my knowledge, if a Bill were taken of the weekly Cuckolds, it wou'd amount to more than the Number of Christnings and Burials put together. (I. ii. 136–40; and see V. i. 9)

The double rhetoric of affirming the Christian cosmos ("Christnings and Burials"), while seeming to reject it, is what we see throughout Poltrot's speeches; its reflection of the rhetoric of living in Restoration England is not difficult to discover.

In some respects the reflection becomes rather specific, especially if we accept Lee's assertion that the play "was a Revenge for the Refusal of the other [*Massacre*]; for when they expected the most polish'd Hero in Nemours, I gave 'em a Ruffian reeking from Whetstone's-Park [a notorious promenade for prostitutes]. . . . He lays about him like the Gladiator in the Park [a nude statue]; they may walk by, and take no notice."[23] The word "they" seems to refer both to those responsible for denying production to *Massacre* and to some group of regular theater-goers who not only read Lafayette's romance (and so expected a different Nemours) but also were hardened to the kind of debauchery symbolized by the nude gladiator in the park. Assuming the play was written in late 1681 or early 1682, then "they" would have been, specifically, the Lord Chamberlain— Henry Bennet, Earl of Arlington—and his Master of Revels, Charles Killigrew, manager of the King's Company after his recently retired father.[24]

In more general terms, "they" would have included the circle of court wits who dominated theatrical taste during the 1660s and 1670s: John Wilmot, Earl of Rochester; George Villiers, Duke of Buckingham; Charles Sackville, Lord Buckhurst, Earl of Dorset and Middlesex; John Sheffield, Earl of Mulgrave; Lord John Vaughan, later Earl of Carberry; Sir Charles Sedley; Sir George Etherege; Henry Savile; Henry Killigrew (half-brother of Charles); and Henry Bulkeley.[25] This not only would explain why libertine behavior had special topicality for Lee at this time but also would help account for the strikingly specific ways in which the wits on stage—Nemours, Tournon, Poltrot, St. Andre, etc.—resemble their actual counterparts in the Restoration court.

Ever since Montague Summers pointed it out in 1935, it has seemed obvious that Nemours somehow represents the Earl of Rochester.[26] For a while one of Rochester's admirers (see the dedication of *Nero*), Lee seems to have shifted from the "Rochester-Shadwell" camp to "the Dryden-Mulgrave axis" sometime after Rochester labelled him "a hot-brained fustian fool" in the "Allusion to Horace" (c. 1675).[27] *Cleve* may therefore be another posthumous satire on Rochester like John Crowne's *City Politiques,* which was banned in June 1682, possibly through pressure brought to bear on the Master of Revels by some of the Earl's friends.[28] The famous dialogue in which Nemours and the Vidam lament the recent death of "Count Rosidore" (Rochester had died in 1680) seems designed to bring the late rake-Lord to mind (I. ii. 89–90, 101–03), and several of the play's lines evoke Rochester's own writings.[29] Moreover, Nemours' closing speech patently ridicules Rochester's deathbed conversion to Anglicanism, as publicized in Robert Parson's *A Sermon preached at the Earl of Rochester's Funeral* and Bishop Burnet's *Some Passages of the*

Life and Death of . . . Rochester (both pamphlets in Dr. Lee's library, below, ch. 1, n. 6):

For my part, the Death of the Prince . . . has so truly wrought a change in me, as nothing else but a Miracle cou'd—For first I see, and loath my Debaucheries—Next . . . I am resolv'd to give satisfaction to all I have wrong'd. . . . This . . . will convince the World of the Ingenuity of my Repentance, because I had the power to go on.

> He well Repents that will not Sin, yet can,
> But Death-bed Sorrow rarely shews the Man. (V. iii. 294–303)

As usual in this play, the satire is double-pronged, for we know that Nemours—his recent wager about bedding the Princess still ringing in our ears—is no more sincere about converting than Lee implies Rochester was.

Yet Nemours is not merely another stage version of Rochester, another Dorimant. For one thing, he does not look like Rochester. St. Andre describes him as "built for Whoring . . . black sanguine Brawny—a Roman Nose—long foot and stiff—calf of a Leg" (I. i. 88–90). If the Jacob Huysman portrait in the National Gallery is lifelike, St. Andre is not describing Rochester. In the Restoration "brawny" meant "Characterized by muscle or muscular strength," and Rochester's physique was characterized by "a slenderness betraying his lack of a robust constitution."[30] If St. Andre is meant to be reminding us of specific courtiers, then he might as well be said to suggest a combination of the dark wiriness of Henry Jermyn, the Duke of York's Master of Horse, and the robustness of the Duke of Buckingham.[31]

There is more than idle speculation involved in linking Nemours with Buckingham and Jermyn—especially with Buckingham. Both men, for a start, had been suitors to the Countess of Shrewsbury and both participated in fatal duels with rivals for her affections. As we shall see, the Shrewsbury affair is paralleled in rather telling ways by the romantic plot of Lee's play. Secondly, if Rochester was the leading "Spirit" of the court wits, Buckingham was their highest ranking member and a man who shared more than his rank with the Duke of Nemours. He too was quick-witted, irreverent, and religiously uncommitted, and his widely ridiculed association with the astrologer "Dr." John Heydon is brought to mind when the Vidam calls Nemours an "Astrologer" (V. iii. 257). Furthermore, he shares with Nem-

ours (as with Dorimant and Rochester) a reputation for juggling "a
dozen intrigues at once"; in fact, "he was the only person in a vicious
age and Court that was publicly censured for women."[32]

Even more striking, just as Nemours indirectly causes the Prince's
death, so "it was Buckingham's bad luck to be known in his own generation and to history as the man who murdered his paramour's husband."[33] The paramour was Anna-Maria Brudenell, who at sixteen
had been married to Francis Talbot, eleventh Earl of Shrewsbury.
Like Lee's Prince, Shrewsbury was "a staid man who found little
pleasure in the constant round of balls, picnics, entertainments, and
plays," and like the Princess of Cleve, Anna-Maria was "eager for the
joys of London, and ripe for intrigue."[34] Until Buckingham made his
conquest in summer, 1666, she apparently kept her virtue; but her
beauty and flirtatiousness kept "a pack of gay dogs . . . panting at her
heels," two of whom, Henry Jermyn and Captain Thomas Howard,
fought bloodily over her.[35] The scandalous openness with which she
and Buckingham indulged their passion finally led the saturnine
Earl's kinsmen to insist on a duel, and he issued the challenge in
January 1667/8. On January 16 the affair was settled at the expense of
two lives, that of Buckingham's second, Sir Robert Holmes, and, two
months later, that of Shrewsbury himself (his wounds having been
maltreated). During these fatal months Anna-Maria had been in
France, probably in a Benedictine convent at Pontoise, where she
had fled in September to escape mounting gossip. But it was rumored
that she had been present at the duel and had fled to avoid scandal—
an order of business that Lee may have had in mind when he wrote
the play.[36]

In any case, while in France, Anna-Maria did what Lee's Princess
hints at doing: she let time work in her lover's favor, so that, in late
spring, 1668, she returned to live openly with Buckingham. This
idyllic liaison—quietly accepted by Buckingham's wife—came to an
unexpected, shocking end in 1674. In response to a petition from the
late earl's teen-aged son, the House of Lords publicly debated the
entire affair and, in the end, reprimanded Buckingham not only for
adultery but also for general immorality and sacrilege. As Anna-
Maria returned to her convent (later to remarry), Buckingham re-
treated to friends, music, chemistry, and the hunt—only to reemerge
as an ally of Shaftesbury in the efforts to prosecute the Popish Plot,
impeach the Earl of Danby (the king's Lord Treasurer), and exclude
the Duke of York from succession to the throne. By this time (1678–

81), however, colorful versions of the Shrewsbury affair, lumped together with Buckingham's ill-advised support for the alliance with France, had become popular material for the street balladeers.[37]

Thus, if Lee was satirizing his literary enemy Rochester, he may also have had in mind Buckingham not only as another member of the group whom he might have blamed for the banning of *Massacre*, but also as a man who had much in common with Nemours. Moreover, Lee may have considered Buckingham as much an enemy to his career as Rochester was, for when the Duke was Chancellor of Cambridge he apparently took an interest in young Lee and "brought him up to town where he never did anything for him."[38] This would have given the young playwright an incentive to depict witty courtiers in the negative terms used in many of his plays, from *Nero* onward, as well as in *Cleve*.

Once the audience had become attuned to a frame of satiric reference comprehending both Rochester and Buckingham, they would naturally have picked up allusions to the more prominent traits of other members of "the merry gang" as well. For example, Nemours' wooing of Marguerite—modelled on Catherine Cleves, daughter of a Huguenot sympathizer—might have reflected rumors that Dorset considered marrying Esther, daughter of the Huguenot Marquis de Governette. And Poltrot's self-proclaimed genius for unpremeditated versifying and for facility with witty comparisons—"I know how to . . . make Similes as fast as hops . . . and as round as a Hoop" (I. ii. 144ff. 189–92)—could be seen as a reference to Sir Charles Sedley, whom Charles II called "Apollo's Viceroy" because of his ready employment of similes. When St. Andre's affectation of martial prowess becomes oppressive, the Vidam charges him to "leave off . . . Lying" and Poltrot adds, "Lord, Lord, how the World is given to Lying!" (I. iii. 43, 52). Perhaps this suggests Henry Killigrew, who was popularly known as "lying Killigrew," an epithet which he himself approved.[39]

Yet the overall effect of such allusions is not so much to pinpoint particular Restoration courtiers as to evoke the ambience created in the popular mind by reports of courtly license. "Citizens, Citizens, look to your Wives, the Courtiers come," cries St. Andre in his sleep (IV. ii. 38–9). And there is much in the play besides possibly esoteric references to keep the courtiers in mind. That distinguished military leaders like le Duc de Nemours and le Maréchal St. André should appear on stage as obscene captains of parlor heroics ridicules the military pretensions of Buckingham, Rochester, Mulgrave, Dorset, Vaughan, Wycherley, Sedley, and Savile. And if so, there is an additional pungency to obscene battle imagery such as "she cock'd me," "the Pan flash'd," "now I go off" (II. iii. 277–81); "let's board'em" and "they carry Chain-shot; Pray Heav'n they do not split us Sister" (III. i. 151–61). That Poltrot has just returned from abroad suggests not only the fops' Grand Tour but also the diplomatic missions of Buckingham, Dorset, Sedley, Etherege, and Savile (the latter two having become professional diplomats for a time). [40]

Upon finding his wife in bed with Bellamore, Poltrot calls the interloper "a Bloody-minded Son of Belial" (V. i. 86–87)—a label certain to remind the audience of Dryden's Miltonic term for the wits in *Absalom and Achitophel*. [41] And another allusion to literary representations of the "merry gang" appears in St. Andre's opening dialogue:

ST. A. How many Bottles last night?
BOY. Five my Lord.
. . . .
ST. A. How many Whores?
BOY. Six my Lord.
. . . .
ST. A. What Quarrels, how many did I kill?
BOY. Not one my Lord—But the night before you Hamstrung a Beadle, and run a Link-man in the Back— (I. i. 94–104)

The effect is similar to that created in many plays where witwouds are depicted. In Etherege's *The Comical Revenge* (1664), for instance, the maid tells of Sir Frederick's night at Mrs. Grace's: he "roar'd out in the streets. . . . march'd bravely at the reere of an Army of Link-boys; . . . wag'd a bloody war with the Constable; and having vanquish'd that dreadful enemy, . . . committed a general massacre on the glass-windows." [42]

Like Etherege, Lee reduces fashionable rakishness to the level of Sir Fopling Flutters, whose real-life equivalents were coxcombs like Sir John Hewitt and Philip Stanhope, second Earl of Chesterfield. But if Etherege's satire is condescending, Lee's is vicious, for by the time he was writing *Cleve* there had been plenty of actual escapades showing that differences between the Chesterfields and Rochesters were not as pronounced as those who publicly ridiculed Stanhope (Etherege, Rochester, Dorset, Sedley) liked to think. [43] There had been many duels and near-duels, and a number of brawls with bloody consequences. Not much time had passed since the heyday of the "Ballers," a notorious nucleus of courtiers headquartered at "Lady" Bennet's brothel, where the girls danced naked (we recall Nemours among the "Naked Nymphs" of the Princess's dream [II. iii. 86 ff]) as the blades plotted mischief. In 1675 a party of such debauchees burst into the Privy Garden at Whitehall and amidst volleys of laughter destroyed the King's phallic-shaped, glass sundial. On at least four occasions between 1663 and 1677 certain of the wits were reported streaking along parks and streets wholly or partially in the nude.[44]

VI *Dimensions of Revenge*

In one respect Lee's "revenge" against the courtly arbiters of dramatic taste was belated. Rochester's death in 1680 symbolized the end of an era of public debauchery. Buckingham had left Whitehall in disgrace; Dorset, Vaughan, and Sedley were beginning to settle down; the rest—except Etherege and Mulgrave—were either dead or relatively quiet.[45] Lee himself had sufficiently vented his contempt for the "merry gang" in previous plays.

Nevertheless, by writing somewhat after the fact, he was able to place his subject into longer perspective and to study its implications in multiple contexts. In the literary context, as Dryden noted in his Prologue and Epilogue, Lee demonstrated that "A Rogue in Mode" like Nemours is not a Dorimant; rather, he is "a filthy Beast, / . . . like the pack of all the rest" and is no more admirable than a "Spaniel Lover" or "Saint-like Fool" such as the Prince of Cleve or his counterparts in contemporary serious drama.[46] Moreover, as the shapeless, prose world of Nemours triumphs over the blank-verse order of the Prince's utopia, we become aware of dark implications created by Lee's use of historical and philosophical contexts. Individuals whose political, military, and religious affiliations were of great consequence in history are made to behave as if politics, war, and the supernatural are joking matters. Yet all the while they unwittingly serve the shadowy political purposes of a Machiavellian queen. Thus, Lee's satire reaches behind the values and behavioral patterns of fashionable society and drama to include a sovereign like Charles II, who regarded moral laxity as irrelevant to religious and political health.

That there is a close connection between morals and politics is only part of Lee's message, however. He also wants it understood, as he usually did, that such earthly doings play a role in the providential design. Tournon serves Queen Catherine's political aims, the Prince serves his principles, and Nemours serves his appetite; but together they act out another chapter in the providentially controlled dialectic between infernal and celestial forces. Through the fallen world of Queen Catherine, and the flesh of Tournon, Nemours, Marguerite, and the fops, the devil destroys icons of piety and order like the Prince and Princess. The result on stage is that mixture of tragedy, comedy, and farce that Lee calls "meer Play"; but in the historical-philosophical world outside the theater, the result is divine comedy: Queen Catherine's victory leads first to civil war, bloody massacres, and assassinations; but eventually it leads to the unified France of her son-in-law Henri IV, who would lay the political foundations upon which "would be built the magnificent . . . monarchy of Louis XIV."[47]

Thus, in the long run Nemours' dissipation is as ineffectual as St. Andre's sleepwalking—as a great military leader dreaming of seducing the chambermaid (IV. ii. 41ff)—or as the Prince's idealism. If the Prince forgets that his soul has links below as well as above, Nemours pretends he has no soul at all. Both views are unrealistic by Restoration standards, for they renounce man's dual nature. They are both acts of pride and therefore offer opportunities for the forces of evil to promote sublunar disorder. That some providential resolution of the resulting conflicts is in store can only be surmised from the historical implications of this play. In Lee's final dramatic essay, *Constantine the Great*, such a resolution is postulated.

CHAPTER 12

Christian Sanity and Social Order:
Constantine the Great; A Tragedy
(1683)

L EE'S last known play ends his decade of professional activity on
an optimistic note that thematically fulfills the promise of *The
Princess of Cleve*. There, as man's fallen nature triumphs over idealism and sanity, history is allowed to hint at a new social, psychological, and spiritual synthesis under the messianic Henri IV. In *Lucius
Junius Brutus* a similar resumption of civic health is foreseen as
superseding the benign surgery of a Cromwellian political physician.
Now, with *Constantine the Great*, Lee uses many of his formerly
effective dramatic conventions to construct a fable that resolves the
kind of discord that ends all previous works except the pastoral *Theodosius*. In that play sanity and social order are reestablished at the
expense of idealized, romantic love (Varanes), irresponsible religious
withdrawal (Theodosius), and power-mongering pagan heroism
(Marcian). A vigorous hybridization of opposing contexts of value is
achieved in the marriage of Pulcheria and Marcian. *Constantine* rings
an instructive variation on this theme as the achieving of order is
symbolized not by the external form of marriage but by the psychological victory *within* Constantine. This self-conquest enables him
simultaneously to cast out the diabolical counsellor, Arius, and to
foster the forces of order and stability in Dalmatius, Crispus, and
Fausta. The move from external to internal synthesis parallels the
earlier shift from conflicts between Nero and Britannicus to conflicts
within the mind of Alexander—with the important difference that
here the subject is triumph, not disaster, a psychological triumph
that is providentially arranged.

I *Plot*

The plot is built of three sub-actions integrated as forces operating to upset the mind and will of the Emperor Constantine. Driving these forces is the evil counsellor-priest, Arius. On the political and religious front, he sends collaborators (Labienus and Eubulus) to foment rebellion among Rome's pagan populace, who resent Constantine's Christian reforms, while he incites the emperor's brother-in-law, Lycinius, to attempt an assassination. On the psychological front, he secretly marries Constantine's favorite son, Crispus, to the luscious Fausta, daughter of the Emperor Maximianus—knowing full well that he himself had earlier betrothed her, sight unseen, to Constantine, after which Constantine had sent Crispus (kept ignorant of the betrothal) to "inspect" the new possession. As these schemes become actions, Dalmatius, the emperor's brother, protects him against Lycinius and the mob, while advising him to retract his death sentence on Crispus (whose martial and political prowess he needs) and to banish Fausta and Arius. In these counsels he is seconded by his spiritual counterpart, Archbishop Sylvester, who seeks the emperor's formal conversion through Christian baptism.

Meanwhile, Annibal, son of Dalmatius, has discovered that his beloved Serena, Fausta's gentler sister, has fallen in love with his best friend Crispus; and Serena, in turn, finds that Crispus is entirely devoted to Fausta. Neither unrequited lover being able to make the necessary adjustments, Annibal provokes a duel with his friend and is killed, and Serena stabs herself to death. Pointing to these disasters as warnings against selfish indulgence of passion, Dalmatius and Sylvester once again urge the dismissal of Arius and Fausta. By now, however, Constantine verges on madness as he struggles to control his feelings for Fausta amid rising turmoils in court and state.

In the final scene, while Fausta prepares to enter the poisoned bath commanded by the enraged emperor, he covertly watches as Arius provides Crispus the means of suicide. This final treachery of Arius at last clears Constantine's vision. Recognizing the foolishness of nursing a middle-aged infatuation for a pagan maiden, and of nurturing a mischievous heretic in the court, he orders Arius executed, blesses the nuptials of Crispus and Fausta, and invokes "the Dews of Heav'n" (V. ii. 334).

II *Dramatic Tradition, History, and Politics*

As Van Lennep and Lee's editors have pointed out,[1] this plot may owe its basic structure and a few of its scenes to Otway's *Don Carlos* (1676), Dryden's *Aureng-Zebe* (1675), and Racine's *Mithridate* (1673). At this point in his career, however, the playwright is more likely to have been remembering his own previous works. Constantine finds himself in difficulties similar to those Mithridates faced; through the machinations of a false priest (Arius) and political malcontents (Eubulus, Labienus and Lycinius), he is driven to compete with his own son (Crispus) for the affections of a beautiful woman (Fausta). Like Mithridates, Alexander, and Theodosius, he is distracted by this amorous dilemma from his imperial duties and, again like Alexander, he threatens the life of the one figure whose martial prowess guarantees social order (Crispus, with the aid of Dalmatius). Finally, like Theodosius, he is psychologically incapacitated to comprehend the voice of true religion (Sylvester). Van Lennep's further suggestion that *Constantine*, like *Nero*, must partly be based on a lost romance, since it departs radically from history,[2] may also be dismissed; Lee's modifications of history seem consistently aimed at developing his own thematic design, which clearly reflects similar designs in earlier plays. What he chiefly does is retain historical characters while ignoring the "accidents" of time and place. He depicts as converging in a significant pattern certain events that actually happened on discrete occasions in different parts of the empire. The artistic procedure reminds us of that used in *Theodosius*.[3]

Not that he avoids bending history a bit even in matters of characterization. The story of Serena and Crispus shows how much he is willing to dilute fact with fiction. Serena is the only main character who appears to have no historical counterpart. She is certainly not Theodora, half-sister of Fausta (by their mother Europia), for Theodora becomes the second wife of Constantius I, and so the mother of Dalmatius and stepmother of Constantine. Her grandson, Hannibalianus, becomes Lee's Annibal. This love-sick youth Lee depicts as dying in a duel with Crispus, while history tells us that he was murdered at least ten years later, in 338 A.D., after Constantine had married him to his eldest daughter Constantia and named him King of Pontus (which then included Cappadocia, where Lee's emperor intends making the boy governor: II. i. 334).

By inventing this affair of unrequited love between Serena and Annibal, Lee does essentially what he did with Sophonisba and Massinissa—and Massina—in *Sophonisba;* with Narcissa and Caesario in *Gloriana;* with Athenais and Varanes in *Theodosius;* Teraminta and Titus in *Lucius Junius Brutus;* and the prince and princess in *The Princess of Cleve.* He provides an example of self-consuming, passionate love, whose failure to harmonize with social necessity is lethal. Annibal refuses to give over an ill-fated love in favor of imperial duties and friendship; Serena is unable to accept the love between Crispus and Fausta as both psychologically natural and politically mandated. That both fall victims to suicidal melancholy (II. i. 106, 118; III. i. 88–90; IV. i. 180ff.) instructively contrasts with what happens in the parallel love triangle involving Crispus, Fausta, and Constantine.

In order to juxtapose this second triangle and the first, Lee needed no fictional characters or situations—only a fictional time scheme and a completely different resolution of conflicts. Fausta was, in fact, a pagan daughter of the Emperor Maximianus. She was, however, betrothed to Constantine (c. 294) before Crispus was born (c. 299) and seems to have been executed for alleged adultery with Crispus in 326, long after she married the Emperor Constantine (307). The instrument of execution was a scalding bath, not the poisoned one that Lee may have borrowed from Otway's *Don Carlos.* Crispus was indeed the Christian son of Constantine (baptized before his father), was for a time heir-apparent to the empire, and gained great popularity as a martial hero. But in history he was executed shortly after Fausta, by some accounts for political treason as much as for adultery.

Lee's reconstruction of these events provides the play with an exemplary resolution of love-rivalry that dramatically contravenes the tragic story of Serena and Annibal. Whereas neither of these lovers can gain a practical view of his dilemma, Constantine learns to control his misdirected passions and therefore to settle his affairs in a manner that is natural (by blessing his son's appropriate match with Fausta), practical (by grafting Maximianus' "Herculian" dynasty to his own "Neo-Flavian" one, while retaining his son's military and political endowments), and, above all, providential (recognizing his own role in the Christian destiny).

Most of the political implications that historians attach to Fausta's liaison with Crispus are shifted by Lee to his third subplot involving Dalmatius, Sylvester, Lycinius, and Arius—all historical figures

whose relationships and activities are changed to suggest parallels
with Restoration English politics. The details of these parallels have
been usefully set forth in an article by Lee's editors, though they do
not show how the political allusions were made possible partly by his
modifications of history, and they overstress the specificity of his
comment on the Tory triumphs of 1681–83.[4] The half-brothers Constantine and Dalmatius are made full siblings who confront a crisis
similar to that faced by Charles II and his brother James, Duke of
York. Their innovative religion (Constantine's new Christianity/
Charles's high-church Anglicanism, with leanings toward James's Roman Catholicism) and strongly monarchical politics (especially as articulated by Dalmatius/James) are challenged by a skeptical and ambitious heretic (Arius, who shares some attitudes and physical
attributes with the Earl of Shaftesbury) aided by an excitable, mal-
contented republican (Lycinius/Algernon Sidney). Like Shaftesbury,
Arius vainly tries to discredit the new religion, incite discord between sovereign and favorite son (Crispus/Duke of Monmouth), and
arrange a royal assassination.

To maintain these parallels, Lee had merely to emphasize one trait
of the historical Lycinius, his hostility toward Christians, but he had
to invent the assassination attempt and to move his execution from
the provinces in 323 or 324 to Rome at the time of Fausta's infidelity
(c. 326–27). Dalmatius, "the Censor" about whom history says very
little (he may actually have been assassinated in 337), is given the
absolutist convictions of the Duke of York (see II. i. 310–14, 355–60),
and Crispus is changed hardly at all to remind us of the brave, charm-
ing Monmouth and of his brief competition with Charles for the favors of Barbara Palmer, Duchess of Cleveland. To qualify Arius for
his role, however, Lee was obliged to bring him to Rome at a time
when his historical original had exiled himself to protest the decisions
made by Constantine's Council of Nicaea. Also, the historical Arius,
a rather obstinately doctrinal figure whose ambitions were mainly
religious, is transformed into one whose chief goals are nihilistic and
political. Perhaps his death in a poisoned bath reflects Lee's awareness that the historical Arius seems also to have died ignominiously,
many years after Crispus: "compelled by a call of nature," he fell
headlong into the lavatory and "burst asunder in the midst."[5]

The play's topicality must not be confused with political allegory,
for its characters and action do not assume a configuration that corresponds with a single pattern in Restoration political life. As usual,

Lee seeks only general relevance, general enough to give him artistic latitude to universalize his theme, yet topical enough to keep the audience alert and to justify Dryden's allusions to the contemporary scene in his epilogue: "Arius . . . / . . . a true Protestant," "Court of Constantine . . . full of . . . / . . . every Trimmer," "their Darling Plot," and "the last Plot."[6] In the play's closing lines, Lee insists on this general relevance by reviving the legend that Constantine was born in Colchester and by having the Emperor remember his youthful Caesarship of his native land (V. ii. 342–45).

III   *From History to Christian Destiny*

Through the historical adaptations discussed so far, Lee unifies his plot and comments on current events. By additional tampering with sources, he endows this commentary with a supernatural dimension, hinting how both Constantine and Charles II act out a providential design. Just before his great victory over the usurper Maxentius in the Battle of Milvian Bridge (312), the historical Constantine had a psychic or spiritual experience which intensified his interest in Christianity. By most accounts he saw in the sky a shining cross over which, or near which, were inscribed the words "in this conquer," and at least one chronicler says attending angels repeated these words aloud. The emperor immediately ordered the insignia marked on his soldiers' standards (and/or shields and helmets), and they proceeded to win the battle.

In Act I, Scene i of the play, this vision, deferred for fifteen years, serves as heaven's prediction of a nonmilitary victory. Within a setting reminiscent of the mural that ornaments the opening scene of *Theodosius*, Constantine dreams of two angels who descend holding a banner on which is emblazoned a bloody cross and the key phrase "*In hoc signo vince.*" They sing that a "Heavenly Doom" decrees he shall suffer "a Torment" in the form of "disturb'd . . . thoughts" before finally overcoming "all the Menaces of Fate." This is symbolized by their banner: its "Emblem of a bleeding Love, / Shall both thy Cross and Triumph prove" (I. i. 1–21). Like Christ, Constantine is predestined to suffer on a cross of love, but his victory is as certain as Christ's Resurrection. He differs from Christ in that his eternal salvation is delayed, and his victory is not over death and the world in general, but over diabolical forces in society and in his own fallen mind.

Interpreting this dream-vision for Constantine is Sylvester, an Archbishop of Rome (i.e., a Pope) whose activities at this time are historically obscure. Legend has it, however, that Sylvester did baptize the emperor, either to purge away his guilt over the execution of Crispus or, earlier, to cure his leprosy and stimulate Christian works like the founding of the Lateran Palace. In any case, Lee seizes the opportunity to make Sylvester the emperor's Christian advisor and thus the spiritual right arm to Dalmatius' civil left, both acting as foils to Arius.

This completes the dramatic pattern which Lee creates by twisting history. By assembling in one time and place historical figures who were scattered around the empire, and issues that had little bearing on one another, he forges a tripartite plot whose actions and motifs work in concert; together, they develop a theme that relates England's fortunes to those of fourth-century Rome and to a timeless heavenly intention. Serena and Annibal exemplify how love breeds destruction when isolated from society. Fausta and Crispus show that such a love, if it recognizes competing commitments, both civil and spiritual, can promote order and sanity. Yet in itself their love, misconstrued and resented by the passion-blinded emperor, becomes a threat to his mental stability. And promoting that threat, along with political and religious unrest, is the diabolical Arius, whose corrosive force is buffered by Dalmatius as civil advisor, Crispus as exemplar of virtuous passion, and Sylvester as steward of Providence.

In society the forces of evil radiate from Arius, and it is clear from the beginning that he is doing the Devil's work. By various other characters he is called snake (I. i. 172; V. ii. 97), devil (I. i. 187; III. i. 204, ii. 224; V. ii. 103, 309), "damn'd one" (III. i. 171), and "Fiend" (V. ii. 311). Like Cassander, he is consciously satanic, as when he exclaims, "Thus far the Devil is the best mounted yet, / And Heresie at least shall win the Race" (III. i. 91–92). But unlike Alexander's arch-enemy, Arius confronts in Dalmatius a more perceptive enemy than Lysimachus or Clytus might have been: Dalmatius, says Arius, has "unravell'd our close Webb of Thought" and "drawn Treason forth, perhaps to hang us all" (II. i. 30–32). It is clear, furthermore, that his satanic machinations are ultimately controlled by Providence. Through the scheming of Arius, Providence arranges Constantine's amorous dilemma, his "bleeding Love," and while it takes the emperor himself some time to realize this, lesser victims quickly perceive the hand of fate in their agonies. Serena, for example, understands that "Passion" has "dethron'd" her "Reason" (II. i. 106), creating "melancholy Thoughts" (II. i. 118), under the influence of "unhappy Stars" (II. i. 97), fate (II. i. 98, 111; IV. i. 50, 54), and the gods (III. i. 10). And before committing suicide, she dimly realizes that Arius, with his "down look, red Hair, and leering Eyes," has something to do with the general "Mischief" that plagues her and others (V. i. 29–30).

That it plagues, without destroying, the key characters other than Serena and Annibal, is what makes this play Lee's most optimistic piece. When Labienus, one of the conspirators, says that, thanks to Arius, "the mischief's Ripe" so that "Fortune points" the "Fate" of Constantine and his family (II. ii. 1–3), and when Arius announces that his "Genius" and that of "the proud imperial Brothers" are "by Nature Mortally oppos'd" (II. i. 9–10), we expect a rehearsal of Alexander's tragedy. As Cassander chooses Philip to execute his projected assassination, so Arius incites the "Melancholy" Lycinius—a "Malecontent" whose "adverse Fortune" has turned his "blood adust"—to stab Dalmatius (II. i. 20–26) and so expose Constantine to the furious rabble. But Dalmatius is more vigilant than Alexander, is more than a match for Lycinius, and Constantine, unlike the Hellenic emperor, withstands the other social and psychological pressures exerted (in his case) by Arius.

He is able to do so, because he is surrounded and protected by worthy men and women whose influences appeal to his better nature. These foes to Arius are the agents of Providence in carrying Constantine through his stormy period. By bolstering his psyche, they help him to achieve that public and private order that Lee's earlier sovereigns sought in vain. Nero, Augustus, Alexander, and Borgia had snuffed out the last vestiges of virtue in their worlds, but Constantine, though almost as weakly human as they, recognizes and respects virtue even when it infuriates him. As the exemplar of civic virtue, Dalmatius early perceives that Arius, the "Civil Villain" (I. i. 172), is doing the Devil's work in fomenting rebellion amongst the rabble, and he advises both Crispus and Constantine to reject Fausta's softening pagan charms, for they are "Death to your Health, and Ruine to your Glory" (III. i. 149). Like Clytus and Marcian, Dalmatius speaks for old Roman Stoicism and patriotism, and senses that Arius's appeal through Fausta to Constantine's passions threatens the emperor's sanity and, hence, the stability of the state.

Dalmatius cannot see that love does have an important place in human affairs, for he is blinded by the particularly inappropriate passion that Constantine, a middle-aged Christian emperor, bears for the youthful and pagan Fausta. That he also fails to see virtue in the chaste, marital love between Fausta and Crispus does not, however, prevent these two from demonstrating the strength of that virtue to Constantine. As a nubile pagan, Fausta does threaten the aging emperor's peace of mind and capacity to foster a Christian state, but with Crispus she is appropriately wed, for their love has time to mature as Crispus grows into the imperial throne and as she grows in Christian conviction. Because of her softening charms and paganism, Fausta does cause "discord" in the "Soul" of Crispus, but he knows that "Time, the Saints and Miracles must win" her (I. ii. 124–27) and that, once consummated, their love will cease to be in conflict with his martial duties and friendship with Dalmatius.

The exemplary influences of Dalmatius, Crispus, and Fausta might not have been enough in themselves to promote Constantine's victory over inner and outer enemies of peace and order. Alexander, after all, has his Clytus, his Lysimachus and Parasatis; Borgia his Machiavel and Bellamira. What these earlier sovereigns lacked was a Sylvester, a strong voice of spiritual advice. Theodosius had such a voice in Atticus, but it was not seconded by Marcian as Sylvester is supported by Dalmatius. Marcian and Atticus, Roman Stoicism and Christian devotion, tugged opposite ways on the soul and psyche of their emperor. Not so Dalmatius and Sylvester. Both have at heart Constantine's sanity—Dalmatius because he thinks it a prerequisite to social order and imperial greatness, Sylvester because he thinks it necessary before spiritual salvation can be achieved. That these are meant to be taken as complementary goals is clear when Dalmatius compares his and Sylvester's joint influence to that of Arius:

> See but the difference of Counsellors;
> What Colours good and bad can give to Reason.
> Had Arius stay'd, by this time you had doom'd
> Your Son to Death; who now have gain'd the Conquest. (V. ii. 133–36)

Dalmatius refers to the "Conquest" over that psychological tempest predicted at the play's beginning, a storm which Sylvester had interpreted as being caused by "a Bosom Foe" governed by the "ill Stars" (I. i. 43, 31) of Providence. On the most literal level, of course, this foe is Arius, the court Devil who is part of the emperor's inner circle of counsellors. But Lycinius, the would-be assassin, says there are several such foes, sent from "Hell," living warmly in the "Bosoms" of the imperial family, and corresponding to pagan "Gods" (II. i. 385–89). In the Christian tradition, especially as interpreted by Milton, the pagan gods are simply masks used by Satan's leading collaborators; and in this play, where Arius is the leading fiend, these bosom foes turn out to be the agents of disruption implanted not only in the rabble outside the palace but, more significantly, in the emperor's mind. They are the unnatural passions for Fausta and the unnatural cruelty toward Crispus which Arius insinuates into Constantine's psyche, and their alliance with Satan's underworld gods is confirmed in the emperor's agonized response to the news of his son's love for Fausta:

> The Thought distracts me; Heav'n remove this Trouble,
> Or I shall run to my old Gods again.
> But . . . I'll bear my Passion cold,
> . . . while the Reins of Reason hold. (III. i. 263–66)

Reason's reins give way more and more from this point on. In Act IV the emperor does call on his "old Gods," and when Sylvester chastises him for doing so, he replies, "forgive me, Saint, / I am eaten up with passion" (IV. i. 88–89). By Act V Constantine calls himself "Madman" (V. ii. 109), while Dalmatius urges that if his "Judgment seems half sunk" it is "not quite drown'd" (V. ii. 114). But in the final scene the joint pleadings of Dalmatius and Sylvester, and the near martyrdom of Crispus and Fausta, at last defeat the influence of Arius, so that what Constantine foresaw in an earlier lucid moment now comes into being:

> So shall the Soveraign pow'r unclouded sway,
> When such Court Devils, shun the glorious Ray,
> And drive like Foggs, before the rising Day. (III. ii. 223–25)

Unlike what happens in *Nero,* here the light of sanity and salvation triumphs over the fogs and darkness of diabolical forces in the emperor's psyche.

The difference is owing to Providence. To show his final confidence in God's justice and in man's consequent potential for good, Lee dramatizes the way Providence can repeat the Fall of Man and the triumph of Christ in the human psyche. While Constantine responds insanely to the false reasoning of the satanic Arius, he tends toward the bestial lust and cruelty that lurk in the bosom of all Adam's sons, and he moves simultaneously away from Christian baptism and toward pagan gods. But it is decreed by Providence, "by the Heavenly Doom" (I. i. 7), that by fostering civic (Dalmatius), interpersonal (Crispus and Fausta), and spiritual (Sylvester) virtue, he will transcend the cross of his psychological torment and emerge "the Savior of [his] . . . Empire" (II. i. 397), the "glorious Image of the Deity" (V. ii. 338). This saving recommitment to his better nature restores not only his sanity but also the order and peace of the empire, and Lee makes certain his audience can apply the lesson to contemporary England. While giving Crispus to Fausta ("and both for ever, in my Bosom live" [V. ii. 347]), Constantine prophesies,

> . . . by my example led;
> Such Love and peace, thru' all the World shall spread,
> And Roman Arts that British Isle adorn. (V. ii. 342–44)[7]

CHAPTER 13

Lee's Artistry

I T is difficult to know whether Lee was innovative when we look at his works as part of more general developments in Restoration serious drama. Certainly, *The Rival Queens* (1676/7) anticipated Dryden's *All for Love* (1677) in restoring blank verse as the dominant form for serious drama. Possibly we can also credit Lee with leading the mid-Restoration movement from awe-inspiring characters and happy endings—typical of tragicomedies and heroic plays of the 1660s—to the more vulnerable and pathetic figures, and to the homicidal or suicidal conclusions, which characterized the tragedies of the later 1670s and 1680s. For the most part, however, he shared the predilections of his fellow playwrights. Like them, he tended to write about "the evils arising from disregard of the royal prerogative,"[1] especially in the era of the Popish Plot and Exclusion Crisis (1678–81), and he too adapted his plots from a combination of history and romance. With Thomas Otway and John Banks, he wrote in the tradition that Eric Rothstein has defined as "late heroic,"[2] wherein protagonists become more flawed and the conflicts between their private and public lives irreconcilable. He probably invented no new subgenres. *Nero, Massacre,* and *Borgia* are villain tragedies growing out of the Elizabethan tragedies of blood and following such Restoration examples as Thomas Porter's *The Villain* (1662) and Nevil Payne's *Fatal Jealousy* (1672). *Sophonisba, Gloriana, Theodosius,* and *Constantine* are sentimentalized variations on the high heroic mode, like Dryden's *Aureng-Zebe* (1675) and Elkanah Settle's *Fatal Love* (1680). *The Rival Queens, Mithridates,* and *Lucius Junius Brutus* are high tragedies in the fashion of Dryden's *All for Love* and Otway's *Venice Preserv'd* (1682). *The Princess of Cleve,* finally, is a hybrid that imbues split-plot tragicomedy (e.g., *Marriage A-la Mode,* 1671) with the satiric savagery of Thomas Shadwell's *The Libertine* (1675) or Otway's *Friendship in Fashion* (1678).[3]

Working within such conventional limits, Lee achieved a dramatic style that is distinctive and that enabled him to gain a unique perspective on contemporary life. The central characteristic of this style, a kind of impassioned lyricism, has long been recognized but never adequately described or given its due as a legitimate mode of dramaturgy.[4] For Lee it is a particularly appropriate mode because it provides a natural approach to his favorite subject: the mental pathology of political leadership and its relation to both social and supernatural phenomena.[5] That the usual result of this union of interest and artistic mode is a more intensely emotional drama than Lee's friend Dryden typically produced is probably not owing to any marked difference in the two playwrights' abilities to design plays. The standard distinction between Dryden the disciplined designer and Lee the wild-eyed expressionist is off the mark,[6] for many of Lee's plays were clearly conceived and ably constructed. It would be more accurate to say that Dryden's dramatic designs are more intellectual, Lee's more lyrical.

In *All for Love*, for instance, the characters work *through* passion toward a philosophical apprehension of their tragic situation. Sensing that his infatuation with Cleopatra has cut him off from the natural, external order of the universe, Antony painfully acquires an alternative philosophy to guide his conduct—an inner sanctuary of values with transcendental criteria of fulfillment, instead of those "Roman" virtues favored by historical destiny. Dryden's characters have to philosophize passion; they feel compelled to make intellectual—as well as political, moral, and emotional—order out of their lives. An Antony's or an Aureng-Zebe's greatest sense of achievement comes not from defeating the enemy, winning love, or ascending a throne, but rather from fulfilling a philosophy of conduct and understanding what he does and feels.[7]

By contrast, what so often happens in Lee's plays is that his characters fail to grasp what is really happening to them. Only the audience can grasp it, and the audience is told more through patterns of action, allusion, and imagery than through discourse. Alexander suffers a conflict between passion and duty that is similar to Antony's, but while he sporadically regrets his weaknesses, he never fully understands how they are destroying him by remote control. He dies without the personal hope Antony gains from philosophical conviction, though he can at least foresee how a different psychological makeup might better qualify a monarch for peacetime leadership.

Likewise, Mithridates does penance and cancels the power his misplaced favor has put into the hands of Pharnaces. But unlike the Emperor in *Aureng-Zebe*, he never comprehends the full implications of his unnatural behavior, so that he fails to save his virtuous and loyal son from the destructive forces which—as so often in Lee—have expanded into the power vacuum.

Rational judgment and courageous virtue are weaker qualities in Lee's plays than they are in contemporaneous ones by Dryden. The courage and idealism of a Britannicus, the "civil brav'ry" of a Scipio, the public spirit of a Brutus—these admirable traits do not save their possessors from death, despair, or inhumanity, respectively. It would appear that Lee's so-called lyrical, impassioned mode of drama was not merely the spontaneous effusion of a verbose and excitable writer; it may have been the outward impress of an almost Calvinistic conviction that the bestiality of fallen man is irremediable except through some form of spiritual grace. Out of the immense reservoir of his own powerful emotions Lee draws the obsessions that define his characters' psyches and drive their actions, while on another level he informs their language and the setting with images and allusions that allow the audience to make both social and supernatural sense of their doings.

This dual vision, conveyed through a bipartite dramatic mode, preserves for the audience an ultimately metaphysical perspective on the action, a perspective that belies the Hobbesian assumptions operative in the personalities and behavior of the characters themselves. A kind of persistent dramatic irony is at work in Lee. Through allusions, imagery, and spectacle, he enables his audience to see onstage phenomena as part of a larger pattern of action. Yet the characters are usually so taken up with satisfying their obsessions that they fail to discern the more significant shapes into which their behavior is falling. Lee carefully contrives his prodigies, his characters' predispositions, and their language, so as to provide the audience with means of assessing—of philosophizing about—events which onstage are passionally, not philosophically, determined. Dryden's lead characters work toward some harmonious adjustment between conduct and theory. Lee's pursue the course of conduct fixed by their personalities, and it becomes the audience's responsibility to understand the philosophical implications of what is going on.

Thus, Lee's plays can be called "lyrical" for two reasons. First, their plots are emotionally, not intellectually, motivated. Unlike

Dryden, Lee is finally interested in how social and political patterns develop out of certain configurations of passion. Second, in Lee's plays the figurative content—imagery, spectacle, allusions—expresses the author's, not his character's, personal explication of what is happening.[8]

As his artistry develops, it is the nature of this explication that changes more than anything else. Lee's political philosophy, for example, does not materially change, notwithstanding prevailing opinions that he oscillated between Whig and Tory attitudes after 1678.[9] As Frances Barbour accurately explained it in one of the least biassed of modern commentaries, "on the whole it seems as if Lee liked the sound of lofty expressions of loyalty and the current phrases relative to divine right, but that, confronted with misdemeanors of a ruler, he would hold the ruler accountable, and in extreme cases would counsel measures of deliverance."[10] Such extreme cases he depicts in most of his plays, and the various forms of deliverance he contemplated are to be found in *Theodosius* (an engrafting of proven virtue onto the royal stock: Marcian/Pulcheria, William/Mary), *Lucius Junius Brutus* (imposition of order by a republican strongman), and *Constantine* (fostering of psychospiritual order within the current monarch).

The fact that these three dramas of deliverance were written in the final three years of Lee's active career suggests the pattern of change which his artistry took. While maintaining throughout his works essentially the same definition of effective sovereignty—judicious leadership founded on self-control, humane compassion, a sense of familial and civic duty, martial prowess, and spiritual humility—Lee gradually developed a vision of cosmic order that modulated into confidence in providential design. With the advantage of hindsight, we can perceive two cycles in this progression. In moving from *Nero* to *Mithridates,* we explore increasingly sophisticated rhythms of psychological disintegration, a disintegration encouraged by demonic forces and exfoliating in social chaos and destruction. We also note a shift from the dividing of opposed obsessions between two or more distinct personalities (Nero/Britannicus, Hannibal/Massinissa/Scipio) to the uniting of conflicting obsessions as aspects of a single, tortured mind (Alexander, Mithridates). Finally, we sense Lee's growing conviction that specific cases of disorder and evil operate as aspects of a more general ecology of sociopolitical relations. In *Nero* and *Sophonisba* we study forms of ruin; in *The Rival Queens* and

Mithridates we perceive that such forms belong to the larger dynamics of sociopolitical ecology: that a sovereign's melancholy or madness amounts to an imbalance of psychological forces which creates a correlative imbalance in the social and political interrelations of his family, court, and state.

To turn from these first five plays to the last six is to start a second, thematically and formally more complex, cycle. The early plays deal in pagan subjects and settings, and they focus upon sublunar phenomena, adding only a hint of infernal cooperation in the various patterns of disorder. In the later plays, except *Lucius Junius Brutus*, the religious scaffolding is overtly Christian, and as infernal powers become more clearly defined, the hand of Providence also comes into better focus. Moreover, the last plays are more definitely topical than their predecessors. While the earlier works always seemed to comment on the Restoration court in the most abstract, oblique ways, the later ones allude to such distinct events as the Popish Plot, the Exclusion Crisis, and the Rye House Plot; to such issues as religious enthusiasm, republicanism, and royal succession; and to such individuals as Cromwell, Shaftesbury, and William and Mary.

Thus, as Lee composes these later plays, he stretches significance in two directions: toward a more specific assessment of contemporary life and toward a more completely metaphysical vision of social and psychological phenomena in general. This reaching for a more comprehensive Christian interpretation develops in a pattern similar to the one leading from *Nero* to *Mithridates*. In the first five plays of the later cycle, the conflicting forces are embodied in separate personalities (Queen Mother/Admiral; Brutus/Tiberius). But in *Constantine*, as in *The Rival Queens* and *Mithridates*, the discordant energies function within the emperor's own divided psyche, while the other characters gain identity as correlatives to these mental conflicts. The general movement in the later plays is a Christian equivalent to the growing sense of "classical" order in the early works. More and more, Lee shows that patterns of depravity and madness are episodes in a providential history whose greater contours, humanly incomprehensible, can only be pointed to by prodigies and the vocabulary of devil-possession. While this metaphysical confidence is conveyed to the audience through Lee's increasingly spectacular staging, accompanied by a highly figurative, allusive language, his characters continue to wrestle with essentially the same egocentric lusts that made a demon of Nero and a witch of Poppea.

Nathaniel Lee's Family*

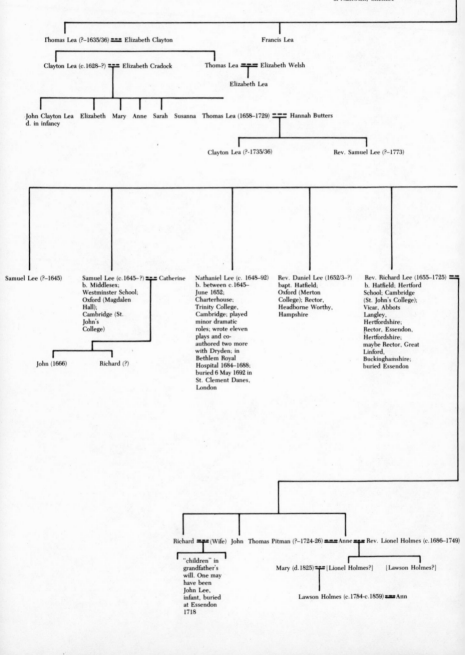

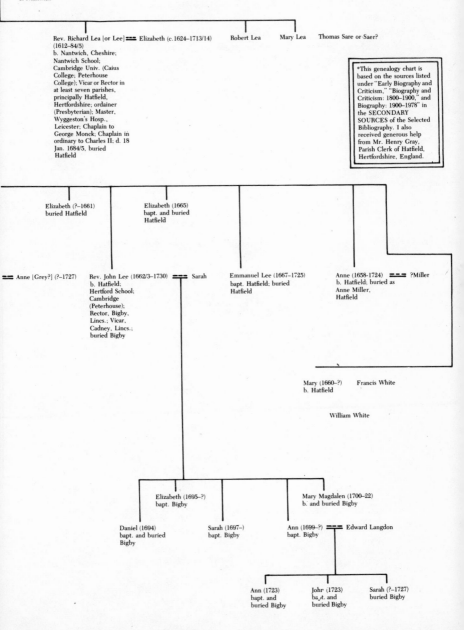

Anne Bickerton (?–c.1647)
daughter of Thomas Bickerton
of Nantwich

Rev. Richard Lea [or Lee] === Elizabeth (c.1624–1713/14)   Robert Lea   Mary Lea   Thomas Sare or Saer?
(1612–84/5)
b. Nantwich, Cheshire;
Nantwich School;
Cambridge Univ. (Caius
College; Peterhouse
College); Vicar or Rector in
at least seven parishes,
principally Hatfield,
Hertfordshire; ordainer
(Presbyterian); Master,
Wyggeston's Hosp.,
Leicester; Chaplain to
George Monck; Chaplain in
ordinary to Charles II; d. 18
Jan. 1684/5, buried
Hatfield

*This genealogy chart is
based on the sources listed
under "Early Biography and
Criticism," "Biography and
Criticism: 1800–1900," and
Biography: 1900–1978" in
the SECONDARY
SOURCES of the Selected
Bibliography. I also
received generous help
from Mr. Henry Gray,
Parish Clerk of Hatfield,
Hertfordshire, England.

Elizabeth (?–1661)   Elizabeth (1665)
buried Hatfield   bapt. and buried
                            Hatfield

=== Anne [Grey?] (?–1727)   Rev. John Lee (1662/3–1730) === Sarah   Emmanuel Lee (1667–1725)   Anne (1658-1724) === ?Miller
                             b. Hatfield;   bapt. Hatfield; buried   b. Hatfield; buried as
                             Hertford School;   Hatfield   Anne Miller,
                             Cambridge   Hatfield
                             (Peterhouse);
                             Rector, Bigby,
                             Lincs.; Vicar,
                             Cadney, Lincs.;
                             buried Bigby

                                                     Mary (1660–?)   Francis White
                                                     b. Hatfield

                                                     William White

                             Elizabeth (1695–?)   Mary Magdalen (1700–22)
                             bapt. Bigby   b. and buried Bigby

              Daniel (1694)   Sarah (1697–)   Ann (1699–?) === Edward Langdon
              bapt. and buried   bapt. Bigby   bapt. Bigby
              Bigby

                         Ann (1723)   John (1723)   Sarah (?–1727)
                         bapt. and   bapt. and   buried Bigby
                         buried Bigby   buried Bigby

Notes and References

Preface

1. *A History of English Drama 1660–1900*, 4th ed. (Cambridge, Eng., 1952), I, 148; hereafter cited as *History*, I.

2. Gerard Langbaine, *An Account of the English Dramatick Poets* (1691), intro. John Loftis (Los Angeles, 1971), II, 321; Samuel Johnson, "Rambler" No. 20, in *The Rambler*, eds. W. J. Bate and Albrecht B. Strauss (New Haven, 1969), III, 112. An obvious exception is Bonamy Dobree, whose unusually negative impression of Lee in *Restoration Tragedy 1660–1720* (Oxford, 1929), pp. 110–31, is countered with enthusiasm by G. Wilson Knight, *The Golden Labyrinth* (London, 1962), pp. 157–67. To sample the full range of critical attitudes, see below, "Early Biography and Criticism," "Biography and Criticism: 1800–1900," and "Criticism and Scholarship: 1900–1978," under *Selected Bibliography*.

3. "Nathaniel Lee's *Sophonisba*," a review in *Englische Studien*, XLVII (1913–14), 96–97.

4. *The Works of Nathaniel Lee*, 2 vols. (1954–55; rpt. Metuchen, N. J., 1968). Hereafter cited as *Works*.

5. The publications about Lee by these and other scholars and critics are listed below, "Criticism and Scholarship: 1900–1978," under *Selected Bibliography*.

6. I continue vainly to search for Lee's literary remains and will happily share my failures with interested scholars. The rewards, on the other hand, of studying performances of Lee's plays are suggested by Philip Parsons, "Restoration Tragedy as Total Theatre," in *Restoration Literature: Critical Approaches*, ed. Harold Love (London, 1972), pp. 59–64. The staging and long-range influence of *The Rival Queens* are surveyed by Nancy Eloise Lewis, *Nathaniel Lee's "The Rival Queens,"* Diss. Ohio State 1957 (Ann Arbor, Michigan, 1975).

7. A task now being undertaken by A. L. McLeod. See his listing of poems in "A Nathaniel Lee Bibliography, 1670–1960," *Restoration and 18th Century Theatre Research*, I, No. 2 (1962), 27–39.

Chapter One

1. Except where otherwise noted, the following narrative of Lee's life judiciously synthesizes information contained in the sources listed below un-

183

der "Early Biography and Criticism" and "Biography: 1900–1978." An up-
dated genealogical chart reflecting my recent research, and that of Mr.
Henry Gray (Parish Clerk of Hatfield), appears in *Appendix*.

2. *Cor Humiliatum & Contritum. A Sermon preached at St. Paul's . . .
Nov. 29, 1663* (London, 1664).

3. *The Recantation of a Penitent Proteus; or, the Changling*, printed together with *The Poring Doctor, or the Gross Mistakes of a Reverend son of
the Church, in bowing to the name of Judas, at St. Paul's, Novemb. 5, 1663*
(London, 1663).

4. *The Manuscripts of Sir William Fitzherbert, Bart., and Others* (London, 1893), Hist. MSS Comm., XIII, appendix VI, 273.

5. See *A Catalogue of the Library of Choice Books . . . Of the Reverend
and Learned Dr. Richard Lee* (1685).

6. For example, it contained the following publications:

a. Relating to Providence and the infernal powers: George Hakewill's *An
Apologie of the Power and Providence of God in the Government of the World*
(1627); Bishop John Wilkins' *A discourse concerning the beauty of Providence*
(1649); Edward Haughton's *The rise, growth and fall of Antichrist* (1652);
John Gaule's *Select cases of conscience, touching witches and witchcraft*
(1646); and something called *Considerations about Witches;*

b. Relating to the history of ancient Rome, the Roman Catholic Church,
and Renaissance France: *"Eusebius his Ecclesiastical History with the Life
of Constantine"* (probably Wye Saltonstall's translation attached in 1636 to
Meredith Hanmer's *Ancient Ecclesiasticall Histories);* Robert Codrington's
1654 translation of *The History of Justine . . . with the Epitomie of the lives
and manners of the Roman Emperors* (of Aurelius Victor); Patrick Symson's
*The Historie of the Church since the dayes of our Saviour Jesus Christ untill
this present age* (1634); *The Glory of their times, or the lives of ye Primitive
Fathers* (by D. Lupton, 1640); and "Epitome of all the Lives of the *French*
Kings" (1639);

c. Relating to seventeenth-century psychology: Bishop Edward Rey-
nolds' *A treatise of the Passions and Faculties of the Soule* (1640); William
Fenner's *A treatise of the affections* (1642); and Meric Casaubon's *A Treatise
concerning Enthusiasme* (1655);

d. Relating to political philosophy: William Sancroft's pseudonymous
Modern Policies, taken from Machiavel, Borgia, and other choise authors
(1652); Matthew Wren's *Monarchy Asserted . . . in vindication of the Considerations upon Mr. Harrington's Oceana* (1660); and William Lucy's *Observations . . . of notorious Errours in Mr. Hobbes his Leviathan and other
his bookes* (1663);

e. Relating to affairs of court and state: William Lloyd's *A Sermon at the
funeral of Sir Edmund-Berry Godfrey* (1678); Robert Parsons' *A Sermon
preached at the funeral of John, Earl of Rochester* (1680); Gilbert Burnet's
Some Passages of the Life and Death of the Right Honourable John Earl of

Rochester (1680); "Collection of State affairs . . . *viz.* Pacquets of Advice to the Men of *Shaftesbury*," "Collection of speeches, Debates . . . about the Popish Plot, . . . Cabal of Jesuits discovered . . . Five Jesuits at *Tiburn*, Vindication of the Earl of *Shaftesbury*, 1682," and *"Alg. Sidney's* Tryal, . . . *Dangerfields'* Narrative, . . . *Titus Oates* of the Exorcismes of the *Papists*, and a Narrative of the Plot against K. *Charles* the 1st."

7. On Lee's Cambridge, see G. M. Trevelyan, *Trinity College* (Cambridge, 1943), pp. 39–50, and James Bass Mullinger, *The University of Cambridge* (1911; rpt. New York and London, 1969), III, 549–665.

8. "On the Death of the Duke of Albemarle," *Works*, II, 551. I shall mention only the poems included in *Works*. McLeod identifies one other in "A Nathaniel Lee Bibliography": "To His Grace The Duke of Ormond" (1685).

9. Told by Dean Lockier to Joseph Spence: see *Observations, Anecdotes, and Characters of Books and Men*, ed. James M. Osborne (Oxford, 1966), I, 280, item 677. See also John Harold Wilson, *A Rake and his Times: George Villiers 2nd Duke of Buckingham* (New York, 1954), pp. 185–88.

10. "An Allusion to Horace, the Tenth Satyr of the First Book," l. 39, in *The Complete Poems of John Wilmot, Earl of Rochester*, ed. David M. Vieth (New Haven and London, 1968), p. 122.

11. *Works*, I, 151.

12. *Works*, I, 219.

13. *Works*, II, 557–58, 11. 47, 50.

14. *The Works of John Dryden*, I: Poems 1649–1680, ed. Edward Niles Hooker and H. T. Swedenberg, Jr. (Berkeley and Los Angeles, 1956), pp. 106–07.

15. See *The Works of John Dryden*, I, 158–62; and II: Poems 1681–1684, ed. H. T. Swedenberg, Jr. and Vinton A. Dearing (Berkeley and Los Angeles, 1972), pp. 185–90, 199–201.

16. "To the Unknown Author of this Excellent Poem," *Works*, II, 559.

17. D'Urfey's epilogue, *Works*, II, 61–63; Wycherley's "To *Nath.* Lee, in *Bethlem*," in *The Complete Works of William Wycherley*, ed. Montague Summers (Soho, 1924), III, 233–37; Duke's prologue, *Works*, II, 323. Lee and Southerne may also have been friends: see the poem on Southerne's death, interleaved in a copy of Langbaine and Gildon's *Lives and Characters of the English Dramatick Poets* (London, 1699), pp. 136–37 (British Library c. 46. d. 16).

18. "To the Prince and Princess of Orange, upon Their Marriage," *Works*, II, 553–56.

19. On this episode of theater history, see the relevant entries in Leslie Hotson, *The Commonwealth and Restoration Stage* (Cambridge, Mass., 1928), pp. 260–61; *The Dictionary of National Biography*, ed. Leslie Stephen and Sidney Lee (London, 1937–38); *The London Stage 1660–1800*, Part I: 1660–1700, eds. Emmett L. Avery and Arthur H. Scouten (Carbondale,

1968), pp. lxii, cxlvii–cxlviii; *The Revels History of Drama in English*, V:1660–1750, ed. John Loftis et al (London, 1976), p. 122; and Robert D. Hume, *The Development of English Drama in the Late Seventeenth Century* (Oxford, 1976), pp. 318–25.

20. Charles Gildon's *The Patriot* (1702) is a bland adaptation.

21. "To the Unknown Authour of this Excellent Poem," *Works*, II, 559, ll. 15–16.

22. *Works,* II, 567, 560–61.

23. *The Life and Times of Anthony Wood*, ed. Andrew Clark (Oxford, 1894), III, 112; Langbaine's *Account*, ed. Loftis, II, 322–23; Wycherley's "To *Nath. Lee*," esp. ll. 32 ff.; Etherege's letter to Dorset, 25 July 1687, in *The Letters of Sir George Etherege*, ed. Frederick Bracher (Berkeley, 1974), p. 135; "Satyr against the Poets," British Library Harleian MS 7317; and see Samuel Derrick (pseud. Thomas Wilkes), *A General View of the Stage* (London, 1759), pp. 297–98, and E. G. O'Donoghue, *The Story of Bethlehem Hospital* (London, 1914), pp. 224–227. Contemporary mental pathology is discussed in Daniel Hack Tuke, *Chapters in the History of the Insane in the British Isles* (London, 1882); Robert R. Reed, Jr., *Bedlam on the Jacobean Stage* (Cambridge, 1952); Lawrence Babb, *Sanity in Bedlam* (E. Lansing, 1959); Michel Foucault, *Madness and Civilization*, trans. Richard Howard (New York, 1965); and Michael V. De Porte, *Nightmares and Hobbyhorses* (San Marino, 1974).

24. Patricia Allderidge, Archivist of The Bethlem Royal Hospital, kindly sent photocopies of relevant pages from the admissions and accounts books, 1684–88, and these are confirmed by parallel entries in the *Calendar of State Papers . . . Domestic* (London, 1960), I, 420 and in the *Liber Literarum* of James II, 4 January 1685 (P.R.O.) and the *Booke of Minutes* of the Board of Greencloth, 23 April 1688 (P.R.O.).

25. "On Their Majesties Coronation," *Works* II, 562–63.

26. *Works*, II, 564. Stroup and Cooke also include two undated songs— "Love's Opportunity Neglected" and "A Song" (*Works*, II, 565–66)—both of which are in the risqué, mock-pastoral mode often used by Rochester, Sedley, and their cohorts.

27. *Letters from the Dead to the Living*, Part II (London, 1703), pp. 130–31.

28. MS notes to Langbaine's *An Account of the English Dramatick Poets* (1691), British Library, c. 28. g.l.

29. Oldys says he heard of the papers a year before his letter, which is dated 23 February 1730/1, in *Report on the Manuscripts of his Grace the Duke of Portland*, VI (London, 1901), 37.

30. The following account of Restoration backgrounds draws from many sources, among which the more generally useful are Basil Willey's *The Seventeenth Century Background* (1934; rpt. New York, 1953); J. Bronowski and Bruce Mazlish, *The Western Intellectual Tradition* (1960; rpt. New York,

1962); H. S. Davies and George Watson, eds., *The English Mind* (Cambridge, Eng., 1964); David Ogg, *England in the Reign of Charles II*, 2d ed., 2 vols. (Oxford, 1955); J. P. Kenyon, *The Stuarts* (1958; rpt. London, 1974); Maurice Ashley, *Charles II* (1971; rpt. St. Albans, 1973); K.M.P. Burton, *Restoration Literature* (London, 1958); James Sutherland, *English Literature of the Late Seventeenth Century* (Oxford, 1969); and John Harold Wilson, *A Preface to Restoration Drama* (Cambridge, Mass., 1965).

31. See J. H. Wilson, *Court Wits of the Restoration* (Princeton, 1948).

32. See "Introduction," *Three Restoration Divines*, ed. Irene Simon (Paris, 1967), pp. i–vi, 1–300.

33. This paragraph slightly modifies and expands David M. Vieth's categories in "Divided Consciousness: The Trauma and Triumph of Restoration Culture," *Tennessee Studies in Literature*, XXII (1977), 46–62.

34. These changes in historical perspective have recently been discussed by Achsah Guibbory, "Dryden's Views of History," *PQ*, LII (1973), 187–204, and J. P. Vander Motten, "The Dramatic Uses of History in the Restoration Period: Some Considerations," *Studia Germanica Gaudensia*, XVIII (1977), 15–29.

35. Robert Burton, *The Anatomy of Melancholy*, cited by S. Blaine Ewing, *Burtonian Melancholy in the Plays of John Ford* (Princeton, 1940), p. 8. For the relation of mental disturbance to cosmic design in Renaissance and Restoration thought, see Reed, Babb, Foucault, and DePorte (above, n. 23).

Chapter Two

1. IV. iii. 22, iv. 63, in *Works*, I, 56, 60; hereafter, references to plays in this edition will be cited parenthetically by act, scene, and line.

2. William Van Lennep thought this digressive episode was a badly integrated piece from some ur ˙ ɪown romance: "The Life and Works of Nathaniel Lee, Dramatist: A Study of Sources," Diss. Harvard 1933, pp. 76–77; hereafter this work will be cited as "Sources."

3. *History*, I, 122; *Works*, I, 22.

4. See Van Lennep, "Sources," pp. 72–90, where he shows how Lee freely alters the easily accessible historians while mostly ignoring earlier tragedies, continental and English, that deal with Nero.

5. James Sutherland's depiction, "a play full of riot, rant, blasphemy, and horror," in *English Literature of the Late Seventeenth Century*, p. 72, is standard.

6. On Prometheus and Phaeton, see relevant entries in *The Oxford Classical Dictionary*, eds. N.G.L. Hammond and H. H. Scullard, 2d ed. (Oxford, 1970); and in *The New Century Classical Handbook*, ed. Catherine B. Avery (New York, 1962).

7. See Rossell Hope Robbins, *The Encyclopedia of Witchcraft and Demonology* (London, 1959), p. 465. Such beliefs, emerging out of Justin Mar-

tyr, Tertullian, Cyprian, and the pseudo-Clementine homilies (see "Devil," *Encyclopaedia Britannica,* 1970 ed., VII, 326), were current but under attack in the Restoration. Lee's wide-ranging knowledge of occult lore could have come from many popular sources: e.g., the *Malleus Maleficarum* (1486), Reginald Scot's *Discoverie of Witchcraft* (1584), James I's *Daemonologie* (1597), accounts of Matthew Hopkins's witch-hunts in the eastern counties (while Dr. Lee was there, 1645–47), John Gaule's and Joseph Glanvill's treatises (some in the Hatfield library; see above, ch. 1, n. 6), and the Cambridge discussions during Lee's undergraduate days (some responding to John Wagstaffe's *Question of Witchcraft Debated,* 1669). In addition to Robbins, see R. H. West's books, *The Invisible World* (Athens, Ga., 1939), pp. 26, 93–94; *Milton and the Angels* (Athens, 1955); and *Shakespeare and the Outer Mystery* (Lexington, Ky., 1968), p. 88; see also Alan MacFarlane, *Witchcraft in Tudor and Stuart England* (London, 1970) and Keith Thomas, *Religion and the Decline of Magic* (1971; rpt. Hammondsworth, Middlesex, 1973).

8. Reginald Scot stresses the historical Nero's interest in the occult: *The Discoverie of Witchcraft,* ed. H. R. Williamson (Arundel, 1964), p. 375. On the sinister implications of "wicker wings," see "Wicker" in the *OED* (1969).

9. See *OED* (1969) under "Dog-star."

10. See "Harpies," *Encyclopaedia Britannica* (1970), II. 123.

11. Cited in Robbins, p. 76. Also, see below, ch. 5, n. 13.

12. Scot, *The Discoverie of Witchcraft,* pp. 342–43. See the discussions of enchanted circles in Cotton Mather's *Magnalia Christi Americana* (1852; rpt. New York, 1967), I, 139; and in C. G. Jung, *Psychology and Alchemy,* trans. R. F. C. Hull, in *The Collected Works of C. G. Jung,* ed. Herbert Read et al., 2d ed. (1953; rpt. New York, 1968), XII, esp. pp. 23, 42, 54, 95–223. See also West, *The Invisible World,* pp. 45–47, 124–30; and K. M. Briggs, *Pale Hecate's Team* (London, 1962), pp. 241, 257–9, 261.

13. *The Golden Labyrinth* (London, 1962), p. 163.

14. Penelope B. R. Doob, *Nebuchadnezzar's Children: Conventions of Madness in Middle English Literature* (New Haven and London, 1974), p. 131.

15. On the changing conceptions of madness, see Reed, Babb, Foucault, and De Porte (above, ch. 1, n. 23).

16. "*Nero* and the Politics of Nathaniel Lee," *PLL,* XIII (1977), 125–35.

17. Anon., "The Fourth Advice to a Painter" (1667), cited by Kastan, p. 127.

18. Kastan, p. 127.

19. Kastan's point, pp. 134–35.

Chapter Three

1. See "An Allusion to Horace, the Tenth Satyr of the First Book," ll. 37–40, in *The Complete Poems of John Wilmot, Earl of Rochester,* ed. Vieth,

p. 122; Henry Fielding, "H. Scriblerus Secundus; His Preface," *The Tragedy of Tragedies; or the Life and Death of Tom Thumb the Great* (London and Dublin, 1731), n. pag.; Adolphus Ward, *A History of English Dramatic Literature to the Death of Queen Anne*, rev. ed. (London, 1899), III, 408–09; Hume, *Development*, p. 313; John Dryden, cited by Stroup and Cooke, *Works*, II, 76; Langbaine, *Account* (1691), ed. Loftis, II, 325–26.

2. *Otway and Lee* (1931; rpt. New York, 1969), p. 66.

3. *History*, I, 723.

4. *Ideas of Greatness: Heroic Drama in England* (New York, 1971), pp. 236–39.

5. For the historical background of this chapter, I rely chiefly on David Ogg, *England in the Reign of Charles II* (Oxford, 1955), esp. chs. I, IV-V, VIII-X, XV-XVII, XIX.

6. Eric Rothstein, *Restoration Tragedy: Form and the Process of Change* (Madison, 1967), pp. 81–85.

7. The best source study is Van Lennep's, pp. 94–120. Waith (pp. 236–39) is more easily accessible but is less thorough.

8. These sources, and other versions of the Sophonisba story, are more fully discussed by Van Lennep.

9. *The Golden Labyrinth*, pp. 159–60.

10. The view of Arthur C. Kirsch, "The Importance of Dryden's *Aureng-Zebe*," *ELH*, XXIX (1962), 160–74.

11. "Introduction," *All for Love*, ed. Vieth (Lincoln, Nebraska, 1972), pp. xxiii-xxv. In reviewing past discoveries of Dryden's literary debts in this play, Vieth, like all other scholars thus far, does not comment on its relation to *Sophonisba*.

12. For imagery relating to the Africans, see I.i.10, 144; II.i. 14–17, ii.106; IV.i.70–75, ii.92,113, iv.150; V.i.5–6, 79, 83, 224–25. Contrasting imagery associated with the Romans appears in II.i.53, 82–86, 99, 172; III.i.28–29, ii.92; IV.i.281–332; V.i.39–41.

13. This chapter is essentially the same as my article, "Hero as Endangered Species: Structure and Idea in Lee's *Sophonisba*," *DUJ*, LXXI (1978), 35–43. I should note that while Thomas R. Edwards (*Imagination and Power* [New York, 1971]) does not discuss Lee, his tracing of "the disappearance of heroic man" in public poems indirectly reinforces my argument.

Chapter Four

1. See the summary of earlier criticism in *Works*, I, 147–48. A typical attitude among more recent critics is Hume's: "basically, the play shows him [Lee] marking time" (*Development*, p. 314). Howard D. Weinbrot has lately called the play a witty melodrama that is "unintentionally comic": *Augustus Caesar in "Augustan" England* (Princeton, 1978), pp. 72–73.

2. See Van Lennep's discussion of sources, pp. 122–34.

3. The name seems taken from Edmund Spenser's *The Faerie Queene* (see *Works*, I, 147).

4. He is stabbed by a group of men, as his father was, but the reasons differ suggestively: what is now seen as worth dying for?

5. Dedicatory epistle, *Works*, I, 151.

Chapter Five

1. And one of his best, according to many prominent critics. See the summary of earlier criticism in *Works*, I, 214–16. The fullest modern assessments appear in Lewis, *Nathaniel Lee's "The Rival Queens"*; Robert Birley, *Sunk Without Trace* (New York, 1962), pp. 40–75; G. Wilson Knight, *The Golden Labyrinth*, pp. 160–63; and P. F. Vernon, "Introduction," *The Rival Queens* (Lincoln, Nebraska, 1970), pp. xxiii–xxvii. Except where otherwise noted, I am indebted to these commentaries only for their enthusiasm.

2. For a closer look at the sources, see Van Lennep, pp. 138–91.

3. In his paper, "Nathaniel Lee's *The Rival Queens* and the Psychology of Assassination," *Restoration: Studies in English Literary Culture, 1600–1700*, II, No. 2 (1978), 10.

4. "Introduction" to *The Rival Queens*, p. xxiv.

5. Antony D. Hammond verges on this point in his unpublished dissertation, "The Development of the Serious Play in the Restoration," Diss. Auckland, 1969, pp. 537–38.

6. See ch. 1, n. 35.

7. On the contractual implications see Vernon's "Introduction," p. xxi.

8. See II. i. 129–31, 162, 221, 420; III. i. 435; IV. i. 283, 353, 358.

9. See Reed, Babb, Foucault, and DePorte (ch. 1, n. 23), as well as Keith Thomas, *Religion and the Decline of Magic* (ch. 2, n. 7), pp. 90–103.

10. See *Paradise Lost*, I. 263.

11. See relevant entries in *The Oxford Classical Dictionary* and *The New Century Classical Handbook*.

12. See above, ch. 2, nn. 7, 8, and 10. "Queen of Devils" seems to refer to Hecate: see K. M. Briggs, *Pale Hecate's Team* (London, 1962), esp. pp. 79 ff.

13. Could Lee have known the folk tale relating how the usually beneficent moon was once dragged into a bog, allowing evil forces free reign until she was released? See Briggs, pp. 228–29. Through the allusions to Diana, this might also have influenced the story of Poppea.

14. Lee may have read the book his father owned, Edward Haughton's *The rise, growth and fall of Antichrist* (1652)—see ch. 1, n. 6. Comprehensive studies of the Antichrist myth are Rev. P. Huchedé, *History of Antichrist*, trans, J.D.B. (1884; rpt. Rockford, Ill., 1976) and Christopher Hill, *Antichrist in Seventeenth-Century England* (London, 1971).

15. Penelope B. R. Doob, *Nebuchadnezzar's Children* (ch. 2, n. 14), p. 151.

16. On Hercules, see relevant entries in *The Oxford Classical Dictionary* and *The New Century Classical Handbook*. Eugene M. Waith does not discuss Lee in *The Herculean Hero* (New York, 1962).

17. Noted in Vieth, "Nathaniel Lee's *The Rival Queens* and The Psychology of Assassination," pp. 10, 12.

Chapter Six

1. "this last Birth . . . is much the Fairest Child," Dedication of *Mithridates* ("To . . . Dorset"), *Works*, I, 291.

2. See the summary of criticism in *Works*, I, 288–89, which reflects wildly differing responses to the play—from Elwin's "tremendous tragic power" to Ward's "a mere story." More recent critics dismiss it in a word or two and are cautious in their assessments. Robert Hume's "has much to recommend it, but is somewhat spoiled by . . . emotional exaggeration" is typical: *Development*, p. 323. See Eric Rothstein, *Restoration Tragedy*, p. 54, and G. Wilson Knight, *The Golden Labyrinth*, p. 163.

3. *Works*, I, 291.

4. See G. Wilson Knight, *The Golden Labyrinth*, p. 163.

5. All his later plays, except *Lucius Junius Brutus* (1680), deal with nominally Christian characters.

6. For guidance in dealing with sources, I rely heavily on Van Lennep, "Sources," pp. 193–220; and on Harold F. Brooks, "Dryden's *Aureng-Zebe*: Debts to Corneille and Racine," *Revue de Littérature Comparée*, XLVI (1972), 5–34.

7. To Appian, Lee may owe the notion that Mithridates murdered three sons, many concubines, and hoards of Romans—including the one down whose throat he poured molten gold (see Van Lennep, pp. 197–99). References to the king's learning perhaps derive from Pliny (Van Lennep, p. 195). Both his cruelty and his knowledge were seventeenth-century legends, as indicated, for instance, in "Hounslow Heath," 11. 16–25, 78–84, *Poems on Affairs of State*, ed. Galbraith M. Crump (New Haven and London, 1968), IV, 171–73.

8. *Works*, I, 292.

9. Dryden seems to have had this trait in mind when, in his Epilogue, he wrote, "Love is no more a violent desire; / 'Tis a meer Metaphor, a painted Fire" (*Works*, I, 364).

Chapter Seven

1. "Sources," p. 323; and see his speculations regarding less likely sources, pp. 265–66, 271–328.

2. Davila's seventeenth-century translators were Charles Cotterell and

William Aylesbury. Bacon's *Essayes or Counsels* (1597) went through more than a dozen editions between 1600–80. Burnet's *Relation* is most easily found in Vol. I of his three-volume *A Collection of Several Tracts and Discourses Written in the Years 1677, to 1704* (London, 1704). For a list of the French pamphlets Lee may have seen, consult Van Lennep, pp. 307–08, 317.

3. Robert D. Hume, *Development*, p. 401, and see pp. 201 and 223; Van Lennep, p. 323; *Works*, II, 5; John Loftis, *The Politics of Drama in Augustan England* (Oxford, 1963), p. 23.

4. "The Satiric Design of Nat. Lee's *The Princess of Cleve*," *JEGP*, LXXV (1976), 120–22.

5. Burnet, *Relation*, p. 9.

6. For detailed comparisons of Davila and Lee, see Van Lennep, pp. 271–318.

7. Roswell Gray Ham, *Otway and Lee*, p. 167.

8. See Van Lennep, p. 309. Like Lee, John Oldham also connected Caesar Borgia with the period of French history involving the St. Bartholomew's Day Massacre. See Satires I (11. 55–61, 203–17) and III (11. 579–95, 657–61) of "Satires upon the Jesuits" in *Poems on Affairs of State*, ed. Elias F. Mengel, Jr. (New Haven and London, 1965), II, 22–29, 63–66. Oldham's allusions to the assassins of the French Kings Henry III and IV parallels Lee's similar allusion in *Borgia* (V. iii. 341–44).

9. See ch. 1, n. 19.

10. See ch. 11, n. 25.

11. Hume, "Satiric Design," p. 122.

12. Maurice Ashley, *Charles II*, p. 268 (ch. 1, n. 30). For the historical background of this chapter, I rely on Ashley and on David Ogg, *England in the Reign of Charles II*.

13. I therefore question Hume's assertion (*Development*, p. 223) that *Massacre* "has no 'parallel' significance."

14. Lines 35–37, *Works*, II, 62.

15. Dedication (to the Earl of Dorset) of *The Princess of Cleve*, *Works*, II, 153.

16. For the imagery interpreting the queen mother's circle, see I. i. 16–17, 22, ii. 54–55, 79, 145, 157–61; II. i. 103, 220–26, 257–68; III. i. 32, 65–67, ii. 11–12, 56–68; IV. i. 24, 61–63, 71–73, ii. 2–3, 19–20, 165; V. i. 104, 167, 213, ii. 5. For imagery representing the admiral, see I. i. 123, ii. 138; III. iii. 45; V. i. 137, ii. 26–27, iii. 29.

17. See *The Oxford Classical Dictionary*.

18. *The Essayes or Counsels, Civill and Morall* (London, 1625), p. 17. The other passages taken from Bacon are I. i. 89–92 (from "of Love") and IV. ii. 111, 130–36 ("Of the true Greatnesse of Kingdomes and Estates").

19. Ashley, *Charles II*, p. 323.

Chapter Eight

1. Earlier criticism is summarized in *Works*, II, 67–70. See Van Lennep, "Sources." In the latest remarks on *Caesar Borgia* Robert Hume calls Borgia and Machiavel "real and interesting" and notes the "gore and horror": *Development*, pp. 201, 348.

2. See Van Lennep, pp. 330–78.

3. "A Relation . . .," in *Nicholas Machiavel's Prince*, trans. Edmund Dacres (London, 1640), p. 293.

4. Robert Ornstein, *The Moral Vision of Jacobean Tragedy* (Madison, 1960), pp. 25–26. And see Edward Meyer, *Machiavelli and the Elizabethan Drama* (1897; rpt. New York, n.d.); Mario Praz, "The Politic Brain: Machiavelli and the Elizabethans," in *The Flaming Heart* (Garden City, N.Y., 1958), pp. 90–145; and Felix Rabb, *The English Face of Machiavelli: A Changing Interpretation, 1500–1700* (London, 1964). The serious stage villains of Kyd, Marlowe, Chapman and others were influenced by Innocent Gentillet's biassed image in the widely read *Contre Nicholas Machiavelli* (1576, trans. Simon Patricke, 1602). Comic Machiavellians also appeared, like Sir Politicke Would-be in *Volpone*, and at least five plays, the second and third no longer extant, present Machiavelli under his own name, as in Lee: the "Prologue" to Marlowe's *The Jew of Malta* (c. 1588), a play called *Machiavel* (1591), Robert Daborne's *Machiavel and The Devil* (1613), Thomas Rawlins's *The Rebellion* (1640), and Aston Cokaine's *Trappolin suppos'd a Prince* (1658).

5. We may speculate on other borrowings as well. In Barnabe Barnes's *The Divel's Charter* (1607) Pope Alexander VI is a Machiavellian who makes a Faustian pact with the Devil, and Borgia has Gandia killed but then murders the assassin in turn by pitching him (not Gandia's corpse, as in Lee) into the Tiber. In *Alphonsus, Emperor of Germany* (c. 1636) the Machiavellian Lorenzo poisons himself with his own poison and the Borgia-like Spaniard, Alphonsus, attempts to poison enemies at a banquet that repeats "Pope Alexander VI's famous feast, with the difference that Alphonsus only pretends to be poisoned himself" (Praz, pp. 121, 127, 143; Meyer, pp. 47, 111, 113, 159; Van Lennep, p. 354). And in *The Jew of Malta* Barabas prepares a poison for Abigail which he hopes will "work like Borgia's wine, / Whereof his sire, the Pope, was poisoned" (III. iv. 94–95, in *The Complete Plays of Christopher Marlowe*, ed. Irving Ribner, New York, 1963).

6. "The 'Just Decrees of Heav'n' and Congreve's *Mourning Bride*," in *Congreve Reconsidered*, ed. H. T. Swedenberg (Los Angeles, 1971), p. 5; and see Williams's similar comments in other articles: *ELH*, XXXV (1968), 540–65; *Tennessee Studies in Literature*, XVII (1972), 1–18; *PQ*, LIII (1974), 676–80; and *Studies in the Literary Imagination*, X (1977), 57–76. The most likely general sources for Lee's interest in Providence were Hakewil's *Apol-*

ogie (1627) and Wilkins's *discourse* (1649), both in his father's library (see ch. 1, n. 6).

7. See Thomas Flanagan, "The Concept of *Fortuna* in Machiavelli," in *The Political Calculus: Essays on Machiavelli's Philosophy*, ed. Anthony Parel (Toronto, 1972), pp. 127–56; Rudolf B. Gottfried, *Geoffrey Fenton's Historie of Guicciardini* (Bloomington, n.d.), pp. 34–42; and Jacob Viner, *The Role of Providence in the Social Order* (Philadelphia, 1972), pp. 4–11.

8. This paragraph synthesizes information drawn from Willard Hallam Bonner, *Captain William Dampier, Buccaneer-Author* (Stanford, Calif., 1934), esp. pp. 50–53; Robert R. Cawley, *The Voyagers and Elizabethan Drama* (Boston, 1938) and *Milton and the Literature of Travel* (Princeton, 1951); Irving A. Leonard, *Books of the Brave* (1949; rpt. New York, 1964); Boies Penrose, *Travel and Discovery in the Renaissance* (Cambridge, Mass., 1952); Howard Mumford Jones, *O Strange New World* (New York, 1965), chs. 1 and 2; Harry Levin, *The Myth of the Golden Age in the Renaissance* (New York, 1969), esp. pp. 59–62; J. H. Elliott, *The Old World and the New* (Cambridge, Eng., 1970); and Percy G. Adams, "The Discovery of America and European Renaissance Literature," *Comparative Literature Studies*, XIII (1976), 100–15.

9. See *The History of Italy*, readably translated by Sidney Alexander (New York, 1969), pp. 9–10, 108–09, 179–82.

10. Before Lee's use, many seventeenth-century literary works used the New World as metaphor for the misuse of human beings and earthly goods: e.g., John Phillips's translation of Las Casas, *The Tears of the Indians* (1656); Davenant's *The Cruelty of the Spaniards in Peru* (1658); and Dryden's *Indian Emperor* (1665). See Cawley, *Voyagers*, pp. 282, 295, 297, 299, 302, 328; Howard Mumford Jones, pp. 46–48; and John Loftis, commentary to *The Indian Emperor*, in *The Works of John Dryden*, ed. Loftis and V. A. Dearing (Berkeley and Los Angeles, 1966), IX, 309–16.

11. See Cawley, *Voyagers*, pp. 290–91, 344–46; Jones, pp. 16–20, 33–36; and Harry Levin, pp. 59–62.

12. *Samuel Butler (1612–1680): Characters*, ed. Charles W. Daves (Cleveland and London, 1970), p. 29. For guiding me to this passage I am grateful to Professor James Gill of the University of Tennessee.

13. Quoted by Cawley, *Voyagers*, p. 338.

14. "Elegie: Going to Bed," ll. 27–28, in *The Metaphysical Poets*, ed. Helen Gardner (Baltimore, 1964), p. 54.

15. *The Life and Death of King John*, IV, ii. 104–05, in *The Complete Plays and Poems of William Shakespeare*, ed. William A. Neilson and Charles J. Hill (Cambridge, Mass., 1942), p. 587.

16. Marlowe in Ribner, ed., p. 179, ll. 20–21.

17. Ibid., pp. 178–79, ll. 1–4.

18. See H. C. Davila, *The Historie of the Civill Warres of France*, trans. William Aylesbury and Charles Cotterell (London, 1647), pp. 817–19; and

Richard S. Dunn, *The Age of Religious Wars* (New York, 1970), pp. 23–31, 132–33.

19. See my extended analysis of suggested specific parallels, in "Lee, Renaissance Conventions, and the Psychology of Providence: the Design of *Caesar Borgia*," *Essays in Literature*, IV (1977), 171; Van Lennep. p. 374; and K. H. D. Haley, *The First Earl of Shaftesbury* (Oxford, 1968), pp. 137, 211–14, 414–16, 440.

20. See Praz, *The Flaming Heart*, pp. 131–40, esp. his reading of Donne's *Ignatius his Conclave* (1611).

Chapter Nine

1. For example, Ham, *Otway and Lee*, pp. 106, 130; Stroup and Cooke, *Works*, I, 14; and Vernon, "Introduction" to *The Rival Queens*, p. xix.

2. See *The Plays of Philip Massinger*, ed. W. Gifford, 2nd ed. (1813; rpt New York, 1966), III, 239–352; *Pharamound; or, The History of France*, trans. J Phillips (London, 1677); and *Moot Plays of Corneille*, trans. Lacy Lockert (Nashville, 1959), pp. 373–428.

Lee's historical knowledge could have come from several sources. Not only were Latin and Greek versions of Theophanes, Eusebius, Socrates, and Evagrius available in many seventeenth-century editions before 1680, but there were also English translations and compilations: the Eusebius in Dr. Lee's library (ch. 1, n. 6), part of Meredith Hanmer's *The Auncient Ecclesiasticall Histories of the first six hundred yeares after Christ . . . by Eusebius, Socrates, and Evagrius* (editions in 1577, 1585, 1607, 1619, 1636, and 1650); W. Caton's *An Abridgement . . . of the . . . Chronologies . . . contained in that famous Ecclesiasticall History of Eusebius* (1661); Pedro Mexia's *The Imperiall Historie: or The Lives of the Emperours*, trans. W. T., rev. Edward Grimeston (1623); and Richard Brathwait's *The Lives of all the Roman Emperors . . . from Julius Caesar, unto the now reigning Ferdinand the second* (1638). Also extant was Louis Cousins's French *Histoire de Constantinople* (1672–74), a trans. from several sources.

3. *Byzantine Empresses*, trans. Harold Bell and Theresa de Kerpely (New York, 1963). For another well annotated, readable account of the reign of Theodosius II, see J. B. Bury, *History of the Later Roman Empire* (1889; rpt. New York, 1958), esp. I, 212–39; II, 1–5.

4. Van Lennep cites these sources but does not closely analyze Lee's modifications (pp. 406–51).

5. See the *OED* (1969) annotation on "morning star," which cites Milton's use of both symbolic senses; and on the Astraea myth, see Harry Levin's *The Myth of the Golden Age in the Renaissance*, esp. pp. 70, 93, 99–100, 112, 143.

6. Pastoralism is stronger in this play than in any of Lee's others. Perhaps he derived the dual, pagan-Christian heritage of pastoral, and its symbolic

potential, from Spenser and Tasso, whom he mentions in the "Prologue" (*Works*, II, 239). All the main characters in *Theodosius* indulge in pastoral fantasizing as a means of escape from tribulations. Their pastoral visions are idyllic or nightmarish, regenerative or penitential, depending on the particular character's cultural background and frame of mind (Varanes: I. i. 116–23; II. i. 383–94; III. ii. 387–90; V. ii. 1–20; Marcian: II. i. 248–53; Pulcheria: III. ii. 87–95; Athenais: III. ii. 56–58; V. i. 69–75, 103–11; and Theodosius: I. i. 170–206). The songs between acts (and the the beginning of V) are pastoral or mock-pastoral comments on the plot: one is composed by Athenais to lament her misfortunes (V. i. 31–57); two descant upon the motif that Arcadia offers no sure refuge from suffering (after I and after II); and one extends the dreams of Varanes (after III). On kinds of pastoralism and on its relation to love melancholy and religious enthusiasm, see Levin, pp. 27–28, 81–82, 128–30; Patrick Cullen, *Spenser, Marvell, and Renaissance Pastoral* (Cambridge, Mass., 1970), pp. 3, 13, 22–23, 152, 185 ff.; B. G. Lyons, *Voices of Melancholy* (1971; rpt. New York, 1975), pp. 4–6, 88, 103; and De Porte, *Nightmares*, pp. 33, 38–39. Lee's use of pastoral motifs is more thoroughly examined in my essay, "Lee's Artistry: *Theodosius* as Tragi-Comedy of Contexts," *Restoration and 18th Century Theatre Research*, forthcoming.

7. See *The Book of Saints*, ed. The Benedictine Monks of St. Augustine's Abbey, Ramsgate, rev. ed. (New York, 1966); and John J. Delaney and James E. Tobin, *Dictionary of Catholic Biography* (New York, 1961). Both Pulcheria and Eudosia were later sainted for their pious good works, while Marcian and Theodosius are still mentioned with reverence by Catholic biographers.

8. *Works*, II, 237–38.

9. Quoted by Arthur Bryant in *King Charles II*, rev. ed. (London, 1964), p. 133. On Frances Stuart, see Cyril Hughes Hartman, *La Belle Stuart* (London, 1924), esp. pp. 221–25.

10. My main sources for the following historical information are Maurice Ashley, *Charles II*, pp. 227–69; and Gerald M. and Lois Straka, *A Certainty in the Succession* (New York, 1973), pp. 75–81. On Lee's politicized audience, see Ham, *Otway and Lee*, 118–30.

Chapter Ten

1. For example, Ham accepts Gildon's belief that the play is "Antimonarchical," written as "a Compliment" to the Whigs: *Otway and Lee*, pp. 129–30; John Loftis speaks of the play's "vehement Whiggism" and "constitutionalism" in his "Introduction" to *Lucius Junius Brutus* (Lincoln, Nebraska, 1967), pp. xiii-xiv, xviii. See also Hume, "Satiric Design," p. 121, and *Development*, p. 344.

2. *Development*, p. 344.

3. The most thorough tracing of sources has been done by Van Lennep, pp. 454–522.

4. While I disagree with his reading of the play's structure and meaning, I am indebted to Antony Hammond's very instructive emphasis on Brutus' imperfections and on the tragic position of Titus and Teraminta. See Hammond's "The Development of the Serious Play in the Restoration (1660–1690)," Diss. Auckland 1969, pp. 596–614.

5. Hume mentions Lee's "political turnabout" ("Satiric Design," p. 121), and Loftis speaks of Lee's "conversion to the Tory position in 1682" ("Introduction" to his edition of *Brutus*, p. xviii); but David Vieth points out (without developing the observation) that Whig propaganda in the play has "self-cancelling aspects" and so should not be overemphasized: "Psychological Myth as Tragedy: Nathaniel Lee's *Lucius Junius Brutus, HLQ*, XXXIX (1975), 58–60, 63.

6. See Cleanth Brooks, "Marvell's 'Horatian Ode'"; Douglas Bush, "Marvell's 'Horatian Ode'"; and Cleanth Brooks, "A Note on the Limits of 'History' and the Limits of 'Criticism'": all in *Seventeenth-Century English Poetry: Modern Essays in Criticism*, ed. William R. Keast (New York, 1962), pp. 321–58. David Vieth has discussed the providential aspects of this poem and Dryden's *Heroique Stanzas* in "Divided Consciousness: The Trauma and Triumph of Restoration Culture," *Tennessee Studies in Literature*, XXII (1977), 48–9.

7. *The Poems and Letters of Andrew Marvell*, ed. H. M. Margoliouth, 2nd ed., 2 vols. (Oxford, 1952), I, ii. 1.26.

8. These vulnerable protagonists are discussed in Frances Barbour's "The Unconventional Heroic Plays of Nathaniel Lee," *University of Texas Studies in English*, XX (1940), 109–16.

9. For guidance to these and other aspects of the Antichrist myth, see ch. 5, n. 14.

10. This chapter essentially repeats my article, "The Tragicomic Design of *Lucius Junius Brutus*: Madness as Providential Therapy," *PLL*, XV (1979), 38–51.

Chapter Eleven

1. I accept Robert D. Hume's conclusions about the play's date: "Satiric Design," pp. 118–23.

2. See *Works*, II, 149–50, and Hume, "Satiric Design," pp. 117–18.

3. *Works*, II, 153, 149.

4. *Works*, II, 227, 153. Part of this variety is borrowed from *The Massacre of Paris:* IV. iii. 163–68 (*Massacre*, V. ii. 58–64) and V. i. 46–47 (*Massacre*, II. i. 11–12). Possibly an entire scene was also borrowed, then cut out after V. iii. 275.

5. See *Works*, II, 150; Sutherland, *English Literature of the Late Seventeenth Century*, pp. 143–44; and Hume, "Satiric Design."

6. *Works*, II, 153.

7. IV. i., in the text edited by Dennis Davison as part of *Restoration Comedies* (London, Oxford, and New York, 1970), pp. 108–15.

8. *The Princess of Cleves . . . by the greatest Wits in France*, trans. "a person of Quality" (London, 1679).

9. Lee omits le Duc de Guise, la Duchesse de Valentinois, Lignerolle, and several framing historical events. See H. K. Kaps, *Moral Perspective in La Princesse de Clèves* (Eugene, Oregon, 1968), pp. 3–38; and Janet Raitt, *Madame de Lafayette and 'La Princesse de Clèves'* (London and Toronto, 1971), pp. 157–58.

10. "Satiric Design," pp. 132–33.

11. *Works*, II, 153.

12. See Michael Alssid, *Thomas Shadwell* (New York, 1967), pp. 107–09.

13. *English Literature of the Late Seventeenth Century*, p. 144.

14. V. iv. 75–80, 112–13, 176–80, in the version ed. Marjorie Hope Nicolson and D. S. Rodes (Lincoln, Nebraska, 1966), pp. 124 ff.

15. "Satiric Design," pp. 136–37.

16. Lee's historical knowledge could have come from the "Epitome" in his father's library (ch. 1, n. 6), from Davila (above, ch. 8, n. 18), from Mezeray's *Histoire de France* (Paris, 1643–51), or from J. de Serres and P. Matthieu, *General Inventorie of the Historie of France*, trans. Edward Grimestone (London, 1607, with many later editions). Useful modern histories include Henry M. Baird's two-volume *History of the Rise of the Huguenots* (1879) and its two-volume sequel, *The Huguenots and Henry of Navarre* (1903), both rpt. New York, 1970; Jean Hérities, *Catherine de Medici*, trans. Charlotte Haldane (New York, 1963); and J. W. Thompson, *The Wars of Religion in France, 1559–1576* (1909; rpt. New York, 1957).

17. See I. i. 3; II. i. 40–41, iii. 20, 215; III. i. 148–50, 167 ff., 246; IV. i. 97–98, 236, ii. 27, 29, 96; V. i. 12, 57, 61, 72, 74–75.

18. For extensions of this garden imagery, see II. ii. 118–19, 134–39, 186–88.

19. On Lee's knowledge of demonology, see ch. 2, n. 7.

20. Rochester's monkey?

21. See ch. 2, n. 7.

22. A source for Dryden's *Secular Masque?*

23. *Works*, II, 153.

24. See ch. 1, n. 19. Charles succeeded his father as manager of the King's Company and as Master of Revels in 1676/7. On the date of composition, see Hume, "Satiric Design," p. 122.

25. For information about these men, see John Harold Wilson's three books: *The Rochester-Savile Letters, 1671–1680* (Columbus, 1941), *The Court Wits of the Restoration* (Princeton, 1948), and *A Rake and his Times:*

George Villiers, 2nd Duke of Buckingham (New York, 1954). See also V. de Sola Pinto, *Sir Charles Sedley 1638–1701* (London, 1927) and Brice Harris, *Charles Sackville, Sixth Earl of Dorset* (Urbana, 1940).

26. *The Playhouse of Pepys* (1935; rpt. New York, 1964), p. 301.

27. David M. Vieth, ed., *The Complete Poems of John Wilmot, Earl of Rochester,* pp. xxix-xxx.

28. Noticed by Hume, "Satiric Design," pp. 129–30.

29. See I. ii. 23–26; III. i. 125–33; IV. i. 203–17 (compare to Vieth's *Poems,* pp. 52–53, 104–12, 116–17) and Hume, "Satiric Design," pp. 129–30, 135–37.

30. *OED* (1969) and Vieth, *Poems.* p. xx.

31. Wilson, *Rake,* pp. 34–35.

32. Ibid., pp. 11, 14, 15, 27, 70–92, 103–05, 125, 137.

33. Ibid., p. 119.

34. Ibid., pp. 33–34.

35. Ibid., pp. 34 ff.

36. Ibid., pp. 112–15.

37. Ibid., pp. 244, 251–54.

38. See above, ch. 1, n. 9.

39. Harris, *Dorset,* pp. 84–85; Pinto, *Sedley,* p. 72; and Wilson, *Rake,* pp. 37–38, 52–53.

40. See Wilson, *Rake;* Vieth's "Introduction" to *Poems;* Harris, *Dorset;* Pinto, *Sedley;* Wilson, *Rochester-Savile;* and Wilson, *Wits,* esp. pp. 47–66.

41. *The Works of John Dryden,* II, 23, 1. 598.

42. I. ii. 78–125, cited by Earl Miner, *The Restoration Mode from Milton to Dryden* (Princeton, 1974), p. 370.

43. On Stanhope and Hewitt, see Pinto, *Sedley,* p. 145, and Harris, *Dorset,* p. 25.

44. This information is synthesized from the books listed above, n. 25. For an overview, see the chronologies in Wilson, *Wits,* pp. 206–17.

45. See Wilson, *Wits,* pp. 198–205.

46. "Prologue and Epilogue to *The Princess of Cleves,*" in *The Works of John Dryden,* II, 188–89: "Prologue," 11. 7, 9–10; "Epilogue," 11. 13, 27.

47. Richard S. Dunn, *The Age of Religious Wars, 1559–1689* (New York, 1970), esp. pp. 20–31.

Chapter Twelve

1. "Sources," pp. 622–25; *Works,* II, 479–80.

2. Van Lennep, "Sources," p. 622.

3. The accessible historical sources which Lee would have found helpful were the narratives of Socrates Scholasticus (trans. Meredith Hanmer) and of Eusebius (trans. Wye Saltonstall and in Dr. Lee's library) in Hanmer's *Auncient Ecclesiasticall Histories* (above, ch. 9, n. 2); the history by Zosimus

in Louis Cousin's French *Histoire Romaine* (Paris, 1678) or in the 1678 Oxford edition in Latin and Greek; the "Epitome" of Aurelius Victor in *The History of Justine . . . out of Trogus Pompeius . . . Together with the Epitome of the lives and manners of the Roman Emperors,* trans. Robert Codrington (London, 1654; this edition in Dr. Lee's library, later ones appearing in 1664, 1671, 1682); and the anonymous *A True History of the lives of the Popes of Rome* (London, 1679). I depend on these and on the following modern sources for the historical information woven into the next several paragraphs: H. M. D. Parker, *A History of the Roman World from A.D. 138 to 337* (New York, 1939); Moses Hadas, *A History of Rome from its Origins to A.D. 529, as told by the Roman historians* (London, 1958); Joseph Vogt, *The Decline of Rome,* trans. Janet Sondheimer (1965; trans. 1967; rpt. New York, 1967); the annotated *Zosimus: Historie Nova: The Decline of Rome,* trans. and ed. James J. Buchanan and Harold T. Davis (San Antonio, Texas, 1967); and John Holland Smith, *Constantine the Great* (New York, 1971). A partial account of the play's historical background is sketched out by Van Lennep, "Sources," p. 621 and in *Works,* II, 607–10.

4. Arthur L. Cooke and Thomas B. Stroup, "The Political Implications in Lee's *Constantine the Great,*" *JEGP,* XLIX (1950), 506–15.

5. A letter of Athenasius, cited by Smith, *Constantine,* p. 259.

6. *Works,* II, 546, and see *The Works of John Dryden,* II, 199–200, 403–06, 463–64. The prologue, a conventional lament for the indigence and ill fortune of poets, is variously attributed to Otway or Lee, most modern scholars favoring the latter; see Ham, pp. 208–09; Van Lennep, "Sources," pp. 630–31; *Works,* II, 506; and Hammond's Diss., p. 633.

7. Stroup and Cooke summarize the few extant critical remarks about this play, none of which is enlightening: *Works,* II, 480–81.

Chapter Thirteen

1. John Loftis, *The Politics of Drama in Augustan England,* p. 155.

2. *Restoration Tragedy,* pp. 77–110.

3. These subgenre labels are adapted from John Harold Wilson, *A Preface to Restoration Drama,* pp. 52–118, and Robert D. Hume, *Development,* pp. 192–224, 269–363.

4. See, for example, Nicoll, *History,* I, 148; Waith, *Ideas,* pp. 241–42; and Hume, *Development,* p. 323.

5. I agree here with G. Wilson Knight, *The Golden Labyrinth,* p. 164.

6. For the usual comparison, see Nicoll, *History,* I, 148; Waith, *Ideas,* pp. 241–42; Sutherland, *English Literature of the Late Seventeenth Century,* p. 78; Wilson, *Preface,* p. 89; and Hume, *Development,* pp. 197–98, 323.

7. The best discussions of Dryden's earlier dramatic style remain Eugene M. Waith's *The Herculean Hero* (New York, 1962), pp. 152–201; Arthur C. Kirsch's *Dryden's Heroic Drama* (Princeton, 1965); Bruce King's *Dryden's*

Major Plays (Edinburgh, 1966); and Anne T. Barbeau's *The Intellectual Design of John Dryden's Heroic Plays* (New Haven, 1970).

8. Rothstein, *Restoration Tragedy*, p. 93, senses this aspect of Lee's artistry as it appears in his language: his visual imagery "clings to the connotative world within the minds of the audience rather than to the created world of the drama."

9. See Hume, "Satiric Design," p. 211; and Loftis, ed., *Brutus*, p. xviii.

10. "The Unconventional Heroic Plays of Nathaniel Lee," *University of Texas Studies in English*, XX (1940), p. 114.

Selected Bibliography

This list excludes sources only tangentially related to Nathaniel Lee's life and works: e.g., primary sources concerning his father's life, less accessible or less useful literary histories, and contextual studies.

PRIMARY SOURCES

I include only modern editions and reprints. Individual plays are listed in the order in which they originally appeared on stage and in print.

The Works of Nathaniel Lee. Ed. Thomas B. Stroup and Arthur L. Cooke. 2 vols. 1954–55; rpt. Metuchen, N.J.: Scarecrow Reprint Corp., 1968.

The Tragedy of Nero, Emperour of Rome. Ed. Richard Horstmann. Heidelberg: Carl Winters, 1914.

Sophonisba, or Hannibal's Overthrow. Ed. F. Holthausen. Kiel: Lipsius and Tischer, 1913.

Sophonisba, or Hannibal's Overthrow. A Tragedy. Pp. 247–316 in *Five Heroic Plays.* Ed. Bonamy Dobrée. London: Oxford Univ. Press, 1960.

The Rival Queens; or, The Death of Alexander the Great. Pp. 130–166 in *Plays of the Restoration and Eighteenth Century.* Ed. Dougald MacMillan and H. M. Jones. 1931; rpt. New York: Holt, Rinehart and Winston, 1962.

The Rival Queens. Ed. P. F. Vernon. Regents Restoration Drama Series. Lincoln: Univ. of Nebraska Press, 1970.

The Rival Queens (1677). Facsimile. Menston, Yorkshire, England: Scolar, 1971.

Lucius Junius Brutus, Father of his Country. A Tragedy. Ed. Byrne R. S. Fone. Bell's British Theatre. 1793–1796; rpt. New York: AMS, 1977. Vol. XI.

Lucius Junius Brutus. Ed. John Loftis. Regents Restoration Drama Series. Lincoln: Univ. of Nebraska Press, 1967.

Lucius Junius Brutus; Father of his Country. A Tragedy. Pp. 99–180 in *Restoration Tragedies.* Ed. James Sutherland. London, Oxford, New York: Oxford Univ. Press, 1977.

Constantine the Great. Ed. Walter Hafele. Heidelberg: Carl Winters, 1933.

SECONDARY SOURCES

1. Modern Bibliographies

LINK, FREDERICK M. *English Drama, 1660–1800: A Guide to Information Sources.* Detroit: Gale Research, 1976, pp. 232–33. A good selected listing.
McLEOD, A. L. "A Nathaniel Lee Bibliography, 1670–1960." *RECTR,* I, No. 2 (1962), 27–29. Collected works, individual plays, poems, and secondary sources.
STRATMAN, CARL J. et al, eds. *Restoration and Eighteenth Century Theatre Research: A Bibliographical Guide, 1900–1968.* Carbondale and Edwardsville: Southern Illinois Univ. Press, 1971, pp. 441–47. Marred by errors but useful.

2. Early Biography and Criticism

ADDISON, JOSEPH and RICHARD STEELE. *The Spectator.* Ed. Donald F. Bond. Oxford: Clarendon, 1965. Vols. I, 128, 166–72, 392, 405; II, 10; III, 11, 358; IV, 40. Depicts Lee as a flawed genius and favorite of the ladies.
Administrative Bonds for Lionel and Lawson Holmes. Lincolnshire Archives. Lincoln. Give clues as to the fate of Lee's literary remains.
AMES, RICHARD. "A Search after Wit; Or, a Visitation of the Authors." London, 1691. Hails Lee's "mad" play on a "mad" subject. See *Poems on Affairs of State.* Ed. William J. Cameron. New Haven and London: Yale Univ. Press, 1971. Vol. V, pp. 1–2.
"Between Nat. Lee *the Tragedian, and* Colley C_____r *the Plagiary." Visits from the Shades.* London, 1704, and partially rpt. in the appendix to the 1965 facs. of Cibber's *Rival Queans* (see below). As Lee complains of ill usage and Cibber congratulates himself, both men are satirized.
Biographia Britannica. London: W. Innys, 1760. Vol. V, 2912 ff. Biographical sketch; suggests Lee became a Fellow at Cambridge.
A Booke of Minutes: Anno primo Rse Jacob Secund, 1684. Board of Greencloth, Monday April 23, 1688. Records Lee's discharge from Bedlam.
BROWN, THOMAS. "From Bully Dawson to Bully W_____." *Amusements Serious and Comical and Other Works.* Ed. Arthur L. Hayward. London: Routledge, 1927, p. 379. Shows a ranting, red-faced Lee.
_____. "The Late Converts Exposed, or the Reason of Mr. Bays's changing his Religion." *A Collection of all the Dialogues written by Mr. Thos. Brown.* London, 1704, p. 197. Shows a paunchy Nat.
_____. *Letters from the Dead to the Living.* Part II. London, 1703, pp. 130–31. Says ruby-face Lee wrote a 25-act play in Bedlam.

Calendar of State Papers . . . Domestic. James II. Vol. I. London: H. M. Stationery Office, 1960, p. 420. Daniel Lee asks financial aid for institutionalized Nathaniel.

A Catalogue of the Library of Choise Books, Latin and English, Of the Reverend and Learned Dr. Richard Lee. n.p., 1685. Possibly indicates some of Nat's early reading.

CIBBER, COLLEY. *An Apology for the Life of Mr. Colley Cibber.* Ed. Robert W. Lowe. London: John C. Nimmo, 1889. I, 105–09, 113–14; II, 327–28. Tells of Lee reading aloud, esp. *The Rival Queens*, which was worthless rant unless acted well.

————. *The Rival Queans, With the Humours of Alexander the Great* (1729). Facsimile. Ed. William M. Peterson. Painesville, Ohio: Lake Erie College Press, 1965. Thoroughly, if not subtly, burlesques Lee's *The Rival Queens.*

CIBBER, THEOPHILUS et al. *The Lives of the Poets of Great Britain and Ireland.* London, 1753. Vol. II, 227–32. Biographical sketch (Lee as neglected genius) and critique of *Brutus.*

COWPER, WILLIAM. *The Correspondence of William Cowper.* Ed. Thomas Wright. London: Hodder and Stoughton, 1904. Vol. IV, 330. Condemns Lee for flattering Dryden.

DENNIS, JOHN. "The Impartial Critick," "Remarks upon . . . Pope's . . . Homer," "Characters and Conduct of Sir John Edgar." *The Critical Works of John Dennis.* Ed. E. N. Hooker. Baltimore: Johns Hopkins Univ. Press, 1939, 1943. Vols. I, 19–22, and II, 121–33, 184, 219. Something on *Oedipus,* on Lee's fire and fustian, his poor acting, his being ill cared for.

DERRICK, SAMUEL (pseud. Thomas Wilkes). *A General View of the Stage.* London, 1759, pp. 297–98. Anecdotal biographical sketch of "poor Nat."

DRYDEN, JOHN. "The Author's Apology for Heroic Poetry and Poetic License" (1677) and "Preface of the Translator, with a Parallel of Poetry and Painting" (1695). *Of Dramatic Poesy and other Critical Essays.* Ed. George Watson. London: Dent; New York: Dutton, 1962. Vols. I, 195–207, and II, 181–208. Shows Dryden's opinion shifting: Lee the versatile artist to Lee the hyper-emotional genius.

————. *The Letters of John Dryden.* Ed. Charles E. Ward. Durham, N.C.: Duke Univ. Press, 1942, p. 72. Anecdote of Lee's Bedlam wit.

————. "To Mr. Lee, on His *Alexander.*" *The Works of John Dryden.* Vol. I. Ed. E. N. Hooker and H. T. Swedenberg, Jr. Berkeley and Los Angeles: Univ. of California Press, 1956, pp. 106–07. Lee as natural artist, master of passions and imagery.

DUNTON, JOHN. "Dunton's Shadow: Or the Character of a Summer Friend—With a Postscript . . . by the famous NAT. LEE, whilst in Bedlam." *Athenianism: or, the new projects of Mr. J.D.* London, 1710. Vol. I, 110. On being neglected.

ETHEREGE, GEORGE. *The Letters of Sir George Etherege*. Ed. Frederick Bracher. Berkeley, Los Angeles, and London: Univ. of California Press, 1974, p. 135. Implies Lee's confinement may have been intermittent.

EVELYN, JOHN. "The Immortality of Poesie." *Poems by several hands*. Ed. Nahum Tate. London, 1685, p. 92. Predicts immortality for Lee's works.

GOULD, ROBERT. "To Julian, Secretary of the Muses." *Poems chiefly consisting of Satyrs*. London, 1689, p. 279. Says Lee is better cared for in Bedlam.

GRAY, THOMAS. *The Letters of Thomas Gray*. Ed. D. C. Tovey. 2d ed., rev. London: Bell, 1909. Vol. I, 96. Notes "Nat Lee's Bedlam Tragedy" of 25 acts.

HOGARTH, WILLIAM. "The Rake's Progress," Plate VIII. *Hogarth: The Complete Engravings*. Ed. Joseph Burke and Colin Caldwell. London: Thames and Hudson, 1968. The "Scene in a Madhouse" shows the letters "LE" etched into the wall above the mad rake: possibly an allusion to Lee.

Institutions Index. P.R.O., London. Lists clerical positions of Daniel, Richard, and John Lee, and of Lionel Holmes.

JACOB, GILES. *The Poetical Register: or, the Lives and Characters of all the English Poets*. London, 1723. Vol. I. 160–63. Slight and derivative (from Langbaine).

JOHNSON, SAMUEL. "Rambler" No. 20. *The Rambler*. Ed. W. J. Bate and Albrecht B. Strauss. New Haven and London: Yale Univ. Press, 1969. Vol. III, 112. Labels Lee a "great" writer. Repeats Dryden's anecdote (above: Dryden, John. *Letters*).

LANGBAINE, GERARD. *An Account of the English Dramatick Poets* (1691). Intro. John Loftis. Los Angeles: Clark Library, 1971. Vol. II. 320–27. Lee as first-rate author but unfortunate man.

Liber Literarum: Annoprimo Rs Jacob Secun—& Gulielmus Tertius, 1685 contin ad 1702. Board of Greencloth, 4th. January 1685. Official letters on maintenance and discharge of Lee the Bedlamite.

"Milton's Apotheosis." *The Gentleman's Magazine*, IX (January, 1739), 20. Frantic Lee pursues Dennis with a whip and is restrained by Dryden.

A New and General Biographical Dictionary. Vol. VII. London, 1762, pp. 434–36. Fairly detailed accounts of life and works.

OLDYS, WILLIAM and EDMUND CURLL. *The History of the English Stage*. London, 1741, pp. 90–91. Lee praises Mohun's rendering of Mithridates.

OLDYS, WILLIAM. Manuscript Notes to a Copy of Langbaine's *Account* (British Library, c. 28. g.l.). Clarifies a few details of Lee's life.

———. "William Oldys to the Earl of Oxford" (23 February 1730/31). *Report on the Manuscripts of his Grace the Duke of Portland*. Vol. VI. London: Eyre and Spottiswoode, 1901, pp. 36–37. On Lee's literary remains.

"On the Poets and Actors in King *Charles* II's Reign." *Gentleman's Maga-zine*, XV (1745), 99. Anecdotes; Lee as well-loved poet.

PARISH REGISTERS of Hatfield and Essendon, Hertfordshire; Bigby, Cad-ney, Somerby-by-Bigby, and Barnetby-Le-Wold, Lincolnshire; St. Leonard, Shoreditch, London; St. Benet, Paul's Wharf, London; St. James, Duke's Place, London; and St. Marylebone, London. Geneal-ogical information about Lee and family.

Poem on Southerne's death. Interleaved in a copy of Langbaine and Gildon's *Lives and Characters of the English Dramatick Poets*. London, 1699, pp. 136–37. Refers to friendship with Lee. British Library c. 46. d. 16.

Poetae Britannici. London, n.d., p. 18. Rpt. Samuel Cobb's *Poems on Sev-eral Occasions*. 3rd ed. London, 1710, p. 20. Lee was driven insane by his own hyperbolical imagination.

PRIOR, MATTHEW. "Satyr on the Poets," "A session of the Poets," "Journey to Copt-Hall." *The Literary Works of Matthew Prior*. Ed. H. Bunker Wright and Monroe K. Spears. 2nd ed. Oxford: Clarendon, 1971. Vol. I, 28–35, 63–65, 72–73. Depicts paunchy, "Dedicating" Lee, the mad poet.

"Remarkable Circumstances that Occasioned the Death of Four English Poets." *Scot's Magazine*, XLIV (1782), 595. Anecdotal.

"Rochester's Ghost addressing itself to the Secretary of the Muses." *Poems on Affairs of State*. London, 1703, p. 131. Lee may have joined Waller and Dryden in helping on Mulgrave's "Essay on Satire."

"Satyr against the Poets." British Library Harleian MS. 7317, p. 64. Portrays the "Brain-sick Poet."

"A Session of the Poets" (1676) and "The Tryal of Skill: or, A New Session of the Poets" (1704). *Poems on Affairs of State: Augustan Satirical Verse, 1660–1714*. Ed. George deF. Lord, Frank Ellis, et al. New Haven and London: Yale Univ. Press. Vol. I (1963), 352–56; Vol. VI (1970), 679–711. Tell of "Murder'd *Nat Lee*," the ranting drunkard.

SPENCE, JOSEPH. *Observations, Anecdotes, and Characters of Books and Men, Collected from Conversation*. Ed. James M. Osborn. Oxford: Clarendon, 1966. Vol. I, 280. Tells of Buckingham's maltreatment of Lee.

STEELE, RICHARD. "Prologue design'd for *Lucius* King of *Britain*, Written by Mrs. *Manley*." *The Occasional Verse of Richard Steele*. Ed. Rae Blanchard. Oxford: Clarendon, 1952. Gives Lee's recipe for appealing to the various social classes in his audiences. Calhoun Winton (*Sir Rich-ard Steele, M.P.* Baltimore: Johns hopkins, 1970, p. 116) guesses Steele was repeating Drury Lane gossip.

––––––. "Tatler" No. 191 (1710). *The Tatler*. Ed. George Aitken. Vol. III. 1899; rpt. Hildesheim and New York: Georg Olms, 1970, pp. 398–400. Praises Cibber's burlesque *Rival Queans* (performed 1710) for showing

Lee's play to be a pernicious distortion of history and a purveyor of immorality.

Wills of Richard Lee, D.D., and Rev. Richard Lee (Hertfordshire County Archives); of Anne Lee (P.C.C.); and of Rev. John Lee (Lincolnshire County Archives). Genealogy and clues to the whereabouts of Nat's literary remains.

WILMOT, JOHN, Earl of Rochester. "An Allusion to Horace, the Tenth Satyr of the First Book." *The Complete Poems of John Wilmot, Earl of Rochester*. Ed. David M. Vieth. New Haven and London: Yale Univ. Press, 1968. Pp. 120–26. Calls Lee a "hot-brained fustian fool."

WOOD, ANTHONY. *The Life and Times of Anthony Wood, antiquary, of Oxford, 1632–1695, described by Himself*. Ed. Andrew Clark. Vol. III, 112. Oxford: Clarendon, 1894. Notes Lee's death.

WYCHERLEY, WILLIAM. "To *NATH. LEE, in Bethlem*." *The Complete Works of William Wycherley*. Ed. Montague Summers. Soho: Nonesuch Press, 1924. Vol. III, 233–37. Now that hot-tempered Lee is well cared for, he can rail at a world that is madder than he is.

3. Biography and Criticism: 1800–1900

BAKER, DAVID ERSKINE, ISAAC REED, and STEPHEN JONES, eds. *Biographia Dramatica; or, a Companion to the Playhouse*. 1812; rpt. New York: AMS, 1966. Vol. I, Part 1, 448–49. Regards Lee as a "very eminent" tragedian.

"Biographical Sketch of Nathaniel Lee, the Poet." *The Monthly Mirror*, XIII (1802), 75–78. Not reliable but contains a supposed portrait.

BYRON, GEORGE GORDON. *The Works of Lord Byron*. Vol. IV: Letters and Journals. 1898–1901; rpt. New York: Octagon, 1966. P. 66. Mentions Lee's 25-act "Bedlam tragedy."

DORAN, JOHN. *"Their Majesties' Servants": Annals of the English Stage from Thomas Betterton to Edmund Kean*. Ed. Robert W. Lowe. London: Nimmo, 1888. Vol. I, 142, 221, 232–33. Lee quit acting because of stage fright and then wrote impassioned, bombastic, spectacular plays that are better than Otway's.

DUNHAM, S. A., *Lives of the Most Eminent Literary and Scientific Men of Great Britain*. London: Longman et al., 1838. Vol. III, 134–45. A full but factually inaccurate depiction of an excessively energetic genius whose "strange" tragedies are best exemplified by *Theodosius*.

FOSTER, JOSEPH, ed. *Alumni Oxonienses*. Vol. III, Early Series. Oxford: Parker, 1891. Fragmentary notice of Daniel Lee.

GARNETT, RICHARD. *The Age of Dryden*. London: Bell, 1895. Pp. 109–13. Not useful.

GIFFORD, WILLIAM, ed. *The Dramatic Works and Poems of James Shirley*.

London: J. Murray, 1833. Vol. I, 1v, n. 9. Lee's acting, appearance, death.

GOSSE, EDMUND. *A History of Eighteenth Century Literature (1660–1780).* London and New York: Macmillan, 1896. Pp. 57–58. Lee was a wretched man whose bombast occasionally reached Miltonic heights.

LEE, SIDNEY. "Lee, Nathaniel." *The Dictionary of National Biography.* Ed. Leslie Stephen and Sidney Lee. 1885–1901; rpt. London: Oxford Univ. Press, 1937–38. Vol. XI, 805–09. Compact and comprehensive, but outdated now.

MOSEN, R. "Über Nathaniel Lee's Leben und Werke." *Englische Studien,* II (1879), 416–39. Factually unreliable, appreciative, with some interesting critical remarks.

"Nat. Lee's Certificate." *N&Q,* I (1849–50), 149. Nat put his *imprimatur* on a copy of verses.

NEVE, PHILIP. "Remarks on the English Poets: Lee." *The Monthly Mirror,* XI (1801), 261–63. Sees Lee as majestic and original.

"Plays, written by Mr. Nathaniel Lee." *The Restrospective Review,* III (1821), 240–68. "His frenzy is the frenzy of a poet."

RYAN, RICHARD. *Dramatic Table-Talk.* London, 1825. Vols. I, 96 and II, 113. Anecdotes.

WARD, A. W. *A History of English Dramatic Literature to the Death of Queen Anne.* New and Rev. Ed. London: Macmillan, 1899. Vol. III, 407–12. Lee had "genuine" if "impure" passion.

4. Biography: 1900–1978

ADSHEAD, HAROLD. "The Mad Playwright of Hatfield." *Hertfordshire Countryside,* X, No. 37 (summer, 1955), 30–31. Popularized account, slight but fairly accurate.

ARMISTEAD, J. M. "Nathaniel Lee and Family: The Will of Richard Lee, D. D." *N&Q,* NS XXIV (1977), 130–31. Lee is named as the second son, after Samuel and before Daniel.

BARKER, G. F. R. and A. H. STENNING, eds. *The Record of Old Westminsters.* London: Chiswick Press, 1928. Vol. II. The item on Samuel Lee seems reliable, but the one on Nathaniel is spurious.

HAM, ROSWELL GRAY. *Otway and Lee: Biography from a Baroque Age.* 1931; rpt. New York: Greenwood Press, 1969. Still the best biography and includes critical remarks on the plays.

HOOKER, E. N., H. T. SWEDENBERG, et al., eds. *The Works of John Dryden.* Vols. I and II. Berkeley and Los Angeles: Univ. of California Press, 1956 and 1972. Contain biographical and bibliographical information related to "To Mr. Lee, on His *Alexander*" and the prologues and epilogues to *Mithridates, Sophonisba, Caesar Borgia, The Princess of Cleve, and Constantine.*

MARSH, B. and F. A. CRISP. *Alumni Carthusiani.* London: private printing, 1913. Useful item on Lee at Charterhouse.

McLEOD, A. L. "Nathaniel Lee's Birth Date." *MLN,* LXIX (1954), 167–70. Posits 1651.

————. "Nathaniel Lee's Portrait." *N&Q,* NS I(1953), 103–05. Attributed to William Dobson, at the Garrick Club.

VAN LENNEP, WILLIAM. "The Life and Works of Nathaniel Lee, Dramatist: A Study of Sources." Diss. Harvard 1933. A thorough biography and source study. Particularly useful on Richard Lee, D.D., and on anecdotes about Nathaniel's personality and manners.

VENN, JOHN and J. A. VENN, eds. *Alumni Cantabrigienses.* Part 1, Vol. III. Cambridge: Cambridge Univ. Press, 1924. Useful sketches, but to be used with caution.

5. Criticism and Scholarship: 1900–1978

ARCHER, WILLIAM. *The Old Drama and the New: An Essay in Revaluation.* Boston: Small, Maynard, 1923. P. 152. Denigrates Lee's artistry.

ARMISTEAD, J. M. "Hero as Endangered Species: Structure and Idea in Lee's *Sophonisba.: DUJ,* LXXI (1978), 35–43. Essentially the same as Ch. 3 above.

————. "Lee, Renaissance Conventions, and the Psychology of Providence: the Design of *Caesar Borgia.*" *Essays in Literature,* IV (1977), 159–73. Longer version of Ch. 8 above.

————. "Lee's Artistry: *Theodosius* as Tragi-Comedy of Contexts." *RECTR,* forthcoming. Longer version of Ch. 9 above.

————. "The Tragicomic Design of *Lucius Junius Brutus:* Madness as Providential Therapy." *PLL,* XV (1979), 38–51. Essentially the same as Ch. 10 above.

AXELRAD, A. JOSÉ. *Le Thème de Sophonisbe dans les principales tragédies de la littérature occidentale.* Lille: Bibliothèque Universitaire, 1956. Surveys French, English, and German plays on the theme form 1500–1913.

BARBOUR, FRANCES. "The Unconventional Heroic Plays of Nathaniel Lee." *University of Texas Studies in English,* XX (1940), 109–16. Lee's criticism of sovereignty is distinctive in its Whiggish tendencies.

————. "William Gilmore Simms and the Brutus Legend." *Midwest Folklore,* VII (1957), 159–62.

BARTHOLOMEW, A. T. "Restoration Drama, III." *The Cambridge History of English Literature.* Ed. A. W. Ward and A. R. Waller. New York: Putnam's; Cambridge: Cambridge Univ. Press, 1912. Vol. VIII, 210–12. Lee is humorless and unreadable, though sometimes broadly effective.

BENSLEY, EDWARD. "*The Tragedy of Nero and Piso's Conspiracy.*" *N&Q,* CXXXVII (1919), 323. Corrects Nicoll (see below).

BIRLEY, ROBERT. "Nathaniel Lee: *The Rival Queens.*" *Sunk without Trace: Some Forgotten Masterpieces Reconsidered.* New York: Harcourt, Brace & World, 1962. Pp. 40–75. The best analysis before Vernon's "Introduction" (above).

BOWERS, FREDSON. "Crux in the Text of Lee's *Princess of Cleve.*" *Harvard Library Bulletin*, IV (1950), 409–11. An unauthoritative omission.

———. "Nathaniel Lee: Three Probable Seventeenth-Century Piracies." *PBSA*, XLIV (1950), 62–66. Of *Rival Queens, Sophonisba, Nero.*

———. "The Prologue to Nathaniel Lee's *Mithridates*, 1678." *PBSA*, XLIV (1950), 172–75. Supports Lee's authorship.

COOKE, ARTHUR L., and THOMAS B. STROUP. "The Political Implications in Lee's *Constantine the Great.*" *JEGP*, XLIX (1950), 506–15. The Popish Plot and Rye House Plot are commented upon.

CROSS, GUSTAV. "Ovid Metamorphosed: Marston, Webster, and Nathaniel Lee." *N&Q*, NS III (1956), 244–45, 508–09. *Oedipus* is indebted to Golding's translation of Ovid.

DOBRÉE, BONAMY. "Nat Lee (1653–1692) and the Tragedy of Humours." *Restoration Tragedy 1660–1720.* Oxford: Clarendon, 1929. Pp. 110–31. Lee is too emotional and operatic.

ELWIN, MALCOLM. "Lee and Otway." *The Playgoer's Handbook to Restoration Drama.* New York: Macmillan, 1928. Lee is the "most unjustly neglected of the old dramatists."

EVANS, G. BLAKEMORE. "Milton and Lee's *The Rival Queens*, 1677." *MLN*, LXIV (1949), 527–28. Echoes.

FLETCHER, HARRIS F. "Nathaniel Lee and Milton." *MLN*, XLIV (1929), 173–75. On Lee's poem on Dryden's *State of Innocence.*

German dissertations (published). See listings in Stroup and Cooke, *Works*, I, 452; McCleod, "A Nathaniel Lee Bibliography"; and Carl J. Stratman et al., eds., *Restoration and Eighteenth Century Theatre Research: A Bibliographical Guide, 1900–1968.*

GHOSH, J. C. "Prologue and Epilogue to Lee's 'Constantine the Great.' " *TLS*, 14 March 1929, p. 207. Dryden's and Otway's, respectively?

GREENE, GRAHAM. "Rochester and Lee." *TLS*, 2 November 1935, p. 697. Nemours as Rochester.

HAMMOND, ANTONY D. "The Development of the Serious Play in the Restoration (1660–1690)." Diss. Auckland 1969, pp. 500–641. The section on Lee usefully evaluates the plays.

HUME, ROBERT D. *The Development of English Drama in the Late Seventeenth Century.* Oxford: Clarendon, 1976. Useful plot summaries and critical insights scattered throughout.

———. "The Satiric Design of Nat. Lee's *The Princess of Cleve.*" *JEGP*, LXXV (1976), 117–38. Sees the play as satire against heroic values and rake-heroes, esp. Rochester.

KASTAN, DAVID S. *"Nero* and the Politics of Nathaniel Lee." *PLL*, XIII (1977), 125–35. Reads the play as a political warning.

KIES, PAUL P. "Lessing's Das befreite Rom and Lee's *Lucius Junius Brutus." JEGP*, XXVIII (1929), 402–09. Discusses Lee's influence on Lessing.

KNIGHT, G. WILSON. *The Golden Labyrinth: A Study of British Drama.* London: Phoenix House, 1962. Pp. 157–67. Section on Lee stresses his psychological subtlety.

———. "The Plays of Nathaniel Lee." *Venture,* I (1960), 186–96. Superseded by the section in *The Golden Labyrinth.*

LAWRENCE, W. J. "Correspondence." *TLS,* 9 November 1935, p. 722. Clarifies Greene's note (above).

LEARY, LEWIS. "St. George Tucker Attends the Theatre." *William and Mary Quarterly,* 3rd Ser., V (1948), 396–98. Lee's *Rival Queens* in New York, 1786.

LEWIS, NANCY ELOISE. *Nathaniel Lee's "The Rival Queens": A Study of Dramatic Taste and Technique in the Restoration.* Diss. Ohio State 1957. Ann Arbor, Michigan: Xerox University Microfilms, 1975. Not helpful on "technique" but useful as a survey of literary tastes and influences, esp. chs. II, IV, and V.

LOFTIS, JOHN. *The Politics of Drama in Augustan England.* Oxford: Clarendon, 1963, esp. pp. 15–23. Puts Lee's political interests into perspective.

MARSHALL, GEOFFREY. *Restoration Serious Drama.* Norman: Univ. of Oklahoma Press, 1975. Esp. pp. 155–79. Analyzes the diction of *Brutus* as representative of contemporary practices. Other Lee plays are mentioned.

MCLEOD, A. L. "The Douai MS. of Lee's *Mithridates." N&Q,* NS VII (1960), 69–70. It is not in Lee's hand.

NETTLETON, G. H. "Dryden, Lee and Otway." *English Drama of the Restoration and Eighteenth Century (1642–1780).* New York: Macmillan, 1914. Pp. 96–99. Lee's promise was snuffed by his enthusiasm and insanity.

NEWELL, GEORGE. "The Tragedy of Nero and Piso's Conspiracy." *N&Q,* CXXXVII (1919), 299–300. Corrects Nicoll (see below).

NICOLL, ALLARDYCE. *A History of English Drama 1660–1900.* Vol. I. 4th ed. Cambridge: Cambridge Univ. Press, 1952. Views Lee as an impassioned tragedian with a poetic gift, flawed but ranking next to Dryden.

———. "The Tragedy of Nero and Piso's Conspiracy." *N&Q,* CXXXVII (1919), 254–56. Distinguishes the anon. play from Lee's. See correctives by Bensley and Newell (above).

PARSONS, PHILIP. "Restoration Tragedy as Total Theatre." *Restoration Literature: Critical Approaches.* Ed. Harold Love. London: Methuen, 1972. Pp. 59–64. Analyzes several Lee plays for their spectacle.

PETERSON, WILLIAM M. "Introduction" to Colley Cibber's *The Rival Queans, With the Humours of Alexander the Great* (1729). Painesville, Ohio: Lake Erie College Press, 1965. Pp. xii-xxii. Usefully summarizes the eighteenth-century reputation of Lee's *Rival Queens*.

PITOU, SPIRE, JR. "French and English Echoes of a Descriptive Passage in Tasso." *MLN*, LII (1937), 265–66. *Theodosius* echoes *Gerusalemme liberata*.

ROTHSTEIN, ERIC. *Restoration Tragedy: Form and the Process of Change.* Madison, Milwaukee, and London: Univ. of Wisconsin Press, 1967. Esp. pp. 77–86, 91–96. Provocative insights into *Sophonisba* and *Lucius Junius Brutus*, esp. their diction and imagery.

SAINTSBURY, GEORGE. "Nathaniel Lee's *Sophonisba*." *Englishe Studien*, XLVII (1913–14), 96–97. Insists Lee's plays have been unjustly neglected.

SANDERS, H. M. "The Plays of Nat Lee, Gent." *Temple Bar*, CXXIV (1901), 497–508. Recommends Lee for powerful emotional effects but notes his lack of subtlety and controlled artistry. Rightly senses Lee is above petty political bias in *Brutus* and commends that play along with *Rival Queens* and *Mithridates*. Misses both formal and thematic virtues of *Sophonisba, Borgia,* and *Cleve*. Factually unreliable.

SCOUTEN, A. H. "Plays and Playwrights." *The Revels History of Drama in English.* Ed. John Loftis, et al. London: Methuen, 1976. Vol. V, 269–72. General survey.

SHERBURNE, GEORGE. "The Restoration and Eighteenth Century (1660–1789)." *A Literary History of England.* Ed. Albert C. Baugh. New York: Appleton-Century-Crofts, 1948. Pp. 757–58. Although somewhat confused in language and imagery, Lee has a "strong, crude" poetic genius.

SKRINE, PETER N. "Blood, Bombast, and Deaf Gods: The Tragedies of Lee and Lohenstein." *German Life and Letters*, XXIV (1970), 14–30. *Nero, Sophonisba,* and *Borgia;* useful for understanding Lee's appeal in Germany.

SMITH, JOHN HARRINGTON. "Dryden's Prologue and Epilogue to *Mithridates*, Revived." *PMLA*, LXVIII (1953), 251–67. Supports Dryden's authorship.

STROUP, THOMAS B. "The Authorship of the Prologue to Lee's *Constantine the Great*." *N&Q*, NS I (1954), 387–88. Ascribes it to Lee, not Otway.

———. "*The Princess of Cleve* and Sentimental Comedy." *RES*, XI (1935), 200–03. This play is an early example.

SUMMERS, MONTAGUE. *The Playhouse of Pepys.* New York: Macmillan, 1935. P. 301. Nemours and Rochester.

SUTHERLAND, JAMES. *English Literature of the Late Seventeenth Century.* Oxford: Clarendon, 1969. Pp. 71–75, 143–44. Concise and revealing, esp. on *Brutus* and *Cleve*.

THORNDIKE, ASHLEY H. *Tragedy*. Boston and New York: Houghton, Mifflin, 1908. Pp. 266–69. Impressionistic.

VIETH, DAVID M. "Psychological Myth as Tragedy: Nathaniel Lee's *Lucius Junius Brutus*." *HLQ*, XXXIX (1975), 57–76. A post-Freudian reading.

————. "Nathaniel Lee's *The Rival Queens* and the Psychology of Assassination," *Restoration: Studies in English Literary Culture, 1660–1700*, II, No. 2 (1978), 10–13.

WAITH, EUGENE M. *Ideas of Greatness: Heroic Drama in England*. New York: Barnes & Noble, 1971. Pp. 235–42. Revealingly analyzes *Sophonisba* and *Rival Queens* in light of previous heroic plays.

WEINBROT, HOWARD D. *Augustus Caesar in "Augustan" England: The Decline of a Classical Norm*. Princeton: Princeton Univ. Press, 1978. Pp. 72–73. Briefly notes *Gloriana* as a witty melodrama that is "unintentionally comic."

WHITE, FELIX. "The Gordian Knot Untied." *TLS*, 11 June 1925, p. 400. Marriage as Gordian Knot in *Theodosius*.

WHITING, GEORGE W. "Political Satire in London Stage Plays 1680–1683." *MP*, XXVIII (1930), 29–43. Brief notices of *Borgia, Brutus,* and *Guise*.

WILSON, JOHN HAROLD. *A Preface to Restoration Drama*. Cambridge, Mass.: Harvard Univ. Press, 1968. Esp. pp. 86–89. Bracing, insightful remarks.

WRIGHT, H. BUNKER. "Prior and Gildon." *N&Q*, NS III (1956), 18–20. Gildon's *Titus and Teraminta* is another adaptation of Lee's *Brutus*.

Index

The historical originals of Lee's dramatic characters are indexed whenever they are stressed, although the characters themselves are not indexed.

Abraham and Isaac, 143
Albemarle, George Monck, Duke of, 18, 21
Alexander VI, Pope, 115
America as New World, 106, 114–18, 121
Andrewes, Lancelot, 19
Anglican parishes, 18, 20, 25
Annesley, Lyttleton, Lieutenant General, 19
Appian, 83–84
Arcadia, 114
Aristotle, 55
Arius, 167
Arlington, Henry Bennet, Earl of, 156
Astraea, 124–25
Augustine, St., 112

Bacon, Francis, 26; *Essays*, 94, 105, 132
"Ballers, The," 161
Banks, John, 174
Barbour, Frances, 177
Barclay, Robert, 28
Barrow, Isaac, 20, 28
Baxter, Richard, 20, 28
Bennet, "Lady," 161
Bethlem Royal Hospital, 24
blank verse, 174
Board of Greencloth, 24
Bouillon, Henri de, 150
Bourbon, Antoinette de, 150
Boutell, Elizabeth, 54
Boyle, Roger: *Parthenissa*, 47
Brown, Tom, 25
Buckingham, George Villiers, second Duke of, 21, 27, 156–61; *The Chances*, 148
Bulkeley, Henry, 156
Bunyan, John, 21, 28, 29; *Grace Abounding*, 21
Burnet, Gilbert, 19–20, 28; *A Relation of the Barbarous and Bloody Massacre*, 94, 96; *Some Passages of the Life and Death of . . . Rochester*, 156–57
Busby, Richard, 19
Butler, Samuel: *Hudibras*, 29; "A Modern Politician," 116

Caesar, Julius, 104
Calvinism, 20, 98, 101–104, 153, 176
Cambridge Platonists, 20
Cambridge University, 18, 20–22, 30
Canon Episcopi, 37
Catherine of Braganza (Queen Consort of England), 25, 128
Cato Uticensis, 104
Catullus, 44, 53
Cerberus, 36
Chapman, George: *The Middle Temple and Lincoln's Inn Mask*, 117
Charles I (King of England), 26
Charles II (King of England), 22, 27, 41, 44, 56–57, 95, 98, 105, 127–29, 159, 161, 167, 168
Charterhouse, 19, 20
Chester Cycle, 40
Chesterfield, Philip Stanhope, second Earl of, 160
Chillingworth, William, 20

Christ, 125–26, 143, 168, 173
circle imagery, 35, 37–39, 41
Clark, Thomas, 54
Clement, Jaques, 120
Cleveland, Barbara Palmer, Duchess of, 167
Cleves, Catherine de, 150–51
Cleves, Francis I de (Duke of Nevers), 150
Cleves, Marie de, 150
Colchester, 168
Coligny, Gaspard II de (Admiral of France), 150
Columbus, Christopher, 106, 114–17
comedy, 138; split-action comedy, 147; libertine comedy, 147
Condé, le Prince de, 150
Constantia, 165
Constantine, 165
Constantius I, 165–66
Cooke, Arthur L., 34, 94, 165, 167
Corneille Pierre, 43, 83; *Sophonisbe*, 46–47, 49; *Pulchérie*, 123
Cosin, John, 18
Cotterell, Sir Charles, 69
Cotton, John, 20
courtiers, 27, 127–28, 151, 156–61
Covent Garden, 28
Cowley, Abraham, 21
Crispus, 165–66
Crog, Antoine de (Prince of Porcien), 150
Cromwell, Oliver, 139, 178
Crowne, John: *City Politiques*, 156
Cudworth, Ralph, 20
Curtius, Quintus: *Wars of Alexander*, 69

Dacres, Edmund, 108
Dalmatius, 165, 167
Danby, Earl of, 28, 158
Daniel, Samuel, 40
Davenant, Sir William, 21; Macbeth, 21; Cruelty of the Spaniards in Peru, 116
Davila, E. C.: *Historie of the Civill Warres of France*, 94, 96, 121
Descartes, René, 26–27
Diana (moon goddess, huntress), 37, 74–76
Diehl, Charles, 123

Donne, John, 19; "Elegie: Going to Bed," 117
Dorset, Charles Sackville, Earl of, 23, 25, 27, 156, 159–61
Dorset Garden, 23
Dreux, Battle of, 150
Dryden, John, 19, 21–23, 29–30, 43, 83–84, 156, 175–77; "To Mr. Lee, on His *Alexander*," 22; prologue and two epilogues to *Mithridates*, 22; prologue to *Caesar Borgia*, 22; prologue to *Sophonisba*, 22, 44–45, 56; prologue and epilogue to *Cleve*, 22; epilogue to *Constantine*, 22, 168; *Oedipus*, 22, 23, 97; *Duke of Guise*, 22–23, 97; "Heroique Stanzas," 29, 139, 142; "Astraea Redux," 30; *The Hind and the Panther*, 30; *Conquest of Granada*, 48, 53–54, 122; *All for Love*, 54–55, 71, 174–75; *Aureng-Zebe*, 54, 65, 84–85, 130, 133, 152, 165, 174–76; *Absalom and Achitophel*, 97, 111, 142, 152–53, 160; *Marriage A-la-Mode*, 147–48, 174; *The Spanish Fryar*, 147
Duke, Richard: prologue to *Lucius Junius Brutus*, 22
Duke Street, 24
Duke's Company, 22–23, 97
D'Urfey, Thomas, 22; epilogue to *Massacre*, 22, 98–99
Dutch fleet, 27

Eden, Richard: trans. Peter Martyr's *Decades*, 114
Eden myth, 96, 102, 104, 114, 116–17, 120–21, 125, 134, 153
empiricism, 26, 28, 30
epicureanism, 27, 147
Este, Anne de (Duchess of Guise and of Nemours), 151
Etherege, Sir George, 21, 24, 27, 156, 160–61; *The Man of Mode*, 29, 148, 157, 160; *The Comical Revenge*, 147, 160
Europa, 153
Exclusion Crisis, 97, 106, 138, 174, 178

Faust, 35

Fausta, 165–66
Fenton, Geoffrey, 108, 111
Festial: A Collection of Homilies, 40
Fielding, Henry, 43
Fire of London (1666), 27
Fletcher, John, 83–84; Valentinian, 84;
    Thierry and Theodoret, 132
Ford, John, 40
Fortune, 110–13
Fox, George, 28
French Civil Wars, 94–96, 120, 150–52
Fuller, Thomas, 19

Ganymede, 154
ghosts, 39, 69, 90, 113
Glanvill, Joseph, 20–21, 28; Philosophi-
    cal Considerations concerning Witches,
    21
Godfrey, Sir Edmund Berry, 98
Godolphin, Sidney, 28
Golden Age, 114, 116, 125
Governette, Esther de, 159
Governette, Marquis de, 159
Grand Tour, 160
Great Chain of Being, 133
Guicciardini: Historie, 108–109, 111, 115
Guise, Francis le Duc de, 151
Guise, Henri le Duc de, 150
Gunning, Peter, 18

Halicarnassus, Dionysius, 132
Halifax, Marquis of, 28
Ham, Roswell G., 43
Hannibalianus, 165
Harleian collection, 25
Harpy, 37, 75
Hart, Charles, 54
Henri II (King of France), 150
Henri III (King of France), 120
Henri IV (King of France), 120, 162–63
Hercules, 56, 60–61, 78–79
"Herculian" Dynasty, 166
heroism and heroic drama, 43–45, 48–57,
    61, 76, 122, 125–26, 128, 147–48, 152,
    174
Hewitt, Sir John, 160
Heydon, "Dr." John, 157
historical sense, 30
Hobbes, Thomas, 27–28, 53, 138, 148,
    176

Holland, Philemon: trans. Livy, Roman
    History, 47
Holmes, Ann Lee Pitman, 25
Holmes, Sir Robert, 158
Homer, 44, 53
Hooke, Robert, 28
Hooker, Richard, 19
House of Lords, 158
Howard, Captain Thomas, 158
Howard, Sir Robert, 21
Huguenots, 95, 130, 150–51, 159
Hume, Robert D., 43, 94–96, 97, 131,
    147–49
Huysman, Jacob (portrait of Rochester),
    157
Hyde, Laurence, 28

Indians (American), 114, 115–16
Infernal powers, 20, 31, 35–39, 52–53,
    74–75, 77, 96, 110, 113–21, 134–35,
    141, 153–55, 168–73, 177–78
Isle of Axholme, 25
Iwain and Gawain, 77–79

James II, King (previously Duke of York),
    24, 128–29, 158, 167
Jermyn, Henry, 157–58
Johnson, Samuel, 17
Joinville, castle of, 150–51
Jove, 60, 74
Jupiter, 60, 64, 74
Jupiter Ammon, 78

Kastan, David S., 41
Kéroualle, Louise de, 98
Killigrew, Charles, 23, 97, 156
Killigrew, Henry, 97, 156, 159
Killigrew, Thomas, 97
King's Company, 23, 97, 156
Knight, G. Wilson, 40, 48
Kyd, Thomas: Spanish Tragedy, 110

La Calprenède: Cléopâtre, 58; Cassan-
    dra, 69–70; Pharamond, 123
La Marck, Robert IV de (Duke of Bouil-
    lon), 150
Lafayette, Madame de: La Princesse de
    Clèves, 147, 149, 151, 156
Langbaine, Gerard, 24, 43
Langdon, Ann Lee, 25

language, 149–50
Lateran Palace, 169
Lee, Anne, 20
Lee, Daniel, 19, 24
Lee, Elizabeth, 19
Lee, Emmanuel, 19
Lee, John, 19, 25
Lee, Mary, 20
Lee, Nathaniel (1649?–92) birth, 20; education, 20–21; family, 17–20; reading, 20–21; early London years, 21–24; contemporaries, 21–25; years of fame, 22–24; in Bedlam, 24; last years, 24–25; literary remains, 25; in his cultural milieu, 30–31; conventionality, 174; distinctive style, 175–77; cycles of artistic development, 177–78.
WRITINGS:
Caesar Borgia, 23–24, 41, 64–65, 81, 96–97, 101, 106–21, 139, 170–71, 174
Constantine, 24, 64–65, 67, 71, 81, 105, 130, 138, 139, 143, 162, 163–73, 177–78
Duke of Guise, The, 23–24, 95, 97, 105, 138
Gloriana, 22, 58–66, 67, 69, 85, 87, 89, 166, 170, 174
Lucius Junius Brutus, 23, 41, 64–65, 71, 95–96, 130–43, 163, 166, 174, 176–78
Massacre of Paris, The, 23, 25, 65, 71, 94–105, 106–107, 120–21, 122, 130, 132, 141–42, 144, 155–56, 174, 178
Mithridates, 23, 64–65, 71, 80–93, 101, 107, 122, 130, 133, 138, 139, 141, 165, 174–75, 177–78
Nero, 21, 30, 32–42, 65, 67, 70–74, 76, 78, 85–87, 101, 130–32, 138–39, 142, 159, 163, 165, 170, 174, 176–78
Oedipus, 23, 97, 107
"On the Death of Mrs. Behn," 25
"On the Death of the Duke of Albemarle," 21
"On Their Majesties Coronation," 24
Princess of Cleve, The, 24–25, 95, 97, 144–63, 166, 174
Rival Queens, The, 22, 41, 54–55, 65, 67–79, 81, 85–87, 101, 122, 126, 130, 138–41, 163, 165, 169–71, 174–75, 177–78
Sophonisba, 22, 30, 43–56, 59, 64–65, 67, 69, 76, 81, 85, 87, 122, 132, 138, 166, 174, 176–77
Theodosius, 23, 64–65, 71, 81, 122–29, 132–33, 138–39, 163, 165–66, 168, 170–71, 174, 177
"To Mr. Dryden, on his Poem of Paradice," 22
"To the Author & Translatour of the following Book," 23
"To the Duke on His Return," 23
"To the Unknown Author of this Excellent Poem," 22–23
Lee, Richard (1612–84/5) birth, 17–18; education, 18; Roman Catholicism, 18; church career, 18–19; wife and children, 19–20; library, 19–20, 30, 184n6
Lee, Richard (1655–1725), 19
Lee, Samuel (c. 1645–?), 19
Lee, Samuel (eighteenth-century headmaster of Newport Grammar School), 17
Lee, Sarah, 25
Lee, William, 17
Literary structures, 29
Livy: *Roman History*, 47, 131
Locke, John, 28
Loftis, John, 94
Louis XIV (King of France), 128, 162
Lucian, 111
Lucretius, 112
Lydgate, John: *Fall of Princes*, 40
lyricism, 175–77

Machiavelli and Machiavellianism, 71, 86, 98, 105–14, 116–17, 119–21, 138, 142, 161; *The Prince*, 108, 110–11; "Sinigallia Tract," 108; *The Discourses*, 110–11, 131
Madness, 24, 32, 40–42, 72–73, 75–79, 118, 131, 139–43, 172, 186n23
Mairet, Jean, 43; *Sophonisbe*, 46, 49
Mancini, Hortense, 98
Marlowe, Christopher, 40; *Massacre at Paris*, 94; prologue to *Jew of Malta*, 119–20
Mars, 60

Marston, John, 43; *The Wonder of Women*, 46–47, 49
Martyr, Peter: *Decades*, 114
Marvell, Andrew, 21; *Horatian Ode*, 139
Mary II (Queen of England), 24, 95, 98, 129, 178
Massinger, Philip: *The Emperour of the East*, 123
Master of Revels, 23, 97, 156
Maxentius, 168
Maximianus, 166
Medea, 75
Medici, Catherine de (Queen and Queen Mother of France), 150–51
Medway (river), 27
Merlin, 36
messiah, 78, 124, 143
Milton, John: *Paradise Lost*, 21–23, 29, 74, 139, 153, 160, 172
Milvian Bridge, Battle of, 168
Mohun, Michael, 54
Monmouth, Duke of, 97, 128, 167
Montmorency, le Duc de, 151
More, Henry, 20; *Divine Dialogues*, 21
More, Sir Thomas: *Utopia*, 116
Moses, 143
Mulgrave, John Sheffield, Earl of, 22, 27, 156, 160–61

Nabbes, Thomas: *Hannibal and Scipio*, 47
Nantwich (Cheshire), 17
nature imagery, 48–50, 55, 63, 81, 87–93, 133–34
Nazi, 119
"New-Flavian" Dynasty, 166
Newport Grammar School, 17
Newton, Isaac, 20
Nicaea, Council of, 167
Nichols, Mr., 18
Nicoll, Allardyce, 34, 43

Oates, Titus, 96, 98
occultism, 20, 36–39, 52–53, 74–75, 77, 84, 91–92, 96, 118–19, 134–35, 141, 153–55, 168–73, 177–78, 187–88 notes 7–12, 193n5
Oldys, William, 25

Orrery, Earl of, 21
Otway, Thomas, 22, 83, 174; *Alcibiades*, 69; *Don Carlos*, 84, 165–66; *Venice Preserv'd*, 127, 174; *Caius Marius*, 132; *Friendship in Fashion*, 174
Ovid, 44, 53
Oxford, Edward Harley, Earl of, 25
Oxford University, 19; Wadham College, 26

Parsons, Robert: *A Sermon preached at the Earl of Rochester's Funeral*, 156
pastoralism, 62–63, 125, 128–29, 195–96n6
patriarchy, 85
Payne, Nevil: *Fatal Jealousie*, 21, 174
Pearson, John, 20
Pembroke, Earl of, 23
Penn, William, 20, 28
Pepys, Samuel, 29
Petrarch, 40
Petty, Sir William, 28
Phaeton, 35–36
Plague (1665), 27
Pliny, 83
Plutarch, 59, 69, 83–84; "Life of Valerius Publicola," 132
Poitiers, Diane de (Duchess of Valentinois), 150
Poltrot, Jean de, le seigneur de Méré, 151
Ponet, John: *Short Treatise of Politicke Power*, 114
Pontoise, Benedictine convent at, 158
Popish Plot, 97, 106, 120, 174, 178
Porter, Thomas: *The Villain*, 174
Privy Garden (Whitehall), 161
progress, idea of, 30
Prometheus, 35, 37
Providence, 20, 29–30, 45, 48, 50–53, 57, 64, 76–77, 81, 91–93, 102–104, 107, 110–13, 118, 120, 122, 124–25, 131, 138–43, 152, 162–63, 168–73, 177–78
psychology of the seventeenth century, 20, 31, 40, 42, 50, 59–60, 67, 70–71, 73, 75–79, 81, 85–86, 89–91, 118, 121, 125, 142, 166, 170–73, 177–78

Quakers, 20, 28

Racine, Jean Baptiste, 83–84; *Mithri-date*, 65, 84, 165; *Britannicus*, 84
Ravaillac, 120
republicanism, 132, 135–38, 178
Restoration England, 25–30, 41–42, 44, 56–57, 97–98, 105, 120–22, 127–29, 143, 155–62, 167–68, 178
Richmond, Frances Stewart, Duchess of, 23, 127–28
Rochester, John Wilmot, Earl of, 21–22, 27, 43, 156–57, 159–61; *Satyr against Reason and Mankind*, 29; "Allusion to Horace," 156
Ronsard, Pierre de, 40
Rothstein, Eric, 44–45, 174
Royal Charles (flagship), 27
Royal Exchange, 27
Royal Society, The, 26, 28
royalism, 132, 134–35, 136, 138, 178
Rye House Plot, 178

St. Albans, 18
Saint André, le Maréchal, 151, 159
St. Bartholomew's Day Massacre, 96, 150
St. Clement Danes, 25
St. Mary's Cambridge, 18
St. Paul's London, 18, 27
Salisbury, Earl of, 20
Sardinia Street, 24
Saturn, 60, 64
"Satyr against the Poets," 24
Saunders, Charles, 22
Savile, Henry, 156, 160
Savoie, Jacque de (Duke of Nemours), 151, 159
Scot, Reginald, 38
Scudéry, Magdeleine de: *Clélie*, 131–32
Sedley, Sir Charles, 21, 27, 156, 159–61; *The Mulberry Garden*, 147
Semele, 75
Seneca: *Hercules Furens*, 125–26
Settle, Elkanah: *The Female Prelate*, 96; *Fatal Love*, 174
Shadwell, Thomas, 21, 156; *Epsom-Wells*, 148; *The Libertine*, 148, 174; *The Virtuoso*, 148

Shakespeare, William, 40, 54, 83, 132; *Hamlet*, 34, 40, 69, 131; *The Tempest*, 36; *Antony and Cleopatra*, 47, 71; *Julius Caesar*, 69; *Richard III*, 84, 110; *Othello*, 106, 108; *King John*, 119; *Romeo and Juliet*, 130, 132
Shaftesbury, Earl of, 28, 97–98, 158, 167, 178
Shrewsbury, Anna-Maria, Countess of, 157–59
Shrewsbury, Francis Talbot, eleventh Earl of, 158–59
Sidney, Algernon, 167
Sirius, 36
skepticism, 30
Solomon, 143
South, Robert, 28
South English Legendary, The, 40
Spanish conquerors, 115–16
Sprat, Thomas, 28; *History of the Royal Society*, 20
star imagery, 38, 51, 75, 88
Stillingfleet, Edward, 19, 28
stoicism, 56, 126, 170–71
Stroup, Thomas B., 34, 94, 165, 167
Suetonius, 59
Summers, Montague, 156
Sylvester, Pope, 169

Taylor, Jeremy, 19
Theatre Royal, 24, 97
Theodora, 165
Tillotson, John, 20, 28
Tomasi, Tomaso: *Vita del Duca Valentino*, 108–109
Tory, 167, 177
Tourneur, Cyril: *The Atheist's Tragedy*, 40
tragedy, 43, 56–57, 63, 78, 85, 95, 99, 101, 103–105, 130, 132, 134, 138, 139, 174
tragicomedy, 130, 174
Tyson, Edward, 24

Utopia, 114, 136

Valois, Marguerite de (Princess Royal of France), 151

Van Lennep, William, 45, 94, 106, 108, 165
Vaughan, John, 156, 160
Vendôme, François de (Vidam of Chartres), 150
venereal disease, 114–15
Venus, 76, 124
Vernon, P. F., 72
Vespasian, 42
Vicar of Bray, 18
Vieth, David M., 54, 72
villain tragedy, 174
Virgil, 44, 53

Waith, Eugene, 43–45, 49
Waller, Edmund, 21
Ward, Sir Adolphus, 43
Webster, John: *The Duchess of Malfi,* 40;

The White Devil, 131
Whichcote, Benjamin, 20
Whig, 130, 177
Wild, Robert, 18–19
Wilkins, John, 20, 28
William III (King of England), 23–24, 95, 98, 129, 178
Williams, Aubrey, 110
Windsor, 128
Wood, Anthony, 24
Wren, Sir Christopher, 28
Wycherley, William, 22, 24; *To Nath. Lee,* in *Bethlem,"* 22; *Love in a Wood,* 147
Wyggeston's Hospital (Leicestershire), 18

Zeus, 75, 154

DATE DUE

DEMCO 38-297